Test Tubes for Global Intellectual Property Issues

Small market economies provide a valuable insight into how a country might balance competing interests in global intellectual property. As developed countries that are also net importers of intellectual property, small market economies have similar concerns to some developing countries. This duality of developed and developing country interests has resulted in some innovative ways of calibrating laws so that they both support national economic and social needs and honour international commitments. In this book, Susy Frankel uses examples from the small market economies of Singapore, New Zealand and Israel to address global intellectual property issues. Those issues include approaching treaty interpretation to assist in implementation of obligations, utilisation of flexibilities and effective dispute resolution, the links between trade and innovation, when and how patent and copyright law can be flexible, the importance of trade marks to small businesses, parallel importing and the protection of traditional knowledge.

SUSY FRANKEL is Professor of Law and Director of the New Zealand Centre of International Economic Law at Victoria University of Wellington.

Cambridge Intellectual Property and Information Law

As its economic potential has rapidly expanded, intellectual property has become a subject of front-rank legal importance. *Cambridge Intellectual Property and Information Law* is a series of monograph studies of major current issues in intellectual property. Each volume contains a mix of international, European, comparative and national law, making this a highly significant series for practitioners, judges and academic researchers in many countries.

A list of books in the series can be found at the end of this volume.

Test Tubes for Global Intellectual Property Issues

Small Market Economies

Susy Frankel

Victoria University of Wellington

CAMBRIDGE
UNIVERSITY PRESS

CAMBRIDGE
UNIVERSITY PRESS

University Printing House, Cambridge CB2 8BS, United Kingdom

Cambridge University Press is part of the University of Cambridge.

It furthers the University's mission by disseminating knowledge in the pursuit of education, learning and research at the highest international levels of excellence.

www.cambridge.org
Information on this title: www.cambridge.org/9781107013148

First published 2015

A catalogue record for this publication is available from the British Library

Library of Congress Cataloguing in Publication data
Frankel, Susy, author.
Test tubes for global intellectual property issues : small market economies / Susy Frankel.
pages cm. – (Cambridge intellectual property and information law ; 29)
ISBN 978-1-107-01314-8 (hardback)
1. Intellectual property – Economic aspects. 2. International trade. I. Title.
K1401.F734 2015
346.04′8–dc23

2014048022

ISBN 978-1-107-01314-8 Hardback

For

Claudia and George

Contents

Foreword

Rochelle Cooper Dreyfuss

From both a theoretical and a practical perspective, this book is an important resource. Ever since the Agreement on Trade-Related Aspects of Intellectual Property Rights (the TRIPS Agreement) set out the minimum standards of intellectual property protection for members of the World Trade Organization (WTO), considerable attention has focused on the wisdom of moving towards a system that is more deeply harmonised and that mandates the recognition of even stronger rights.

For the most part, the debate centres on questions of technological development. To many, countries that are behind the technology curve gain little from strong protection, even when it is offset by market access for their own products. The products developing countries sell (raw commodities, manufactures) are priced competitively and therefore earn rather scant returns, while the 'knowledge products' developing countries must buy (pharmaceuticals, manufacturing equipment, educational materials) are patented, copyrighted and trade marked – and priced well above marginal cost. International obligations to impose high standards of intellectual property protection can therefore cause considerable injustice, for these rights siphon funds from poor countries to rich ones. At the same time, proponents of raising worldwide standards point to the post-TRIPS success of the BRICs (Brazil, Russia, India and China) and suggest that strong protection will benefit other developing countries as well. Intellectual property laws can create powerful inducements to domestic innovators. Furthermore, they promote technology transfer, help establish local creative industries and motivate governments to prioritise activities that move their countries to the intellectual frontier.

While this conversation is interesting and important, lost in it is another dimension of the harmonisation issue: market size. Based on the debate set out above, one might think that the interests of all advanced economies would be in alignment, for any country that innovates at world-class levels can reap supra-competitive returns from the global market. This book dispels that notion. Its careful analysis of patent, copyright, trade mark and related law in three economies – New Zealand, Singapore and Israel – demonstrates why small market economies do (or should) develop their own approach to the design of intellectual property laws and institutions.

For theoreticians of international intellectual property law, these insights are provocative. Ultimately, the book suggests that true harmonisation is an unreasonable goal and that achieving distributive justice is not merely a transitional problem, solved as soon as all WTO countries catch up. Under this view, the BRICs' success in benefiting from TRIPS derives not only from their greater responsiveness to intellectual property incentives (as proponents of strong protection suggest) or from the fact that they were on the cusp of becoming robustly innovative at the time TRIPS came into force (as the other side claims), but, at least in part, because their markets are potentially as large as those of the United States, the European Union and Japan. As a result, there is enough local demand to spur creative production across a wide spectrum of endeavours. Moreover, there is sufficient domestic capacity to satisfy the bulk of the population's creative needs.

In contrast, advanced small market economies may, because they are relatively affluent, demand a range of sophisticated, high-quality products – blockbuster films, advanced therapeutics, fashionable attire – that local industry will never be in a position to fully supply. Because these nations are reliant on foreign sources, their interests in the conditions under which intellectual products can be *imported* will often reflect the interests of developing countries. But because local demand is often insufficient to support the creative production of which these countries are capable, they are heavily dependent on making sales abroad. Thus, their *export* interests will largely parallel those of the developed world. Finally, because these countries are already advanced, their interests are unlikely to change significantly over time. The flexibilities in TRIPS are, in short, not a temporary phenomenon that can be phased out in successive negotiations as all markets mature. Rather, they are necessary to do justice to the needs of the varied economies engaged in international trade in creative products.

But this presents a puzzle: if intellectual property rules are harmonised, creators – irrespective of their location – should be acting in response to global, not local, demand. And users – no matter where they live – should be drawing on worldwide supply. Why, then, should the size of national markets matter at all? A partial answer is that full harmonisation has yet to occur. But again, the book suggests that the problem may not be temporary. Local culture and policies determine how potential innovators are educated, the sorts of activities investors will support and the creative opportunities that are most evident to intellectual property-intensive industries. Local taste determines the feedback innovators most immediately receive. Furthermore, industries benefit from clustering and small markets can maintain fewer clusters. The sectors that do develop become salient in the economy, but other countries will not always share a strong interest in devising intellectual property rules that promote or support them. The example provided is the traditional knowledge of the Māori, for which New Zealand has developed its own sui generis domestic legislation. While New Zealand has also taken a leading role in promoting international protection, its achievements fall far short of the success large economies have enjoyed in seeing rights recognised in their special knowledge products (the inclusion of geographical indications in TRIPS, which benefits mainly the European Union, is an illustration).

From a practical point of view, the book is even more important. As it notes, small market economies can suffer from inadequate case law and too few specialist adjudicators. But the experiences of New Zealand, Singapore and Israel that are collected here can inform other small market economies of ways to deal both domestically and internationally with the issues arising uniquely within these nations. Thus, the book emphasises the importance of research: of deep knowledge of the country's industrial base, including what endeavours attract foreign investment, which local industries are primed to flourish, where importation is likely the only long-term solution, how national industries fit into emerging global value chains and which intellectual property rights are crucial to local producers. These factors affect such issues as which subject matter to protect and through which intellectual property right to protect it, the appropriate height of the inventive step, the right term of protection, what should count as infringement, the proper rules on parallel importation (international exhaustion) and the benefits of subsidisation. The book describes laws that demonstrate how to handle the disjuncture these countries experience between import and export interests. It also provides a valuable discussion on the compatibility of the suggested approaches with international law.

Negotiators should also pay heed to the lessons of this book. Increasingly, international intellectual property law making is becoming regional and plurilateral, with several small market economies included. (New Zealand and Singapore, for example, participate in the Anti-Counterfeiting Trade Agreement and the Trans-Pacific Partnership Agreement, both of which are intended to raise the level of intellectual property protection.) In these venues, the representatives of small market economies can suffer from the 'elephant bumping' illusion: at a bargaining table with elephants, they assume that they too are elephants, and that their countries will benefit from the rules proposed by the representatives of much larger economies. The book demonstrates why small market negotiators must be careful. And also why their participation is of global importance: not only do small market economies share interests with developing countries, but, to some extent, they also act as stand-ins for interests (such as user interests) that are overshadowed in the political economies of nations with larger markets.

Now that Susy Frankel has demonstrated that there is a limit to harmonisation, it behoves the international intellectual property community to find an approach to the global economy that is capable of greater nuance. Possibilities include tiers of protection, menus of choices and flexibilities, user rights, supplementing the floors of protection in minimum standard regimes with ceilings. Procedural reforms – international agreements on conflicts of law, jurisdiction, case consolidation and recognition of judgments – should also be on the table, for they would make the worldwide distribution of intellectual products and the global enforcement of intellectual property rights more efficient, while leaving ample space for cultural diversity and market differentials.

Preface

Since I began teaching and researching international intellectual property law, I have observed that frequently large players in the global debate about the scope and details of international intellectual property show little concern for promoting the interests of others around the globe. At the same time, they seek to extract maximum intellectual property related gains from those others. Perhaps this is simply a luxury resulting from being a powerful nation or a part of a relatively significant economic zone. Much intellectual property is created and innovated in the large countries of the developed world and for that we have to thank the creators and innovators of Europe and North America. The large countries of the developing world are, however, now significant players in intellectual property and have in many ways posed serious challenges to the developed world's approach to intellectual property. Developed and developing countries are of course many and varied. Small market economies are different again. They are dependent on global connectedness and they seek to trade with all. They are conscious of international differences and strive to retain their unique culture and identity. Such countries do not have the power to bring about global change or the luxury to 'go it alone'. From an intellectual property perspective, they are often like test tubes, that is, places for experimentation and legal innovation in how to reconcile the competing interests of globalisation and national autonomy inwith their law making. The experiments in these test tubes may sometimes be designed legal innovations and at other times less well planned. This book presents some experiences from these test-tube experiences.

There have been several stages in this project and there are many people to thank. I am extremely thankful to the New Zealand Law Foundation for funding much of the research. Research assistance has spanned several years and included students, past and present, of Victoria University of Wellington, Jessica Lai, Anne O'Driscoll, Danielle Thorne, Thomas McKenzie, Sereana Perry, and especially Rachel Collins. Thanks to Jessica Lai for more recent proofing assistance and comments.

Academic colleagues from around the world have generously commented on aspects of this project at various stages of its development; for that thanks in particular to Graeme Dinwoodie, Peter Drahos, Jane Ginsburg, Wee-Loon Ng Loy, Niva Elkin Koren, Ruth Okediji and Peter Yu. Special thanks to Daniel Gervais for comments on many chapters and discussions about the issues raised therein. Finally, I am especially grateful to Rochelle Dreyfuss for reading and commenting on this book and for her constant encouragement and support.

Abbreviations

ABS	access and benefit sharing
CBD	Convention on Biological Diversity of 1992
EPA	Economic Partnership Agreement
EWCA	Court of Appeal of England & Wales
EU	European Union
FDI	foreign direct investment
FTA	free trade agreement
GATS	General Agreement on Trade in Services
GATT	General Agreement on Tariffs and Trade
GI	geographical indication
IP	intellectual property
IPONZ	Intellectual Property Office of New Zealand
NZ	New Zealand
SCM	Agreement on Subsidies and Countervailing Measures
TCE	traditional cultural expression
TRIPS	Agreement on Trade-Related Aspects of Intellectual Property Rights
WCT	WIPO Copyright Treaty
WIPO	World Intellectual Property Office
WIPO-IGC	WIPO Intergovernmental Committee on Intellectual Property and Genetic Resources
WPPT	WIPO Performances and Phonograms Treaty
WTO	World Trade Organization

1 The unique position of small market economies

> IP for Development is an emphatic articulation of the notion that IP is not an end in itself but rather is a tool that could power countries' growth and development. WIPO, as the lead United Nations agency mandated to promote the protection of intellectual property through cooperation among states and in collaboration with other international organizations, is committed to ensuring that all countries are able to benefit from the use of IP for economic, social and cultural development. Implied in this are the notions of balance, accessibility and reward for creativity and innovation.[1]

> [T]he principle of proportionality is one of the more basic principles underlying the multilateral trading system, although there is no explicit reference to it in WTO law. However, the basic idea of proportionality, i.e. the due balancing of competing rights, is reflected several times in WTO agreements.[2]

How should a country use intellectual property for its own development? How should a country ensure its local publishing industry can produce high-quality literature, works of art and creative products and that its consumers have access to such goods from overseas at affordable prices? How can a country ensure that it has a local film industry or a local sound-recording industry and that its citizens have good access to movies and music from Hollywood and London? How can a country ensure that its own authors and copyright owners are able to thrive and produce works for the local culture? How can the environment be favourable to creating works of authorship that are both unique to that culture and have the potential to, but not necessarily need to, transcend national boundaries? How should a country ensure that its citizens can purchase high-quality pharmaceuticals even when they are not manufactured locally? How can a country retain its publicly funded health service and

[1] WIPO, 'Intellectual Property for Development', available at www.wipo.int/ip-development/en/agenda/.
[2] M. Hilf, 'Power, Rules and Principles – Which Orientation for WTO/GATT Law?', *Journal of International Economic Law*, 4 (2001), 111–130, at 120–121.

subsidised pharmaceutical systems? How can a country encourage research and development within its borders and also ensure that technology is transferred from overseas? How can local businesses ensure that their brands and trade marks help them achieve a competitive edge in the global marketplace? How can businesses be structured so as to achieve optimum gains from intellectual property when the local market is of a small scale and the international market may give better returns?

These are but a few questions that many nations' intellectual property policy makers and lawmakers may ask. These are not easy questions to answer and the answers will not be the same for all countries, or even for all intellectual property issues within a single country or regional grouping of countries. The relationship between protecting intellectual property and using intellectual property for economically, culturally and socially desirable outcomes, both within a country and across national borders, is at the heart of global issues in intellectual property.

In much of the literature, and in the political arena, the debate over the parameters of intellectual property is characterised as a contest between the intellectual property 'haves', predominantly developed countries, and the intellectual property 'have-nots', some developing countries and least-developed countries.[3] Such characterisation has many flaws. Of course, a degree of generalisation may be necessary, but in reality the 'have-nots' are not without intellectual property. They may lack access to developed world intellectual property and its related products because of both availability and cost, but they may have their own intellectual property, which may or may not be recognised at the international level. One such example is the protection of traditional knowledge, which is discussed in Chapter 9 in this book. In addition, large developing countries also compete in certain industries with large developed countries. The generic pharmaceutical industry is an example. The picture is not simple.

Small market economies

In this global intellectual property debate, there are groups of countries that wield very little international political power but often display ingenuity in balancing competing interests in the intellectual property field

[3] These terms are used by the United Nations. There is no general rule for the designations 'developed' or 'developing' country. Usually Europe, Canada and the United States in North America, Singapore and Japan in Asia and Australia and New Zealand in Oceania are considered 'developed'. For international trade purposes, Israel is a developed country. See United Nations, 'Standard Country or Area Codes for Statistical Use', Series M, No. 49, Rev. 4 (United Nations Publication, Sales No. M.98.XVII.9), available at http://unstats.un.org/unsd/methods/m49/m49regin.htm.

and consequently have sometimes demonstrated a unique approach in their intellectual property laws. These are the small market economies. These economies exhibit unique features which are relevant to how they balance competing interests in intellectual property. They are developed but small, so import much intellectual property, have consumers who can pay high prices and are pockets of innovative activities that are fed into the global value chain. The following three 'political' quotes are illustrative.

> Another outstanding feature . . . is to note that Israel is spending more money on research and development (as a percentage of GDP) than any other country. The success of the Israeli high-tech sector is well-known. Those of us who use Skype may recall that the VoIP technology (the Voice over the Internet Protocol) was invented in Israel. Israel has also highly-developed desert agriculture with a lot of expertise in irrigation and water conservation. The drip irrigation that we all know was developed on an Israeli kibbutz. In short, there is probably a lot that Members can learn from Israel when it comes to innovation. So may I put the question to you, what is the Israeli recipe for stimulating innovation and growth, and what benefits do you see for trade?[4]

> In 2007, P&G chose Singapore as the location for its first perfume manufacturing facility in Asia. As a plant which would lead the implementation of new process workflows and technologies for P&G worldwide, it plays a prominent role in driving the company's global perfume business. The Singapore facility is P&G's most technologically-advanced plant, with state-of-the-art innovations such as advanced real-time inventory and production control systems that monitor the production process and reflect changes instantly.[5]

> Ingenuity and innovation are characteristics Kiwis are renowned for, and the tourism industry in New Zealand is no exception. The Hamilton Jet, the ski plane, bungy, blokart and Zorb are all examples of Kiwi inventions that have pushed traditional boundaries of travel and embody the Kiwi sense of adventure. These examples have provided more unique ways to experience some of New Zealand's most scenic locations. New Zealand continues to push innovation in a range of other fields, from its traditional export industries such as agriculture and dairy, to newer growth areas such as fresh cuisine and award-winning wine.[6]

This book is concerned with how small market economies balance competing interests in intellectual property law and what the approach of such economies shows about global issues in intellectual property law. The book does not suggest that small market economies always come up with the perfect solution or can solve global intellectual property issues.

[4] Summary of Israel Trade Policy Review (WT/TPR/M/272), available at www.keionline.org/node/1576.

[5] Future Ready Singapore, 'Proctor & Gamble Innovating for Asian Consumers', available at www.edb.gov.sg/content/edb/en/case-studies/pg.html.

[6] 'Kiwi Innovation', available at http://media.newzealand.com/en/story-ideas/great-kiwi-inventions/.

Rather, an examination of how small market economies deal with intellectual property issues reveals some techniques and legal innovations that are effective experiments in balancing global issues.

Small market economies take international commitments seriously. They are not at liberty to ignore their international obligations and they do not do so. Such 'luxuries' can be the vice of large economies. Indeed, small market economies are critically aware of their international obligations and seek to comply with them. Much of this is because these countries cannot go it alone. They make up for what they lack in size, and the consequent issues of scale, by utilising the experience and where possible the marketplaces of the world. These countries are highly dependent on international trade.

Policy makers and lawmakers in small market economies often pay considerable attention to the detail of international law. New Zealand, for example, has brought disputes to the World Trade Organization (although not about intellectual property) and has participated as a third party in many disputes. It has never, however, had a dispute brought against it. This could be for any number of reasons, but the domestic approach shows significant concern with complying with international trade agreements. Singapore's record at the World Trade Organization is also that it has never had a dispute brought against it.[7] Small market economies are good global citizens and in varying degrees are highly dependent on international trade for their economic survival. This attention to the detail of international obligations is also found in small market economies' approach to intellectual property. This makes them good test tubes for finding the balance between competing interests because, from the outset, balancing national interests with global commitments is an integral part of the policy- and law-making process. To understand the process of weighing and sometimes accommodating the competing interests involved in intellectual property, it is necessary to consider some aspects of the 'developed versus developing countries' debate and the international intellectual property law framework.

Developed versus developing interests

Global issues in intellectual property law are many. There are issues about both the level of protection and the detail of protection. While the United States and the European Union, as substantial producers of intellectual

[7] New Zealand has been the complainant in eight cases, the respondent in none and participated as third party in over 30 disputes. Singapore has once been a complainant, never a respondent and a third party in over ten disputes, see World Trade Organization, 'Disputes by Country/Territory', available at www.wto.org/english/tratop_e/dispu_e/dispu_by_country_e.htm.

property and related products and services, are often in agreement that relatively high levels of intellectual property protection are desirable, there are many areas in which they disagree over what that protection should entail. Two examples are whether exclusions should be allowed from the scope of what is otherwise patentable[8] and whether databases that are not original creations should be protected.[9]

Although these disagreements[10] between the EU and the United States give rise to significant disputes, these large economies are frequently allies in the push for increased intellectual property standards globally. That allegiance is seen in regard to the major international agreements, such as negotiation for the Agreement on Trade-Related Aspects of Intellectual Property Rights (TRIPS Agreement),[11] and the EU and US approaches to negotiating TRIPS-plus free trade agreements (FTAs),[12] or in the case of the EU's so-called economic partnership agreements (EPAs).[13]

[8] The EU, for example, excludes patents which are contrary to *ordre public* and 'plant or animal varieties or essentially biological processes for the production of plants or animals' and 'methods for treatment of the human or animal body by surgery or therapy and diagnostic methods practised on the human or animal body', see European Patent Convention, art 53, as amended by the Act revising the European Patent Convention of 29 November 2000. Such exceptions are compliant with the WTO, Agreement on Trade-Related Aspects of Intellectual Property Rights, Marrakesh Agreement Establishing the World Trade Organization, Annex 1C, 1869 UNTS 299; 33 ILM 1197 (adopted on 15 April 1994, entered into force 1 January 1995), 'TRIPS Agreement', arts 27:2 and 27:3.

[9] The TRIPS Agreement, above n 8, art 10.2 provides that members shall protect databases that are original creations. In addition, the EU provides a right to prevent databases from unfair extraction, see Directive 96/9/EC of the European Parliament and of the Council of 11 March 1996 on the legal protection of databases. Disagreement exists over whether this is a TRIPS-plus or a sui generis right which is separate from TRIPS. Some commentators have argued that such protection is intellectual property and ought to be subject to the national treatment obligations of the TRIPS Agreement. See P. B. Hugenholtz, 'Implementing the European Database Directive', in Jan J. C. Kabel and Gerard J. H. M. Mom (eds.), *Intellectual Property and Information Law – Essays in Honour of Herman Cohen Jehoram*, (Kluwer, The Hague/London/Boston, 1998), pp. 183–200 and J. H. Reichman and P. Samuelson, 'Intellectual Property Rights in Data?', *Vanderbilt Law Review*, 50 (1997), 49–166 at 51.

[10] The difficulties over agreeing to a framework for the protection of audio-visual works make an example. The dispute at the WTO over exceptions to copyright is another example. See WTO Panel, *United States – Section 110(5) of the US Copyright Act*, WT/DS160/R, adopted 27 July 2000.

[11] See discussion of the Uruguay Round of negotiations leading to TRIPS, D. J. Gervais, *The TRIPS Agreement: Drafting History and Analysis*, 4th edn (Sweet & Maxwell, Croydon, UK, 2012), paras 1.19–1.22.

[12] The United States has openly stated that its policy is to use bilateral FTAs in order to increase intellectual property standards. For a discussion of the strategic use of bilaterals, see S. K. Sell, *Private Power, Public Law: The Globalisation of Intellectual Property Rights* (Cambridge University Press, 2003), at Chapter 6, 'Life after TRIPS Aggression and Opposition', at 121.

[13] The European Commission states that EPAs 'between the EU and African, Caribbean and Pacific (ACP) regions are aimed at promoting trade between the two groupings – and

Developing countries, particularly China, India and Brazil, have generally been against this push for increased standards because high standards of intellectual property protection can hinder development of local industry and local research.[14] There are, however, an increasing number of intellectual property owners in these countries. China topped some aspects of the World Intellectual Property Office (WIPO) patent statistics in 2012 and 2013.[15] As countries become less intellectual property users and more producers and creators of intellectual property, their approach to protection may change.[16]

One central example of the developed versus developing country debate is the numerous issues over pharmaceutical patents, including the availability of patents for second and subsequent uses of known pharmaceuticals[17] and the general affordability of and access to medicines. Underlying this sort of developed versus developing country debate is a series of tensions which may be presented as broad questions. These include:

- How should the frequently competing interests of developed and developing countries be balanced, or accommodated in a way that allows certain flexibilities, in international intellectual property law so that

through trade development, sustainable growth and poverty reduction'. See 'Economic Partnerships', available at http://ec.europa.eu/trade/policy/countries-and-regions/development/economic-partnerships/.

14 See R. C. Dreyfuss, 'The Role of India, China, Brazil and Other Emerging Economies in Establishing Access Norms for Intellectual Property and Intellectual Property Lawmaking' (30 July 2009), IILJ (Institute for International Law and Justice) Working Paper 2009/5, NYU School of Law, Public Law Research Paper No. 09–53, available at SSRN, ssrn.com/abstract=1442785 or dx.doi.org/10.2139/ssrn.1442785.

15 See 'Patent Statistics', available at www.wipo.int/ipstats/en/statistics/patents/.

16 This has certainly been the experience of the past, where countries such as the United States have had low protection until they developed their economies. One commentator has said, for example, 'In the nineteenth century in the US and on the continent, infringement and unauthorized borrowing were an important part of American industrial development. The British were the authors of much copyright piracy because they prohibited the sharing of British technological patents with American infant industries. US entrepreneurs borrowed, adapted and stole British patented processes whenever they could.' See D. Drache, 'Trade Development and the Doha Round: A Sure Bet or a Train Wreck?', Centre for International Governance Innovation, Working paper no 5 (March 2006), at 25, available at https://www.cigionline.org/publications/2006/3/trade-development-and-doha-round-sure-bet-or-train-wreck; Professor Gervais discusses the stages of development and their relationship with the movement from accessing intellectual property, to imitation, to developing local intellectual property in D. J. Gervais, 'IP Calibration', in D. J. Gervais (ed.), *Intellectual Property, Trade and Development*, 2nd edn (Oxford University Press, 2014), pp. 86–114.

17 Under the TRIPS Agreement, above n 8, art 27.1 members must make patents available in all fields of technology. The TRIPS Agreement does not define this any further. In some countries, when a new use of a known pharmaceutical is found, it may be patentable. Other countries reject this approach. New Zealand, Singapore and Israel protect new uses of known pharmaceuticals. For a general discussion, see S. Frankel, *Intellectual Property in New Zealand*, 2nd edn (Lexis Nexis, Wellington, 2011), at 412–416.

countries can appropriately adjust their domestic law to meet their economic and social needs?

- How should the players in the global system, whether they are large or small, or developed or developing countries, maximise their ability to produce and use intellectual property?
- Does the global intellectual property system make it possible for all to utilise intellectual property or does the system disadvantage intellectual property users and those more heavily reliant on importing intellectual property?
- Does the system favour those whose economy is involved substantively in the initial development of patented inventions and copyright creations?
- Does the international regime encourage innovation or is international patent law a stumbling block for some aspects of innovation?
- Does the international copyright regime support authors or does it hinder much creativity, ensuring that mostly only large creative industries flourish?

These issues are very contentious and not likely to be easily resolved. They have even evoked the suggestion that intellectual property law's existence is, or aspects thereof are, under threat.[18] There are perhaps threats to the ability of the international system for the time being to reach agreement on some core matters, but those threats do not extend to the foreseeable demise of the intellectual property system. The system may be on shaky ground in some areas and the multilateral negotiations have come to a standstill. This has meant that in recent years the international system has only addressed parts of the law that need change rather than the broader intellectual property picture. At the core of these tensions, however, lies a very strong and well-established international intellectual property regime and at the centre of that regime is the World Trade Organization (WTO) TRIPS Agreement[19] and the WIPO agreements, particularly the Berne Convention for the Protection of Literary and Artistic Works[20] and the Paris Convention for the Protection of Industrial Property[21] (both have also been incorporated into the TRIPS Agreement).[22]

[18] See, for example, R. C. Denicola, 'Mostly Dead? Copyright Law in the New Millennium', *Journal Copyright Society USA*, 47 (2000), 193–208, at 207 and G. S. Lunney Jr., 'The Death of Copyright: Digital Technology, Private Copying, and the Digital Millennium Copyright Act', *Virginia Law Review*, 87 (2001), 813–920, at 815.

[19] TRIPS Agreement, above n 8.

[20] Berne Convention for the Protection of Literary and Artistic Works (Paris text), 1161 UNTS 3, 24 July 1971 ('Berne Convention').

[21] Paris Convention for the Protection of Industrial Property, 828 UNTS 303 (adopted on 20 March 1883, entered into force 16 April 1970), as revised at Stockholm (14 July 1967) ('Paris Convention').

[22] TRIPS Agreement, above n 8, art 9.

An introduction to the international intellectual property law framework

The TRIPS Agreement is a formidable collection of minimum standards supported by the WTO and its dispute settlement regime.[23] The TRIPS Agreement is in many ways unique within the body of WTO agreements. It is the only WTO agreement structured around agreed minimum standards to be implemented in domestic law.[24] The TRIPS Agreement has, perhaps remarkably, been amended since it first came into being.[25] Also, members of the WTO have added to their international intellectual property obligations in many ways outside of the TRIPS Agreement framework, including through other multilateral agreements and by way of FTA commitments between two or sometimes more parties.[26]

At the time of its creation in the mid-1990s, the TRIPS Agreement was the international high water mark in intellectual property protection. Yet, in a relatively short period of time, it has become the baseline for intellec-

[23] The WTO dispute settlement regime applies to all WTO agreements and is incorporated into the TRIPS Agreement, above n 8, art 64. The procedure of dispute settlement is governed by the Understanding on Rules and Procedures Governing the Settlement of Disputes, Marrakesh Agreement Establishing the World Trade Organization, Annex 2 (1994) 1869 UNTS 401, 15 April 1994 ('DSU').

[24] The TRIPS Agreement is an instrument that members agree will have an impact on behind-the-border regulation. In other words, the mere act of signing up to TRIPS is a recognition that some degree of autonomy over intellectual property regulation is given up. The degree of autonomy is limited by the requirement of compliance with the agreement; see TRIPS Agreement, above n 8, art 1.1. For a discussion of the 'TRIPS story' and the narratives of 'coercion', 'ignorance and bargaining' and 'self-interest', see Gervais, above n 16.

[25] The amendment was the introduction of Article 31 bis, which allows members of the TRIPS Agreement to manufacture and import, under compulsory licence, certain pharmaceuticals in specified circumstances. This amendment followed the Doha Declaration on Public Health; see WTO Ministerial Conference, Fourth Session, Doha (9–14 November 2001), *Declaration on the TRIPS Agreement and Public Heath*, WT/MIN(01)/Dec/2 and Implementation of Paragraph 6 of the Doha Declaration on the TRIPS Agreement and Public Health, 2 September 2003, WT/L/540 and Amendment of the TRIPS Agreement, 8 December 2005, WT/L/641. Implementation required that two-thirds of the WTO members ratify the Article by 1 December 2007, which did not happen. The deadline was extended to 31 December 2009, 31 December 2011, 31 December 2013, and the latest General Council decision of 26 November 2013, WT/L/899, extended the deadline to 31 December 2015. Until then, a 'waiver' has been in place since 2003; WTO General Council, 'Implementation of Paragraph 6 of the Doha Declaration on the TRIPS Agreement and Public Health' (WTO Doc. WT/L/540 and Corr.1, 2003). See also C. M. Correa, 'Supplying Pharmaceuticals to Countries without Manufacturing Capacity: Examining the Solution Agreed Upon by the WTO on 30 August 2003', *Journal of Generic Medicines,* 1 (2004), 105–119.

[26] See Chapter 2 for further discussion of FTAs.

tual property protection globally.[27] The twentieth-century opponents of the TRIPS Agreement have now become its twenty-first-century advocates (the exception are least-developed countries that have extended time-frames to comply with TRIPS).[28] Even if some developing countries still regard TRIPS compliance as problematic, its demanding standards are closer to their interests than the TRIPS-plus standards that are settled or are on the negotiating agenda in bilateral or plurilateral FTAs.

There are some broad effects of the TRIPS Agreement and other international intellectual property agreements. One, as mentioned above, is that there are minimum standards of intellectual property protection globally. However, it is important to appreciate that global intellectual property standards are far from uniform. The standards are minimum requirements for national intellectual property protection. Countries will enact those standards in different ways.[29] Some countries will maximise flexibilities of and exceptions to those standards which other countries may have limited or no flexibilities for. Some countries will have increased standards. Others still will have a mix of increased standards and increased flexibilities and exceptions.

There are broadly three ways in which the minimum standards can result in different laws in different countries. First, because the terms used in the agreement in many instances are not defined, they are open to differing interpretations by national legislatures and courts and can be implemented in different ways. An example is the scope of 'inventive step' in patent law.[30] Apart from 'inventive step' meaning something consistent with the TRIPS Agreement's object and purpose, no definition is found in that agreement or any other multilateral agreement as to its parameters.[31] Therefore, it has different meanings in different legal systems. The second way in which different countries may have differing levels of protection, despite the existence of minimum standards, is that those standards may be increased by some, but not all, members of TRIPS. The TRIPS Agreement expressly states that its members may

[27] It seems likely that if discussion returns to the multilateral level, the baseline for that discussion will be the norms created through FTAs rather than the agreed multilateral norms.

[28] Least-developed countries do not have to fully comply with the TRIPS Agreement until at least 2015; see 'Extension of the Transition Period under Article 66:1 for Least Developed Country Members', IP/C/64, 12 June 2013.

[29] TRIPS Agreement, above n 8, art 1.1.

[30] TRIPS Agreement, above n 8, art 27.1 requires that patents are available for invention provided they are new, have an inventive step and are capable of industrial application. No definition of 'inventive step' is given.

[31] Some level of inventive step must be required to comply with the agreement. See also Chapter 5.

provide more extensive protection than what is found in the agreement.[32] The third mechanism that results in different national laws is that many international intellectual property agreements allow for carve-outs from some protections.[33] Fair use for research or parody, for example, may be legitimate carve-outs from the scope of copyright's exclusive rights. Experimental use of an invention may be a legitimate exception from patent rights, and descriptive use is a legitimate limitation on the exclusive rights of a trade mark owner.[34] But such exceptions are mostly optional and therefore not uniform in national laws.[35] In addition, in some FTAs, the ability to utilise the TRIPS Agreement flexibilities has been curbed.[36]

Balancing and calibration techniques: increased protection and flexibilities

Creating more extensive protection and framing exceptions to intellectual property protection involves a careful assessment of the interests of owners and users, other third-party interests and the overall public good. The ultimate result may balance those interests (in the sense of something for everyone) or choose one interest over the others so as to calibrate[37] the

[32] TRIPS Agreement, above n 8, art 1.1.

[33] Carve-outs in the form of exceptions and limitations are for the most part optional and must comply not only with the framework for the carve-out but also with the minimum standards of any agreement. In the case of the TRIPS Agreement, above n 8, carve-outs for patents are found in arts 27.2, 27.3 and 30. Article 30 is also known as a three-step test, which also provides the framework for exceptions for copyright in art 13 and art 9(2) of the Berne Convention (which is incorporated into the TRIPS Agreement) and art 17 for trade marks. Versions of the test are also found in the WIPO Copyright Treaty (WCT), 36 ILM 65 (1997) (adopted 20 December 1996, entered into force 6 March 2002), and the WIPO Performers and Producers of Phonograms Treaty 36 ILM 76 (1997) (adopted 20 December 1996, entered into force 20 May 2002). For a general discussion, see C. Geiger, D. J. Gervais and M. Senftleben, 'The Three-Step-Test Revisited: How to Use the Test's Flexibility in National Copyright Law' (18 November 2013), available at SSRN, ssrn.com/abstract=2356619 or dx.doi.org/10.2139/ssrn.2356619.

[34] This is expressly mentioned as an example in the TRIPS Agreement, above n 8, art 17.

[35] Although the exceptions are not uniform, many copyright laws, for example, incorporate exceptions for research and private study, education, libraries and archives.

[36] See, for example, the Australia–United States Free Trade Agreement (signed 18 May 2004, entered into force on 1 January 2005), where the parties agree to limit parallel importing in art. 17.9:4, which provides that 'Each Party shall provide that the exclusive right of the patent owner to prevent importation of a patented product, or a product that results from a patented process, without the consent of the patent owner shall not be limited by the sale or distribution of that product outside its territory, at least where the patentee has placed restrictions on importation by contract or other means.' In the leaked text of the Trans-Pacific Partnership Agreement (TPP), there are proposals for limiting exceptions. The leaked texts are available at tppinfo.org/resources/leaked-texts-country-info/.

[37] For discussion of the 'calibration phase' of the TRIPS Agreement, see Gervais, above n 16.

law to local needs. Legislative processes, although they consider some of these issues and competing interests, rarely have the luxury of looking beyond the particular statute at issue. Sometimes in smaller markets, however, that is exactly what happens. Some small market economy approaches to defining exclusive rights and providing appropriate carve-outs are far from perfect, but an examination of these economies' legislation reveals some unique experiments that are designed to benefit small market economies.

All nations may seek to achieve a balance in their domestic intellectual property laws that suits their domestic needs. Some openly state that this is their goal. The New Zealand government has said, for example, in relation to an amendment of copyright law:[38]

> The key principle that guides the development of copyright policy is the enhancement of the public interest – copyright laws must benefit New Zealand as a whole. While the term 'balance' is frequently used when discussing copyright policy, this balance is about the wider public interest, rather than simply achieving a middle ground between the competing aims of creators, owners and users of copyright works.

Others may have different goals. The same balancing discussion is found at the international level. However, the international issues of balance are perhaps more extreme. As mentioned above, there is considerable debate, for example, about the role patent law plays in access to patented pharmaceuticals and the availability of affordable medicines. This debate has reached serious proportions and remains substantively unresolved despite amendment to the TRIPS Agreement.[39] If one turns from patent to copyright, challenges are present there as well. The ability to protect works globally is challenging. Equally so is the ability to use flexibilities legitimately on the Internet, which is a matter of significant debate.[40] The ability to be flexible at the domestic law level depends not only on technical expertise but also on the extent of the relevant international obligations and the flexibilities that accompany those obligations.

At the international level, the terms 'flexibilities' and 'exceptions' (sometimes also 'exclusions' and 'exemptions') are variously used. Their place in

[38] Ministry of Economic Development, 'Digital Technology and the Copyright Act 1994 – Position Paper' (December 2002), Ministry of Business, Innovation and Employment, available at www.med.govt.nz/business/intellectual-property/pdf-docs-library/copyright/copyright-new-technologies-amendment-act-2008/position-paper-pdf, at 24.

[39] See above n 25.

[40] See, generally, P. B. Hugenholtz and R. L. Okediji, 'Conceiving an International Instrument on Limitations and Exceptions to Copyright, Final Report', 6 March 2008, available at www.ivir.nl/publicaties/hugenholtz/finalreport2008.pdf and S. Frankel, 'The International Copyright Problem', forthcoming 2014.

the international framework as a structural matter, as well as substantively, is important. If everything is categorised and conceived of as an exception, it tends to suggest (even if it is not exactly so) that rights owners are losing something. Intellectual property flexibilities may be an exception, but they may also be, as discussed above, a way of defining a minimum standard obligation to provide a right that is appropriate to local circumstances. In achieving a balance or calibration, it is important to conceive of the intellectual property system as having rights and exceptions not as binary and uncompromising opposites but as parts of a system with mutual dependencies.

International negotiations

The international debate is unfolding in a variety of ways and in a variety of institutions and relationships among them, including at the multilateral, plurilateral and bilateral levels. At the multilateral level, there are negotiations at the WTO, about the TRIPS Agreement (these are stalled at the time of writing),[41] and at WIPO. WIPO's ongoing negotiations include the protection of traditional knowledge in relation to genetic resources and traditional cultural expressions,[42] a concluded treaty for copyright exceptions for the visually impaired and ongoing negotiations for copyright exceptions.[43] Other multilateral fora, which are mainly focused on issues beyond intellectual property but which have a substantial intellectual property related agreement or discussion, include the Convention on Biological Diversity[44] and its Nagoya Protocol,[45] various human right instruments[46]

41 This round of negotiations is known as the Doha Round. In late 2013, there was some partial success in fields other than intellectual property. In intellectual property it was agreed that least-developed countries would not be required to comply with the TRIPS Agreement until 2015; see above n 28.

42 See discussion in Chapter 8.

43 Marrakesh Treaty to Facilitate Access to Published Works for Persons who are Blind, Visually Impaired, or Otherwise Print Disabled, adopted by the Diplomatic Conference, 27 June 2013, available at www.wipo.int/edocs/mdocs/diplconf/en/vip_dc/vip_dc_8.pdf.

44 Rio Convention on Biological Diversity 1760 UNTS 79; 31 ILM 818 (opened for signature 5 June 1992, entered into force 29 December 1993), 'CBD', available at www.cbd.int/.

45 The Nagoya Protocol is a supplementary agreement to the CBD; Nagoya Protocol on Access to Genetic Resources and the Fair and Equitable Sharing of Benefits Arising from their Utilization to the Convention on Biological Diversity (UN Doc. UNEP/CBD/COP/DEC/X/1, adopted on 29 October 2010). According to the CBD website, '[i]ts objective is the fair and equitable sharing of benefits arising from the utilization of genetic resources, thereby contributing to the conservation and sustainable use of biodiversity'.

46 See L. R. Helfer, 'The New Innovation Frontier? Intellectual Property and the European Court of Human Rights', *Harvard International Law Journal*, 49 (2008), 1–52; See also L. R. Helfer and G. W. Austin, *Human Rights and Intellectual Property: Mapping The Global Interface* (Cambridge University Press, 2011).

and the World Health Organization,[47] to name a few. At the plurilateral level, there has been an intellectual property enforcement agreement, Anti-Counterfeiting Trade Agreement, known as ACTA,[48] and emerging trade negotiations, which include intellectual property chapters. A significant plurilateral negotiation of this nature is the Trans-Pacific Partnership.[49] Additionally, bilateral trade agreements including intellectual property chapters have proliferated since the formation of the TRIPS Agreement.[50]

Many of the international issues may be debated in member countries at the domestic level as well. On some of these issues, small market economies often reach a unique accommodation because of their position with a foot in both the developed and developing country camps. They are developed countries but also net users of intellectual property. The net-user status in some ways makes them more like developing countries.

The position of small market economies

Small market economies share features that make them unique when compared to other economies. They are market economies and are part of the developed world. Consumers in small market economies also have high standards of living and demand products of the same quality as those found in large developed countries. Small market economies, therefore, have much in common with developed countries, whose overall approach to intellectual property is to provide protection for the scientific, technological and creative industries that form a significant part of those countries' economies. Obvious examples of such developed countries are the United States and many member states of the EU. Together, these large market economies are broadly net producers of intellectual property products. That is, they create for domestic consumption more intellectual property and related products than they import. Small market economies are not net producers of intellectual property. They are almost certainly net users because more intellectual property is imported than exported. In this way, small market economies have something in common with developing countries that are also net importers of intellectual property and rely heavily on technology transfer to establish local industries. In sum,

47 World Health Organization, 'Intellectual Property Rights', available at www.who.int/trade/glossary/story055/en/index.html.
48 Anti-Counterfeiting Trade Agreement, 15 April 2011, available at www.ustr.gov/acta. ACTA will probably never come into force.
49 See above n 36; C. L. Lim, D. K. Elms and P. Low, *The Trans-Pacific Partnership: A Quest for a Twenty-first Century Trade Agreement* (Cambridge University Press, 2012).
50 See discussion in Chapter 2.

small market economies stand uniquely with a foot in each of the developed and developing world camps. This has resulted in small market economies structuring aspects of their intellectual property laws, sometimes in unique ways, in order to find a balance between domestic interests and foreign intellectual property constraints. Such countries grapple in their national laws with what might be described at the international level as a competition between developed and developing country perspectives.

The scope of this book

This book draws on examples primarily from three small market economies: New Zealand, Singapore and Israel. These countries have many differences both geographically and politically, but also some commonalties. First, New Zealand and Singapore have populations of fewer than 6 million people and have a similar market size. Israel has an approximate population of 8 million. When I began this project, I also included Norway as a small market economy. That was because New Zealand and Norway have very similar patent and trade mark statistics at WIPO.[51] Research has revealed that Norway's approach to intellectual property, while interesting, is not helpfully analogous to those approaches that are exhibited by the other three examples. Perhaps this is because of Norway's approximate relationship with the rest of Europe and particularly the EU. There are other small market economies, but those such as Denmark and Finland, which are part of the EU, are less useful or comparable as examples for exactly that reason. By comparison to the United States and the EU, Canada and Australia may consider themselves small, but for the purposes of this book their market size is much greater than the small economies of New Zealand, Israel and Singapore. However, examples from Canadian and Australian intellectual property law are, where appropriate, also discussed in this book.

The political and geographic situations of New Zealand, Singapore and Israel are very different, but each country has many areas of intellectual property law that are uniquely designed in order to achieve what those countries see as balance. This book does not describe the laws of these countries in individual chapters. Rather, it uses examples from their laws to show how small market economies approach some aspects of intellectual property law and what the global community can learn from these approaches.

[51] See 'Patent Statistics', above n 15.

Another feature of the small market economies discussed in this book is that much of their law is adopted from other countries with quite different economic situations; however, in the last decade in particular, these countries have developed a more local-needs-based policy and interpretative approach to intellectual property law.

This book engages with economic and other policy discourses in intellectual property, but its primary focus is the law and policy as framed by national laws and international obligations. This book, through analysis of the competing interests found in small market economies, discusses not so much what an optimal intellectual property law for a small market economy is, but rather how issues can be balanced or calibrated in order to potentially achieve the best outcome or equilibrium between competing interests. The balance and adjustment that any country achieves with intellectual property will be different because stages of development, and consequently the appropriate levels of intellectual property protection and flexibilities, will differ.[52] But this sort of appropriate fit for circumstances, based on global minimum standards, is only possible if the necessary flexibility is recognised at the international level.[53] The analysis of examples drawn from small market economies, therefore, is in turn used to discuss how global issues in intellectual property might be effectively balanced.

There is no one solution for intellectual property protection. Put differently, there can be no one-size-fits-all intellectual property law. Differing economic and cultural conditions around the world mean there will be inevitable differences in intellectual property law and doubtless in other areas of law as well. This book does not suggest that one harmonised intellectual property standard can be found. Rather, it illustrates how a better balance might be achieved in some aspects of global intellectual property law and how this balance is already at work in several small market economies. But, as discussed above, small market economies do, like other countries, sometimes get it wrong or even do not know what to do. Thus, the book also includes suggestions as to how the laws might be improved.

Chapter 2 explains and analyses the international framework in which all countries operate intellectual property laws. In particular, it discusses the TRIPS Agreement, WIPO agreements and FTAs. The chapter explains the parameters of those agreements and the extent to which such agreements allow the balancing of competing interests in intellectual property law. The chapter also discusses the limits of those agreements.

[52] See, generally, Gervais, above n 16. [53] See Hugenholtz and Okediji, above n 40.

Chapter 3 discusses the legal rules of interpretation of international agreements. These are found in the Vienna Convention on the Law of Treaties (VCLT).[54] While the rules are well known, the method and scope of their application, in relation to intellectual property in particular, is relatively new. Better interpretation of international agreements is important not only for better outcomes but also as guidance for domestic lawmakers who wish to understand and comply effectively, but not necessarily unduly restrictively such as not using appropriate flexibilities and exceptions, with international agreements.

Next, Chapter 4 examines how science, technology, innovation and cultural policies impact intellectual property law in national regimes and how that, in turn, is reflected in international agreements. Countries that seek to develop or maintain domestic intellectual property businesses often try to subsidise those businesses. International agreements, particularly those of the WTO, permit subsidies and domestic support only in situations that do not discriminate against the goods or services of other WTO members or that are expressly permitted in the WTO agreements. Chapter 4 discusses that framework and explains how such industries might be legitimately subsidised and what, arguably, is not compliant with the WTO.

The book then turns to consider the three core areas of intellectual property law: patents, copyright and trade mark law. Chapter 5 looks at patent law flexibilities and the relationship between patent term extension, regulatory review exceptions and experimental use. This chapter also discusses how patent law rationales are framed on territorial concepts of research and development, manufacture and distribution and how that territorial mechanism does not reflect the role that small market economies may have in patent-related global value chains.

Chapter 6 discusses approaches to copyright. Digital technology and the Internet continue to challenge, and necessitate changes to, copyright law. This is a vast area. The focus of this chapter is on small market economy examples of approaches to copyright, including how the laws of Singapore and Israel, in particular, have moved from a delineated permitted use approach to exceptions to a combined fair use[55] with guidelines and permitted use approach. Also discussed is New Zealand's approach of allowing access to copyright works, even if that involves circumventing technological protection mechanisms, while

[54] Vienna Convention on the Law of Treaties, 23 May 1969, 1115 UNTS 331, 8 ILM 679 (adopted 22 May 1969, entered into force 17 January 1980) ('VCLT').

[55] Fair use is usually primarily associated with US law, and permitted acts with the United Kingdom and its former colonies.

circumvention for copying is always prohibited. Another New Zealand experiment that this chapter considers is its Copyright Tribunal's jurisdiction relating to repeat infringement online.[56]

Chapter 7 focuses on trade marks, which have expanded their scope to incorporate what are sometimes referred to as expressive[57] and functional values.[58] Trade marks are perhaps the 'cheapest' form of intellectual property. They are usually less expensive to register than patents because they are more easily examined.[59] For many small businesses, trade marks have become their primary intellectual property tool. Patents are too expensive and copyright is not always suitable. This practice of heavy reliance on trade marks seems to be prevalent in small market economies and this chapter discusses that phenomenon.

Small market economies parallel import. This is broadly because their market size often makes it effective to do so. In Chapter 8, the approach of Singapore, New Zealand and Israel to parallel importation is discussed. As test tubes of the international exhaustion question, these economies illustrate the delicate balancing act between supporting local businesses and reducing prices through parallel importation. The reaction of the United States to these parallel import policies has not been positive and that is also discussed.

Chapter 9 provides an insight into traditional knowledge protection. Here the examples are largely drawn from New Zealand, where the debate over the protection of traditional knowledge is advanced in global terms. New Zealand is often a leader in recognising indigenous peoples' rights, and so some might say that this is a unique feature of New Zealand. The debate over traditional knowledge has not yet led to complete legal change in New Zealand.[60] The New Zealand-based discussion, however, of the global effects and issues relating to the protection of traditional

[56] At the time of writing, I am the Chair of the New Zealand Copyright Tribunal.

[57] For a discussion of the many uses of trade marks, see R. Dreyfuss, 'Reconciling Trademark Rights and Expressive Values: How to Stop Worrying and Learn to Love Ambiguity', in G. B. Dinwoodie and M. D. Janis (eds.), *Trademark Law and Theory: A Handbook of Contemporary Research* (Edward Elgar Publishing, Cheltenham, 2008), pp. 261–293.

[58] See, generally, A. Firth, 'Signs, Surfaces, Shapes and Structures – The Protection of Product Design under Trade Mark Law', in Dinwoodie and Janis, above n 57, pp. 498–523.

[59] Trade marks are, according to the TRIPS Agreement, registrable provided that they, among other criteria, are capable of distinguishing one trader's goods from those of another trader; see TRIPS Agreement, above n 8, art 15. Patent examination requires extensive knowledge of the prior art relevant to the field. Prior art is relevant to the criteria of novelty and inventive step/non-obviousness, which are requirements for patents, TRIPS Agreement, art 27.1. Of course, some trade mark cases require extensive evidence, but broadly patents are more expensive to obtain and enforce.

[60] See discussion in Chapter 8.

knowledge is a manifestation of the global issues, which are debated at the WTO,[61] WIPO[62] and the CBD.[63] In this way New Zealand is, as the title of this book suggests, a test tube for the global issues around the protection of traditional knowledge. In this chapter, I suggest that one of the reasons for the New Zealand approach to traditional knowledge is that as a small market economy there is considerable need, or perhaps incentive, to work through these issues in a way that is different from that followed by larger developed economies with indigenous peoples, such as Australia, Canada and the United States.

In the final chapter, the book draws together the themes fully discussed in the other chapters. This chapter highlights the overall conclusions of each chapter and how they link to one another to form parts of a cohesive and optimal intellectual property law framework. The focus in the final chapter is on what the international community can learn from the small market economy experience.

61 See, generally, the 'Article 27.3b, Traditional Knowledge, Biodiversity', available at www.wto.org/english/tratop_e/trips_e/art27_3b_e.htm, accessed 22 November 2013. See also Gervais, above n 16, paras 1.79–1.94.

62 See WIPO, 'Traditional Knowledge', available at www.wipo.int/tk/en/.

63 CBD, above n44.

2 Trading in intellectual property

The TRIPS Agreement and free trade agreements

> While it may be good rhetoric for proponents of strong protection to argue that the TRIPS Agreement establishes a comprehensive intellectual property regime for all members of the WTO . . . it makes little sense from a normative, prescriptive or pragmatic perspective.[1]

> The current phase ... is a *calibration phase*, which operates on two different, yet related levels. *Domestically*, calibration allows countries and regions to tailor policy to their potential strengths in innovation while alleviating negative welfare costs. At the level of *international norm-making*, calibration supports attempts to reflect both the need for minimum common denominators and the need to tailor innovation-related rules and policies. Finding a proper admixture of international IP disciplines (which, for many WTO members, meant foreign because TRIPS rules are a reflection of intellectual property notions largely developed in the 'West') and endogenous contextual realities *requires* calibration.[2]

> I explicitly treat development as a pseudonym for a complex network of benefits associated with economic growth and human social capital. The integral role of technological change in national growth prospects requires that the nature and causes of technology production remain critical considerations ... specifically the relationship between IP protection and technology creation.[3]

The above three quotes encapsulate the role of international intellectual property agreements, particularly the Agreement on Trade-Related Aspects of Intellectual Property Rights (TRIPS Agreement),[4] not as a

[1] G. B. Dinwoodie and R. Dreyfuss, *A Neofederalist Vision of TRIPS: The Resilience of the International Intellectual Property Regime* (Oxford University Press, 2012), at 14 ('*A Neofederalist Vision of TRIPS*').

[2] D. J. Gervais, 'IP Calibration', in D. J. Gervais (ed.), *Intellectual Property, Trade and Development*, 2nd edn (Oxford University Press, 2014), pp. 86–116, at 87.

[3] R. L. Okediji, 'History Lessons for the WIPO Development Agenda', in N. Netanel (ed.), *Intellectual Property and Developing Countries* (Oxford University Press, 2009), pp. 137–162, at 140–141.

[4] WTO, Agreement on Trade-Related Aspects of Intellectual Property Rights, Marrakesh Agreement Establishing the World Trade Organization, Annex 1C, 1869 UNTS 299; 33

fixed supranational set of rules[5] but as a set of minimum standards and an international framework that shapes, but does not prescriptively govern, national intellectual property laws. Put differently, minimum standards govern international intellectual property and those minimum standards result in some, but far from complete, harmonisation of rules. The recognition and operation of national autonomy in order to achieve appropriate domestic calibration reflects both domestic and international goals, which include development goals.[6] Development goals may very well look different depending on where in the world the development is taking place and the overall level of development in that place. Development is often used to refer to the growth factors in developing countries which will lead those countries towards developed country status. Developed countries are also involved in development, even if it is further along the development spectrum.[7]

It can be difficult to calibrate intellectual property rules exactly for development, as development will likely depend on factors that are additional to those rules, including higher education, clustering of innovators and creators, and access to financing.[8] The existence of these other factors is important and will likely contribute to the rationales for framing an appropriately calibrated intellectual property law. Those other factors should not, however, become a reason to not fully address the intellectual

ILM 1197 (adopted on 15 April 1994, entered into force 1 January 1995) ('TRIPS Agreement').

[5] Many never thought it was this, but its history seemed to have painted it that way in some commentaries, perhaps because – as the Dinwoodie and Dreyfuss quote from *A Neofederalist Vision of TRIPS*, above n 1, suggests – that would have been convenient for proponents of strong rights.

[6] Both the WTO and WIPO have established development goals; see WTO, 'Millennium Development Goals, The Doha Development Agenda', available at www.wto.org/english/thewto_e/coher_e/mdg_e/dda_e.htm and WIPO, 'Development Agenda for WIPO', available at www.wipo.int/ip-development/en/agenda/. Gervais, above n 2, however, notes that establishing broad development goals internationally is not the same as implementing them locally. For a case study, see A. Kapczynski, 'Harmonization and Its Discontents: A Case Study of TRIPS Implementation in India's Pharmaceutical Sector', *California Law Review*, 97 (2009), 1571–1649.

[7] After all, the reason for protecting patents, for example, is the progress of science and technology, which is a central feature of economic development.

[8] Similar discussions of the role of intellectual property in regard to foreign direct investment can be found in the literature. Intellectual property rules may encourage investment, but they are not always necessary to encourage investment; see K. E. Maskus, 'The Role of Intellectual Property Rights in Encouraging Foreign Direct Investment and Technology Transfer', *Duke Journal of Comparative and International Law*, 9(1) (1998), 109–161; L. Branstetter and K. Saggi, 'Intellectual Property Rights, Foreign Direct Investment, and Industrial Development', NBER Working Paper No. 1539, October 2009; P. K. Yu, 'Intellectual Property, Economic Development, and the China Puzzle', in D. J. Gervais (ed.), *Intellectual Property, Trade and Development: Strategies to Optimize Economic Development in a TRIPS Plus Era* (Oxford University Press, 2006), pp. 173–220.

property question. International intellectual property norms should allow for flexibilities and appropriate adjustments at the domestic level so that at least intellectual property is not a barrier to development, even if it cannot be realistically pinpointed as the sole contributor to that goal.[9]

There is much written about the TRIPS Agreement: how it came into being, what it has achieved and still might achieve.[10] This chapter will not repeat that discussion; rather, it will look at aspects of the TRIPS Agreement and the intellectual property chapters in free trade agreements (FTAs) from the small market economy perspective.[11]

There are some notable features of small market economies and FTAs. The first is that these economies, particularly Singapore and New Zealand, enter into many FTAs. As stated in the Introduction, these countries are significantly dependent on international trade. Consequently, that they pursue trade agreement opportunities is not necessarily surprising. As is also found in some other countries, there has been a very strong political belief that entering into such agreements is beneficial for the progress of trade liberalisation and their country's trade in particular. Part of the relevant provision in the General Agreement on Tariffs and Trade (GATT Agreement) supports this aim.[12]

> The contracting parties recognize the desirability of increasing freedom of trade by the development, through voluntary agreements, of closer integration between the economies of the countries parties to such agreements. They also recognize that the purpose ... of a free-trade area should be to facilitate trade between the constituent territories and not to raise barriers to the trade of other contracting parties with such territories.

[9] 'Intellectual property can always be characterized as a barrier to trade because the very existence of an intellectual property right can be used to prevent the import or export of a product. The status of the TRIPS Agreement as a covered agreement in the WTO has the effect of recognizing intellectual property, within certain agreed limits, as an "acceptable barrier". The significance of the trade barriers that intellectual property can create is that over-protecting intellectual property can be an inhibitor to the free flow of technology and the progress of science globally. If in practice real barriers were created, then neither the objectives of intellectual property law nor international trade would be met. Over-protecting intellectual property does not achieve the barrier-lowering objectives of international trade, but in fact inhibits it. The TRIPS Agreement in its preamble makes it clear that it should be read in a way that is consistent with free trade. In fact, any other interpretation would be at odds with the WTO context' (citations omitted). See S. Frankel, 'The WTO's Application of "the Customary Rules of Interpretation of Public International Law" to Intellectual Property', *Virginia Journal of International Law*, 46 (2005), 365–428, at 374–375 ('*WTO's Application of the Customary Rules*').

[10] See D. J. Gervais, *The TRIPS Agreement: Drafting History and Analysis*, 4th edn (Sweet & Maxwell, London, 2012) ('*Drafting History and Analysis*').

[11] See the Introduction for an outline of that perspective.

[12] General Agreement on Tariffs and Trade (GATT), 30 October 1947, 55 UNTS, 194, art XXIV.4.

That FTAs can be beneficial is contested[13] and it is widely accepted that there are difficulties with the GATT allowance of FTAs.[14] Some say that FTAs damage the system.[15]

Israel, Singapore and New Zealand enter into FTAs with larger economies and also with smaller economies. Some of these arrangements have been described as overtly and predominantly political, such as the US–Israel FTA.[16] Others may build on existing alliances such as the Australia and New Zealand FTA with ASEAN[17] and negotiations with Pacific Island countries.[18]

Small market economies, and Singapore and New Zealand in particular, have an eclectic set of intellectual property obligations in their FTAs. This is broadly reflective of the view, discussed above, that intellectual property rules should be appropriate for the level of development. Consequently, when entering into FTAs with developing countries, Singapore and New Zealand have not tended to add extensive intellectual property obligations to those of the TRIPS Agreement.[19]

[13] In relation to New Zealand, see, for example, J. Kelsey, *The New Zealand Experiment: A World Model for Structural Adjustment?* (Auckland University Press, 1995).

[14] See P. Artiran, 'A Different Approach to the External Trade Requirement of GATT Article XXIV: Assessing "Other Regulations of Commerce" in the Context of EC Enlargement and Its Heightened Regulatory Standards', in M. Lewis and S. Frankel (eds.), *International Economic Law and National Autonomy* (Cambridge University Press, 2009), pp. 216–240.

[15] See J. Bhagwati, *Like Termites in the Trading System: How Preferential Agreements Undermine Free Trade* (Oxford University Press, 2008) ('*Like Termites in the Trading System*'). See also J. Bhagwati, 'Why the TPP Is Undermining the Doha Round', Eaber and Saber newsletter 2013, available at www.eaber.org; see also discussion below.

[16] United States–Israel Free Trade Agreement (signed 22 April 1985, entered into force 1 January 1995), available at www.ustr.gov/trade-agreements/free-trade-agreements/israel-fta. Described as overtly political in Bhagwati, *Like Termites in the Trading System*, above n 15.

[17] ASAEN–Australia–New Zealand Free Trade Agreement (signed 27 February 2009, in force for all states from 10 January 2012), available at www.asean.fta.govt.nz/.

[18] 'The original Pacific Agreement on Close Economic Relations (PACER), finalised in 2001, envisages the gradual trade and economic integration of the economies of the Forum members in a way that is fully supportive of sustainable development of the Forum Island Countries and contributes to their gradual and progressive integration into the international economy. PACER Plus negotiations for a regional trade and economic integration agreement were launched by Pacific Islands Forum Leaders at their 40th Meeting in August 2009.' See www.mfat.govt.nz/Foreign-Relations/Pacific/Trade/index.php.

[19] Obligations which extend those in the TRIPS Agreement are often referred to as TRIPS-plus obligations. These obligations must be extended to all members of TRIPS on national treatment and most-favoured nation basis. Extra obligations outside of the scope of the TRIPS Agreement do not have to be provided on this basis. Consequently, the distinction between what is and what is not TRIPS-plus can be important. For a discussion of what TRIPS-plus means, see S. Frankel, 'Challenging TRIPS-plus Agreements: The Potential Utility of Non-Violation Disputes', *Journal of*

They sometimes do add to TRIPS Agreement obligations in agreeing to provide technical assistance or allowing the protection of traditional knowledge, whereas, when entering into FTAs with the developed countries, TRIPS-plus provisions are found.[20] This phenomenon, which is more prevalent in Singapore's FTAs than New Zealand's or Israel's FTAs, is further discussed below.

Depending on who is the other party, the hegemonic relationship, and consequently the likely outcome of the deal, changes.[21] When entering into non-multilateral trade agreements with even smaller economies, these small market economies have been the demanders, but such demands are not necessarily intellectual property related.[22] When entering into agreements with larger economies, small market economies have sometimes accepted intellectual property related terms for other trade-related benefits, which if assessed independently of those other supposed benefits would not be economically credible in the small market economy.[23] However, because these intellectual property concessions may bring benefits in other areas, small market economies use intellectual property as a kind of expedient trade-off.[24] This trade-off approach is usually attributed to developing countries.[25] This is one way

International Economic Law, 12(4) (2009) ('*Challenging TRIPS-plus Agreements*'), 1023–1066, at 1031–1036.

[20] To date, New Zealand does not have an FTA with the United States or the EU, who are the main demanders of TRIPS-plus standards. Until recently, the relationship with Australia has not included intellectual property. This changed when they agreed to complete FTAs together with others. See, for example, the FTA with ASEAN, above n 17.

[21] See P. Drahos, 'When the Weak Bargain with the Strong: Negotiations in the World Trade Organization', *International Negotiation*, 8 (2003), 79–109, where he discusses how developing countries are in a better position to pursue multilateralism than bilateralism, but that multilateralism may also be problematic.

[22] New Zealand, for example, is often a demander of the services relating to the education sector of the GATS Agreement. For a critical perspective, see J. Kelsey, *The Political Economy of Trade in Services Agreements* (Routledge-Cavendish, Oxford, 2008).

[23] Costing regulatory measures is complicated. For a discussion of the ways in which cost–benefit analysis and other tools can be used, see C. Nixon and J. Yeabsley, 'Voyage of Discovery: How Do We Bring Analytical Techniques to State Driven Behaviour Change?', in S. Frankel and J. Yeabsley (eds.), *Framing the Commons: Cross Cutting Issues in Regulation* (Victoria University Press, Wellington, 2014), pp. 140–175.

[24] For a discussion of how New Zealand might agree to patent term extension even though studies show it will cost millions, see S. Frankel, M. Lewis, C. Nixon and J. Yeabsley, 'The Web of Trade Agreements and Alliances and Impacts on Regulatory Autonomy', in S. Frankel and D. Ryder (eds.), *Recalibrating Behaviour: Smarter Regulation in a Global World* (LexisNexis, Wellington, 2013), pp. 17–62, (*Recalibrating Behaviour*).

[25] See, for example, the discussion of intellectual property as a trade-off in H. G. Ruse-Khan and others, 'Principles for Intellectual Property Provisions in Bilateral and Regional Agreements', *International Review of Intellectual Property and Competition Law*, 44 (2013), 878–883. See also S. Sell, *Private Power, Public Law: The Globalization of*

in which small market economies may, out of necessity, function more like developing countries, with some limited negotiating power,[26] rather than functioning like developed countries. Both of these aspects of small market economies and FTAs will be discussed in this chapter. Before that, it is necessary to outline the relevant features of the TRIPS Agreement and the legal features of FTAs.

Key features of the TRIPS Agreement

Applying dispute settlement to intellectual property

The TRIPS Agreement is part of the World Trade Organization (WTO) agreements and as such applies the WTO dispute settlement process to intellectual property.[27] The WTO members sit as the Dispute Settlement Body (DSB).[28] The DSB adopts as rulings (or can chose not to adopt) recommendations of dispute settlement panels and the Appellate Body. Panels are appointed on an ad hoc basis for each dispute. The Appellate Body is a standing body. The Dispute Settlement Understanding (DSU) governs the overall procedure of dispute settlement at the WTO.[29] Dispute settlement provides a forum for resolving conflicts over interpretation of the TRIPS Agreement. Strictly speaking, rulings of the DSB do not have precedent value in the sense of being binding on the making of future decisions.[30] They do, however, have considerable influence on other disputes and, importantly, on how national legislatures and policy makers interpret the Agreement.[31]

Intellectual Property Rights (Cambridge University Press, 2003), where the introduction begins by discussing why Chile went from refusal to agreement to protect pharmaceutical patents.

26 This would not include least-developed countries because small market economies could, like some developing countries, actually gain from such a trade-off.

27 TRIPS Agreement, above n 4, art 64.

28 This is made up of representatives of the members of the WTO.

29 Understanding on Rules and Procedures Governing the Settlement of Disputes, 15 April 1994, Marrakesh Agreement Establishing the World Trade Organization, Annex 2 (1994) 1869 UNTS 401 ('DSU').

30 The report of a WTO dispute is only binding between the parties to the dispute. However, WTO reports are treated increasingly as having precedential value. The Appellate Body has said that cogent reasons should be given if panels depart from its decisions; see Appellate Body Report, *United States – Final Anti-Dumping Measures on Stainless Steel from Mexico*, WT/DS344/AB/R, 30 April 2008, at para 160.

31 The interpretation of TRIPS in this dispute settlement regime is discussed in Chapter 3.

Structural features of TRIPS

The TRIPS Agreement begins with several paragraphs of preamble and then moves into general provisions, which are followed by substantive minimum standards. The preamble and general provisions are important structural features of the Agreement.[32] The preamble captures many broad aims of the Agreement as a whole and recognises certain unique features about the TRIPS Agreement. These include the role of the TRIPS Agreement as a trade agreement; the role of the GATT[33] as an influence on TRIPS; the need to protect and enforce intellectual property; the recognition that intellectual property rights are private rights which should be protected; the role of intellectual property in not creating trade barriers; and the need for recognition of the underlying policy objectives of national intellectual property systems.

The general provisions, which form the first section of the Agreement, apply the non-discrimination principles of national treatment[34] and most-favoured nation (MFN)[35] to intellectual property law. MFN's most significant impact relates to FTAs. This is further discussed below. National treatment is a principle which was well developed in international intellectual property before the TRIPS Agreement. National treatment is the core structural principle of the Berne Convention[36] and the Paris Convention.[37] National treatment simply means that all rights holders, whether nationals or foreigners, must be treated the same before national courts, tribunals, administrative bodies and registries – that is, without discrimination – with regard to intellectual property rights. Other structural features of the TRIPS Agreement include the objectives and principles, particularly those set out in Articles 7 and 8.[38]

[32] I have argued that some TRIPS-plus FTAs effectively violate these objectives; see Frankel, *Challenging TRIPS-plus Agreements*, above n 19.

[33] GATT, above n 12. [34] TRIPS Agreement, above n 4, art 3.

[35] TRIPS Agreement, above n 4, art 4.

[36] Berne Convention for the Protection of Literary and Artistic Works, 24 July 1971 (Paris Text), 1161 UNTS, p. 3 ('Berne Convention'), where national treatment in bilateral treaties took different forms of material and formal reciprocity. See S. Ricketson and J. Ginsburg, *International Copyright and Neighbouring Rights: The Berne Conventions and Beyond*, 2nd edn (Oxford University Press, 2005), at 25–27. There are a few exceptions to national treatment in the Berne Convention; see Ricketson and Ginsburg, at 319–321.

[37] Paris Convention for the Protection of Industrial Property ('Paris Convention') (Stockholm Text 1967), 828 UNTS, p. 303.

[38] For a discussion of Articles 7 and 8, see Frankel, *WTO's Application of the Customary Rules*, above n 9, 365–431; P. K. Yu, 'The Objectives and Principles of the TRIPs Agreement', *Houston Law Review*, 46 (2009), 797–1046.

Aspects of these structural features were hard won in the negotiation process.[39] The objective and principles are an embodiment of developing countries' concerns in particular. A key example is that members may 'in formulating or amending their laws and regulations, adopt measures necessary to protect public health and nutrition, and to promote the public interest in sectors of vital importance to their socio-economic and technological development'.[40] Subsequently, the way in which these principles have been interpreted and how they interact with the core obligations of the TRIPS Agreement have been under some scrutiny. These Articles are directed at recognising the flexibilities of the agreement and the scope of compatible exceptions. They are a counterforce to the notion that the TRIPS Agreement is a supranational code of protection. Articles 7 and 8, however, are not stand-alone exceptions to TRIPS.[41] They are part of the general provisions. They do, however, provide a strong normative basis which is directly relevant to the framing of exceptions (within the rules set out in other parts of the agreement). They are a strong policy statement and guide.[42]

Importantly, the general provisions of the TRIPS Agreement also include a provision that requires that members of the WTO to comply with the Agreement.[43] Also, members are 'free to determine the appropriate method of implementing the provisions' in their domestic law and they may have more extensive protection.[44] Both the power of and constraint of this Article were recognised and confirmed in the Panel Report of the dispute over enforcement of intellectual property in China.[45] The WTO Panel said,[46]

> The first sentence of Article 1.1 sets out the basic obligation that Members 'shall give effect' to the provisions of this Agreement. This means that the provisions of the Agreement are obligations where stated . . . The second sentence of Article 1.1 clarifies that the provisions of the Agreement are minimum standards only, in that

[39] Dinwoodie and Dreyfuss therefore suggest that the idea that developing countries were forced into the TRIPS Agreement is questionable; see *A Neofederalist Vision of TRIPS*, above n 1, at 22.

[40] TRIPS Agreement, above n 4, art 7.

[41] Significantly, Article 8 uses the phrase 'provided that such measures are consistent with the provisions of this Agreement'. In other words, Article 8 cannot override the provisions of the Agreement.

[42] See S. Frankel and D. J. Gervais, 'Plain Packaging and the Interpretation of the TRIPS Agreement', *Vanderbilt Journal of Transnational Law*, 46 (2013), 1149–1214 ('*Interpretation of TRIPS*'), at 1203; see also Chapter 3.

[43] TRIPS Agreement, above n 4, art 1.1. [44] TRIPS Agreement, above n 4, art 1.1.

[45] WTO Panel Report, *China – Measures Affecting the Protection and Enforcement of Intellectual Property Rights*, 20 March 2009, WT/DS362/R.

[46] *China – Measures Affecting the Protection and Enforcement of Intellectual Property Rights*, above n 45, at 7.513.

it gives Members the freedom to implement a higher standard, subject to a condition. The third sentence of Article 1.1 does not grant Members freedom to implement a lower standard, but rather grants freedom to determine the appropriate method of implementation of the provisions to which they are required to give effect under the first sentence.

This three-part framework of Article 1.1 is the way in which the TRIPS Agreement requires minimum standards protection but preserves national autonomy over flexibility – including both increased levels of protection and recognised exceptions – and implementation of those minimum standards.

Subject matter coverage

The Agreement requires that members provide minimum standards in key fields of intellectual property law (copyright, trade marks and patents) and related rights (including geographical indications, performers' rights and the protection of integrated circuits).[47] The coverage is broad but there are gaps, as not all aspects of all subject matter are covered and there are not minimum standards for all details of all topics. These gaps become important when interpreting the Agreement. The rules of interpretation mean that the Agreement should be interpreted as it is written and, therefore, any gaps cannot be filled in by way of interpretation.[48] The gaps are also recognisable because they may relate to topics on which no agreement was reached in the TRIPS Agreement negotiations or to topics that TRIPS did not anticipate and are, therefore, simply not addressed in the Agreement. An example of a topic about which agreement was not reached is whether intellectual property rights should be exhausted nationally. Because no agreement was reached, TRIPS provides that exhaustion issues cannot be brought to dispute settlement.[49] Traditional knowledge is an example of a topic that is not addressed in TRIPS.[50]

[47] TRIPS Agreement, above n 4, art 1.2 provides 'For the purposes of this Agreement, the term "intellectual property" refers to all categories of intellectual property that are the subject of Sections 1 through 7 of Part II.' These include copyright and related rights, trade mark, geographical indications, industrial designs, patents, layout designs (topographies) of integrated circuits, protection of undisclosed information and control of anti-competitive practices in contractual licences.

[48] See Chapter 3 for interpretation.

[49] TRIPS Agreement, above n 4, art 6, provides: 'For the purposes of dispute settlement under this Agreement, subject to the provisions of Articles 3[national treatment] and 4 [most-favoured nation] nothing in this Agreement shall be used to address the issue of the exhaustion of intellectual property rights.'

[50] Although protection of traditional knowledge is not directly addressed in the TRIPS Agreement, TRIPS has some considerable impact on the protection of traditional knowledge. See Chapter 9.

The Agreement incorporates parts of the Berne Convention[51] and the Paris Convention.[52] The incorporation of the Berne Convention forms the basis of TRIPS Agreement copyright protection. The TRIPS Agreement adds computer programs[53] and original databases[54] as copyright protectable subject matter. It also adds the three-step test for exceptions.[55] Although TRIPS incorporates aspects of the Paris Convention, it adds considerably to the requirements for substantive protection of patents,[56] trade marks[57] and designs.[58] The TRIPS Agreement also incorporates parts of the Rome Convention for Performers' Rights Producers of Phonograms and Broadcasting Organizations.[59] In this way, the TRIPS Agreement builds on the existing international regime of intellectual property law rather than rewriting it from scratch. As well as new additions to substantive standards of intellectual property, TRIPS added enforcement obligations[60] and subjected intellectual property to dispute settlement for the first time.[61]

There are gaps in TRIPS coverage, but that does not mean that the Agreement is static. On the contrary, it uses a number of terms which are open-textured in nature and are part of the Agreement's overall structure, which allows it to evolve as intellectual property itself evolves, subject to some limits.[62] The meaning of invention, as the subject matter of patent law, for example, is not defined. Consequently, countries have a degree of autonomy over its definition. I say degree because they must protect inventions. The autonomy over definition does not extend to non-protection of inventions. 'Invention' in the TRIPS Agreement in some jurisdictions means inventions in fields not yet known, as well as those that are not such giant leaps forward. In other jurisdictions, courts have interpreted fields that raise new policy issues as matters that interpretation of invention cannot decide patentability of but that, rather, the legislature must create a law about.[63]

[51] Berne Convention, above n 36. [52] Paris Convention, above n 37.
[53] TRIPS Agreement, above n 4, art 10.1. [54] TRIPS Agreement, above n 4, art 10.2.
[55] TRIPS Agreement, above n 4, arts 13 and 30 for example.
[56] TRIPS Agreement, above n 4, arts 27–34.
[57] TRIPS Agreement, above n 4, arts 15–21.
[58] TRIPS Agreement, above n 4, arts 25–26. [59] TRIPS Agreement, above n 4, art 1.3.
[60] See TRIPS Agreement, above n 4, part III.
[61] Under the Berne and Paris Conventions, disputes could be taken to the International Court of Justice, but this was never done. See R. C. Dreyfuss and A. F. Lowenfeld, 'Two Achievements of the Uruguay Round: Putting TRIPS and Dispute Settlement Together', *Virginia Journal International Law*, 37 (1997), 275–334.
[62] As discussed in Chapter 3, this raises thorny issues for interpretation of the Agreement.
[63] See, for example, *Commissioner of Patents* v. *President and Fellows of Harvard College et al.* [2002] 4 SCR 45, 2002 SCC 76 (Can.); *Wellcome Foundation Ltd* v. *Commissioner of Patents* [1983] NZLR 385 (NZCA).

This evolving nature of intellectual property was recognised in the WTO dispute settlement process when a panel took into account developments at the World Intellectual Property Organization (WIPO) that related to copyright norms.[64] The decision can be critiqued for the manner in which it did this,[65] but the overall approach of recognising that copyright concepts are not static has considerable merit.[66] That said, there are some limits to the evolutionary approach to interpretation. Sometimes new agreements may be needed, such as the WIPO agreement on copyright, which addressed some Internet-related issues.[67] The existing Berne Convention framework, incorporated into TRIPS,[68] while covering the subject matter of much of digital copyright – such as artistic, literary and musical works – does not cover all copyright issues that could not be predicted at its most recent revision in 1971. There is a difference

[64] In WTO Panel Report, *United States – Section 110(5) of the US Copyright Act*, WT/DS160/R, 27 July 27 2000, the panel sought and considered factual information from WIPO about the WIPO Copyright Treaty, *infra* note 67, see para 1.7. At para 6.70, the panel said, 'we discussed the need to interpret the Berne Convention and the TRIPS Agreement in a way that reconciles the texts of these two treaties and avoids a conflict between them, given that they form the overall framework for multilateral copyright protection. The same principle should also apply to the relationship between the TRIPS Agreement and the WCT. The WCT is designed to be compatible with this framework, incorporating or using much of the language of the Berne Convention and the TRIPS Agreement. The WCT was unanimously concluded at a diplomatic conference organized under the auspices of WIPO in December 1996, one year after the WTO Agreement entered into force, in which 127 countries participated. Most of these countries were also participants in the TRIPS negotiations and are Members of the WTO. For these reasons, it is relevant to seek contextual guidance also in the WCT when developing interpretations that avoid conflicts within this overall framework, except where these treaties explicitly contain different obligations' (citation omitted).

[65] At the time of the decision, the WIPO Copyright Treaty was not yet in force. The panel noted this, *United States – Section 110(5) of the US Copyright Act*, above n 64, at 6.67–6.68.

[66] The nature of intellectual property as laws that regulate creativity and innovation means that the subject matter of the law is inherently dynamic and that the law ought to be as flexible as possible to manage that dynamism without continuous legislative amendment. That does not mean that the law will not need to be amended from time to time. Indeed shifts in technology and science mean that courts or legislatures (this will depend on the jurisdiction) must address significant issues when they arise. See S. Frankel, 'Lord Cooke and Patents: The Scope of "Invention"', *Victoria University of Wellington Law Review*, 39 (2008), 73–98.

[67] World Intellectual Property Organization Copyright Treaty, 36 ILM 65(1997) (adopted 20 December 1996, entered into force 6 March 2002), and WIPO Performers and Producers of Phonograms Treaty 36 ILM 76 (1997) (adopted 20 December 1996, entered into force 20 May 2002).

[68] Legitimate interests are protected under TRIPS, but legitimate expectations, insofar as such words appear to relate to non-violation complaints, are not enforceable under TRIPS. For a discussion of this distinction and how it is related, in WTO terms, to the distinction between legitimate interests and legitimate expectations, see Frankel and Gervais, *Interpretation of TRIPS*, above n 42.

between recognising the evolving nature of intellectual property and filling the gaps in existing agreements. This is an important distinction, which, while sometimes fine, is the kind of distinction that a proper interpretation of TRIPS should navigate.[69] That navigation incorporates an understanding and discussion of the object and purpose of the TRIPS Agreement.

The object and purpose of the TRIPS Agreement

What amounts to the object and purpose of the TRIPS Agreement is a large topic, which is also discussed in Chapter 3.[70] Here it is important to note that in addition to the preamble and Articles 7 and 8, discussed above, the object and purpose of the TRIPS Agreement is not singular. The Agreement is a negotiated outcome between differing interests, and consequently it encapsulates competing aims and values. TRIPS obliges members to provide in their national laws certain minimum standards of protection, and it allows for the possibility of flexibilities and exceptions which enable members to balance competing interests in their national laws. Consequently, the objects and purposes of the TRIPS Agreement are multiple. These objects and purposes include the following: providing protection for intellectual property rights, allowing countries to have flexibilities in those rights, allowing countries to create exceptions to those rights, the values explicitly stated in Articles 7 and 8, bringing dispute settlement to international intellectual property law and, more generally, creating a nexus between intellectual property and other trade topics of the WTO.[71]

The legal rules of free trade agreements

The nexus between trade and intellectual property is not new. The eighteenth- and nineteenth-century debates about copyright and patents

[69] DSU, above n 29, art 3(2) provides: 'The dispute settlement system of the WTO is a central element in providing security and predictability to the multilateral trading system. The Members recognize that it serves to preserve the rights and obligations of Members under the covered agreements, and to clarify the existing provisions of those agreements in accordance with customary rules of interpretation of public international law. Recommendations and rulings of the DSB cannot add to or diminish the rights and obligations provided in the covered agreements.' DSU, above n 28, art 19(2) affirms this and further states that 'in their findings and recommendations, the panel and Appellate Body cannot add to or diminish the rights and obligations provided in the covered agreements'.

[70] See Chapter 3.

[71] See Frankel, *WTO's Application of the Customary Rules*, above n 38, at 390–400.

feature a discourse on trade.[72] Once intellectual property works started to regularly travel across borders, this led to the call for protection of that intellectual property in foreign lands. This call galvanised negotiations, which led to the Berne Convention and the Paris Convention.[73] The linkage between trade and intellectual property is long-standing, but the effects of the combination of intellectual property and the WTO have raised global intellectual property standards and brought the added dimension of making international intellectual property a legalised rules-based relationship. As a newcomer to the legal rules of international trade, the TRIPS Agreement adopted some structural features from other trade agreements, particularly the General Agreement on Tariffs and Trade (GATT).[74] One such provision is most-favoured nation (MFN).[75] Just as GATT (goods) and TRIPS (intellectual property) are different, the function and effects of MFN are different. This is particularly important when looking at to how FTAs function.

GATT permits certain FTAs on the basis that 'duties and other restrictive regulations of commerce ... are eliminated on substantially all trade'.[76] An equivalent provision in the General Agreement on Trade in Services (GATS)[77] allows agreements to be entered into between members to liberalise trade in services, provided that such agreements, among other conditions, have 'substantial sectoral coverage'.[78] The rationale of allowing these agreements is simple; such moves are valued as trade-enhancing.[79] Professor Bhagwati disputes that rationale, claiming that such agreements are 'piggybacking on sentiment for free trade', but undermine it because they create preferences.[80] Bhagwati likens FTAs (he prefers the term 'preferential trade agreements') to termites that

[72] See B. Lauriat, 'The Copyright Commission and Free Trade', in *The 1878 Royal Commission on Copyright: Understanding an Attempt at Victorian Copyright Reform* (unpublished doctoral thesis, Oxford University, 2013), 144–191.

[73] For the history of the Berne Convention, above n 36, see Ricketson and Ginsburg, above n 36, pp. 41–83. See M. Richardson, 'Patents and Exhibitions', *The Journal of World Intellectual Property*, 12 (2009), 402–421, for the history of exhibitions and the development of the Paris Convention's approach to exhibitions and patents.

[74] The preamble of the TRIPS Agreement, above n 4, states, 'Recognizing, to this end, the need for new rules and disciplines concerning: (a) the applicability of the basic principles of GATT 1994 and of relevant international intellectual property agreements or conventions'.

[75] GATT, above n 12, art 1. [76] GATT, above n 12, art XXIV, 8(b).

[77] General Agreement on Trade in Services (GATS), WTO Agreement, 1869 UNTS 183; 33 ILM 1167 (signed 15 April 1994, entered into force 1 January 1995), Annex 1B, art 5.

[78] GATS, above n 77, art 5.

[79] See, generally, J. H. Jackson, 'Regional Trade Blocs and GATT', available at http://deepblue.lib.umich.edu/.

[80] Bhagwati, *Like Termites in the Trading System*, above n 15, at 28–30.

undermine the trading system.[81] The destructive nature of FTAs, he argues, is particularly evident because countries that enter into them can claim an MFN exemption.[82] That is, the same tariff rate or sectorial coverage does not need to be given to those outside the agreement. That introduces a new level of protectionism and also potential trade diversion.[83]

No exception equivalent to MFN exception can be found in the TRIPS Agreement. One might think that because the MFN exception does not apply to intellectual property, it overcomes Bhagwati's point[84] that FTAs create protectionism because the tariff and other barrier reductions are not open to third parties. Unfortunately, the nature of the TRIPS Agreement framework, which requires its members to have minimum standards of protection, means that the usual effects of MFN do not apply and FTAs with intellectual property chapters create a one-way effect of increasing rights.[85]

Drafts of the TRIPS Agreement included in the MFN article something close to an MFN exemption. This provision was not included in the Uruguay Round draft of 1991.[86] The relevant draft exemption from the application of MFN stated,[87]

> Exempted from this obligation are any advantage, favour, privilege or immunity accorded by a party ... exceeding the requirements of this Agreement and provided in an international agreement to which the party belongs, provided that such agreement is open for accession by all parties to this Agreement, or provided that such party shall be ready to extend such advantage, favour, privilege or immunity, on terms equal to those under the agreements, to the nationals of any other party so requesting and to enter into good faith negotiations to this end.

So what might have happened if the MFN provision in TRIPS had such an exemption? We can only speculate, but such an exemption likely would not have prevented countries from agreeing to more extensive protection. An exemption may have encouraged countries to keep those

[81] Bhagwati, *Like Termites in the Trading System*, above n 15.
[82] GATT, above n 12, art XXIV.
[83] See discussion in Bhagwati, *Like Termites in the Trading System*, above n 15, at 63-72.
[84] See above n 80 and the related discussion.
[85] See, for example, P. Drahos, 'Expanding Intellectual Property's Empire: The Role of FTAs', available at www.grain.org, where, at 11, he coins the phrase 'the global ratchet' for intellectual property.
[86] For an explanation of the drafting history of the TRIPS Agreement and the significance of each of these drafts, see Gervais, *Drafting History and Analysis*, above n 10, at 10–26.
[87] Draft Agreement on Trade-Related Aspects of Intellectual Property Rights, including trade in counterfeit goods contained in the 'Dunkel Draft' (mtn.tnc/w/fa) 20 December 1991: see Gervais, *Drafting History and Analysis*, above n 10, at 103.

extra protections between themselves in some instances. It is possible that this would have been desirable. However, those in favour of harmonisation would not likely agree.

The reason that FTAs which increase intellectual property rights are problematic is that a more extensive repertoire of intellectual property is often not trade-enhancing; rather, it will likely increase trade barriers and can also create barriers to innovation. Some might say that these consequences arise because intellectual property is not a trade issue. Bhagwati, for example, specifically says royalty collecting is not trade.[88] Similar arguments were made when TRIPS was negotiated, but 20 years of the TRIPS Agreement has somewhat cemented the linkage, even if the details are not static. Consequently, if we accept that intellectual property is, or has certainly become, a trade issue, it does not mean that we need to accept that it should be subject to FTAs. This is particularly so because FTAs can undermine some of the purposes of intellectual property law.[89]

Even if intellectual property had not become a WTO multilateral trade issue, this would not have necessarily meant that intellectual property chapters in FTAs would not have occurred. It is likely that they would have. In any event, the multilateral platform has given those pursuing increased protection a solid and advanced base to work from. It has also given those who seek more balance in intellectual property some principles, such as the flexibilities and Articles 7 and 8, to draw on.[90] The problem is the ongoing attempts in FTAs to do away with or significantly curb those flexibilities and stated objectives and principles of the TRIPS Agreement.

In the intellectual property context, FTAs have mostly proven to be problematic rather than beneficial or trade-liberalising. The greatest consequence of that is that FTAs are used progressively and strategically to increase intellectual property standards.[91] Yet, more intellectual property protection is not necessarily trade-enhancing or supportive of innovation. It can serve to protect some industries, but that may harm other intellectual property interests.[92] As noted above, some have suggested that global

88 Bhagwati, *Like Termites in the Trading System*, above n 15, at 73.

89 Frankel, *Challenging TRIPS-plus Agreements*, above n 19, where I discuss how FTAs undermine the structural and general provisions of the TRIPS Agreement.

90 See Chapter 3.

91 See, generally, S. Frankel, 'The Legitimacy and Purpose of Intellectual Property Chapters in FTAs', in Ross Buckley, Vai Io Lo and Laurence Boulle (eds.), *Challenges to Multilateral Trade The Impact of Bilateral, Preferential and Regional Agreements* (Wolters Kluwer, The Netherlands, 2008), pp. 185–199 (*'Intellectual Property Chapters in FTAs'*).

92 See further discussion in Chapter 3.

intellectual property rules are only about protecting royalties;[93] however, the aims of global intellectual property agreements are more detailed than that suggests. The goals of global intellectual property agreements include ensuring international royalty flows, but the goals are multiple – including matters such as technology transfer and access to intellectual property works[94] – and amount to more than just the rent-seeking behaviour of some businesses. Increased protection can, however, operate against the core goals of intellectual property such as innovation and creativity.[95] Almost 20 years of having the TRIPS Agreement rules has demonstrated that the consequences of predominantly bilateral increases in intellectual property standards, through FTAs, are far–reaching and extend intellectual property's function beyond incentivising innovation. The consequences have brought aspects of intellectual property under critical scrutiny and are arguably also out of line with intellectual property and trade goals. The role of MFN in this is complex, but it certainly is an ill fit. As Professors Ricketson and Ginsburg cite, in the Berne Convention negotiations MFN was considered to be 'un empruent malhereux' (an unfortunate borrowing), which the Berne negotiators consequently did not borrow.[96]

In the goods context, MFN primarily operates as a tool to drive tariffs and other barriers down,[97] but in the intellectual property context, it operates almost exclusively as a tool to increase protection.[98] Preventing discrimination between foreigners is the main function of MFN. As intellectual property laws are enacted domestically, MFN can prevent countries from applying reciprocity to obligations; that is, providing the same relevant protections to foreigners and foreign works as are provided in the country of origin. This is important for intellectual property, but in

[93] Bhagwati, *Like Termites in the Trading System*, above n 15.

[94] See Dinwoodie and Dreyfuss, *A Neofederalist Vision of TRIPS*, above n 1. For a discussion of the drafting history relating to technology transfer, see Gervais, *Drafting History and Analysis*, above n 10, paras 1.20–1.24, Frankel, *WTO's Application of the Customary Rules*, above n 9.

[95] The objects and purposes of TRIPS beyond providing protection are discussed in Chapter 3.

[96] Ricketson and Ginsburg, *The Berne Conventions and Beyond*, above n 36, at 38 citing Alcide Darras, 'Du Droit des Auteurs et des Artisites dans les Rapports Internationaux' (Paris 1887), at 555. See also Dinwoodie and Dreyfuss, *A Neofederalist Vision of TRIPS*, above n 1, at 103.

[97] If one country provides a lesser or no tariff to another country, then without an MFN exception the lowest rate has to be applied to imports from all countries.

[98] The increase of intellectual property protection was not the overtly stated basis on which the MFN provision was included in the TRIPS Agreement. The drafting history of the TRIPS Agreement suggests that primarily the inclusion of MFN in the TRIPS context was justified so as to apply 'GATT disciplines to intellectual property' – see Gervais, *Drafting History and Analysis*, above n 10, at 2.73.

a practical sense MFN had not proved necessary to achieve this outcome. This is because usually the combination of national treatment (foreign works and right holders must be treated the same as domestic equivalents) and internationally agreed minimum standards has the same effect. There are some exceptions to national treatment which allow reciprocity.[99]

The two structural features of national treatment and minimum standards bring a platform of agreed behind-the-border regulation, making discrimination between foreigners, in a country's laws, less likely. This is demonstrated by the pre-TRIPS era in which, as noted, MFN was not a tool of multilateral intellectual property agreements. Consequently, as noted, there was no MFN provision in either the Berne Convention or the Paris Convention.[100] Both of these treaties, however, encouraged 'special arrangements' for increased protection between members.[101]

As a general principle of international law, states are free to negotiate TRIPS-plus protection among themselves, unless they contract not to do so. A contract not to do so has not been part of the pre- or post-TRIPS Agreement intellectual property framework,[102] which explicitly provides for the ability to employ higher standards.[103]

Although MFN allows for FTAs to increase intellectual property standards, the possibility of increases through bilateralism existed and was used well before the TRIPS Agreement. Indeed, out of control, bilateralism is often credited as being the cause of the Berne and Paris Conventions. So why is the inclusion of MFN in TRIPS problematic?

99 TRIPS Agreement, above n 4, art 3, which also preserves the national treatment exceptions found in the Berne Convention, above n 36 and the Paris Convention, above n 37.

100 The only exception would be where a foreigner has a better intellectual property right than domestic nationals. Such instances are rare. However, in those instances, MFN operates to make sure that there is equal treatment between foreigners.

101 Berne Convention, above n 36, art 20, which provides: 'The Governments of the Countries of the Union reserve the right to enter into special agreements among themselves, in so far as such agreements grant to authors more extensive rights than those granted by the convention, or contain other provisions not contrary to this convention', and Paris Convention, above n 37, art 19, which provides: 'It is understood that the countries of the Union reserve the right to make separately between themselves special arrangements for the protection of industrial property, in so far as these agreement do not contravene the provisions of this Convention.' Those special arrangements are permitted exemptions under the TRIPS Agreement, above n 4, art 3 on National Treatment.

102 Some, however, have suggested that it should be; see H. G. Ruse-Khan and A. Kur, 'Enough is Enough – The Notion of Binding Ceilings in International Intellectual Property Protection', Max Planck Institute for Intellectual Property, Competition & Tax Law Research Paper Series No. 09–01 (8 December 2008), available at SSRN: ssrn.com/abstract=1326429 or http://dx.doi.org/10.2139/ssrn.1326429, (*Enough is Enough*).

103 TRIPS Agreement, above n 4, art 1.1.

Part of the answer is that the addition of MFN increases the spill-over effect from bilateralism into countries outside the FTA and eventually to international norms.[104] In addition, the strength of the TRIPS Agreement in its WTO setting, complete with dispute settlement procedures, seems to have made this flow of increases to international norms more likely.[105]

There have been several calls to stop the tide of FTAs and the damage they do.[106] Suggestions include guidance to ameliorate their effects.[107] Another suggestion is placing maximum standards in the agreement.[108] This does not seem likely to happen; consequently, the solution would seem to be to ensure countries can utilise the flexibilities in the TRIPS Agreement.

Arguably, because of intellectual property's unique status and precarious balancing issues, it is the very subject matter that should be subject to multilateral agreement only. Multilateral norms can develop but they should not change by bypassing multilateral negotiation through bilateral or plurilateral agreements. To borrow from Bhagwati's termites analogy,[109] intellectual property chapters in FTAs are like parasites on the TRIPS Agreement. Sometimes the parasite and the host can coexist, other times the parasite takes over to the detriment of the host.

Singapore's and New Zealand's FTAs

This section takes a closer look at Singapore's and New Zealand's intellectual property chapters in FTAs. New Zealand[110] and Singapore[111] each have entered into several FTAs with both commonalities and differences in substance, perhaps unsurprisingly, depending

[104] A similar phenomenon occurs with investment treaties; see S. W. Schill, 'Multilateralizing Investment Treaties through Most-Favored-Nation Clauses', *Berkeley Journal of International Law*, 27 (2009), 496–569.

[105] Frankel, *Intellectual Property Chapters in FTAs*, above n 91.

[106] A moratorium on international intellectual property rule-making was suggested by K. E. Maskus and J. H. Reichman, 'The Globalization of Private Knowledge Goods and the Privatization of Global Public Goods', in K. Maskus and J. Reichman (eds.), *International Public Goods and Transfer of Technology under a Globalized Intellectual Property Regime* (Cambridge University Press, 2005), pp. 3–45, at 36–39.

[107] See Ruse-Khan, above n 25. The same issue of the journal contains several commentaries on the principles.

[108] Ruse-Khan and Kur, *Enough Is Enough*, above n 102.

[109] Bhagwati, *Like Termites in the Trading System*, above n 15.

[110] New Zealand has entered into eight FTAs and has 12 under negotiation. See www.mfat.govt.nz.

[111] Singapore has 18 FTAs in force with 24 trading partners. See www.fta.gov.sg.

on who is the other party.[112] This is in contrast to the US FTAs and the EU EPAs, which, although not identical, have template features. Singapore's FTAs, entered into as an ASEAN[113] member, for instance, have no intellectual property obligations. These include agreements between ASEAN and China, India, Japan and Korea. Singapore's agreements, as a stand-alone country rather than as part of ASEAN, with Korea, Japan and India do include intellectual property obligations, but focus on cooperation and information exchange rather than on increasing TRIPS substantive norms. The India–Singapore Comprehensive Economic Cooperation Agreement,[114] for example, provides for mutual cooperation in all fields of intellectual property and for collaboration on training programmes, symposia and the like. Likewise, New Zealand also has entered into FTAs wherein it agrees to provide technical and educational cooperation.[115] Singapore's agreement with Japan[116] refers to mutual collaboration and cooperation over education and awareness programmes. More substantively, Singapore agreed to facilitate and give reciprocal treatment to patent applications filed in Singapore, which correspond to applications that have been filed in Japan. A similar arrangement exists with Korea.[117] Other FTAs that Singapore has entered into, as discussed below, have considerable TRIPS-plus standards.

[112] There are also investment-related commitments in free trade agreements and other investment agreements. These sometimes include intellectual property as an investment asset. The importance of these commitments is emerging with investment claims being made in relation to Australia's plain packaging law; see *Philip Morris Brand Sàrl (Switz.), Philip Morris Products S.A. (Switz.) and Abal Hermanos S.A. (Uru.)* v. *Oriental Republic of Uruguay*, ICSID Case No. ARB/10/7, and Canada's patent law, see *Eli Lily* v. *The Government of Canada*, Notice of Intention to Submit a Claim under NAFTA, available at http://www.italaw.com/sites/default/files/case-documents/italaw1531.pdf.

[113] ASEAN was first formed in 1967 with six member countries: Brunei, Indonesia, Malaysia, Philippines, Singapore and Thailand, and was subsequently joined by Cambodia, Laos, Myanmar and Vietnam. The ASEAN grouping does not have intellectual property agreements among its members.

[114] India–Singapore Comprehensive Economic Cooperation Agreement (signed on 29 June 2005, entered into force 1 August 2005).

[115] See, for example, New Zealand–Hong Kong Closer Economic Partnership Agreement (signed 29 March 2010, entered into force 1 January 2011), art 6; New Zealand–China Free Trade Agreement (signed 7 April 2008, entered into force 1 October 2008), chapter 14; New Zealand–China Closer Economic Partnership Agreement (signed 19 April 2005, entered into force 1 July 2005), art 7.8 and 12.5.

[116] Singapore–Japan Economic Partnership Agreement (signed 13 January 2002, entered into force 30 November 2002).

[117] Korea–Singapore Free Trade Agreement (signed 4 August 2005, entered into force 2 March 2006), provided for Singapore to grant the Korean Intellectual Property Office the status of prescribed patent office (PPO), adding it to its current pool of recognised patent offices. This means an applicant for a patent in Singapore can rely on the search

A notable feature of New Zealand's and Singapore's FTAs is that several of them are overlapping. The two countries have a bilateral FTA between them and they are also both parties to the ASEAN–Australia–New Zealand FTA (AANZFTA)[118] and to an FTA which also involves Chile and Brunei (known as P4).[119] In the New Zealand and Singapore FTA there is no intellectual property chapter. AANZFTA, contains the broad statement that 'each Party confirms its commitment to reducing impediments to trade and investment by promoting deeper economic integration through effective and adequate creation, utilisation, protection and enforcement of intellectual property rights'.[120] Some of its detailed provisions are designed to bring some of the ASEAN members up to a higher standard of intellectual property protection. In regard to copyright, the agreement requires communication rights for authors, criminal enforcement measures for wilful infringement and that the parties 'foster the establishment of appropriate bodies for the collective management of copyright'.[121] There are also provisions about central government agencies undertaking to use only legitimate software and to encourage regional and local governments to maintain or adopt similar measures.[122] For trade marks, each party 'shall maintain a trademark classification system and provide high quality trademark rights. In addition, each Party shall protect trademarks and recognise geographical indications.'[123]

In the P4 agreement, New Zealand and Singapore agree that their existing bilateral FTA remains in force. They have created an arrangement wherein exporters from both countries can choose the better of the treatment afforded under either agreement. The stated purpose of this is to ensure that 'no trader is left worse off'.[124]

In the P4 Agreement Chile, Brunei and Singapore agreed to accede to the WIPO Internet Treaties, the WCT (WIPO Copyright Treaty) and the WPPT (WIPO Phonograms and Performances Treaty), which provide for enhanced copyright protection. New Zealand agreed to ensure

and examination results of a similar patent application that has been filed with KIPO (with requisite English translations to be furnished).

118 ASEAN–Australia–New Zealand Free Trade Agreement, above n 17.

119 Trans-Pacific Strategic Economic Partnership Agreement (signed 18 July 2005, entered into force 28 May 2006 (New Zealand and Singapore); 12 July 2006 (Brunei); 8 November 2006 (Chile)).

120 ASEAN–Australia–New Zealand Free Trade Agreement, above n 17, chapter 13, art 1.

121 ASEAN–Australia–New Zealand Free Trade Agreement, above n 17, chapter 13, art 5.

122 ASEAN–Australia–New Zealand Free Trade Agreement, above n 17, chapter 13, art 6.

123 ASEAN–Australia–New Zealand Free Trade Agreement, above n 17, chapter 13, art 7.

124 Ministry of Foreign Affairs and Trade, 'Trans-Pacific Strategic Economic Partnership (P4) Agreement', available at www.mfat.govt.nz/Trade-and-Economic-Relations/2-Trade-Relationships-and-Agreements/Trans-Pacific/2-P4.php.

steps to enhance its copyright regime to address the substance of these treaties.[125] Somewhat uniquely, the parties agreed that they may[126]

(a) provide for the international exhaustion of intellectual property rights;
(b) establish that provisions in standard form non-negotiated licenses for products do not prevent consumers from exercising the limitations and exceptions recognised in domestic intellectual property laws;
(c) establish provisions to facilitate the exercise of permitted acts where technological measures have been applied; and
(d) establish appropriate measures to protect traditional knowledge.

P4 is an open accession agreement and provided the platform from which the Trans-Pacific Partnership (TPP) negotiations were launched.[127] Singapore also has a trade agreement with the United States but New Zealand does not. They are both, however, members of the negotiations for the TPP[128] and the Regional Economic Cooperation Partnership (RCEP).[129]

Compared to New Zealand, Singapore has entered into some considerable TRIPS-plus obligations through separate FTAs with Australia[130] and with the United States[131], an agreement together with Switzerland, Liechtenstein, Norway and Iceland (EFTA)[132] and an agreement with the EU.[133] All of these FTAs agree to accession to the WIPO Internet Treaties.

Singapore made many TRIPS-plus commitments in its FTA with the United States. Its reason for doing so is that the agreement allows 'Singapore to rank... as a true safe haven in Asia, poised to attract greater

[125] New Zealand's stance is discussed in Chapter 4.
[126] Trans-Pacific Strategic Economic Partnership Agreement, above n 119, art 10.3:3.
[127] M. Lewis, 'The Trans-Pacific Partnership: New Paradigm or Wolf in Sheep's Clothing?', *Boston College International and Comparative Law Review*, 34 (2011), 27 at 31–32.
[128] Ministry of Foreign Affairs and Trade, 'Trans-Pacific Partnership (TPP) Negotiations', available at www.mfat.govt.nz/Trade-and-Economic-Relations/2-Trade-Relationships-and-Agreements/Trans-Pacific/index.php.
[129] This is an agreement between ASEAN (which includes Singapore) and six others: Australia, China, India, Japan, the Republic of Korea and New Zealand. It does not to date include intellectual property in any detail. See Frankel et al, *Recalibrating Behaviour*, above n 24 for a comparison of New Zealand's interest in both potential agreements.
[130] Singapore–Australia Free Trade Agreement (signed 17 February 2003, entered into force 28 July 2003).
[131] Singapore–United States Free Trade Agreement (signed 6 May 2003, entered into force 1 January 2004).
[132] Singapore–European Free Trade Assocaition Free Trade Agreement (signed 26 June 2002, entered into force 1 January 2003).
[133] EU Singapore Free Trade Agreement (signed September 2013, not yet in force).

foreign investment and trade in key industries'.[134] It may have achieved this, but it is questionable as to whether this investment has resulted in greater research in Singapore; rather, there is evidence that the investment is aimed to make Singapore a hub of distribution.[135] Such a role maybe economically beneficial, but it is a different purpose of increased standards in intellectual property law than the enhancing innovation theory.

The Singapore–US FTA extends the term of copyright protection.[136] It also requires compliance with WIPO Internet treaties, gives owners control over temporary and transient copies and interactive and other transmission modes, requires measures relating to technological protection mechanisms (TPMs)[137] and rights management information (RMI) and requires US-style notice and takedown procedures and safe harbours for Internet Service Providers (ISPs).[138] In trade marks, non-visual marks (these are sound and scent marks) must be registrable and well-known trade mark protection must cover dissimilar goods and services, whether registered or not.[139] For patents, the agreement requires that subject matter must include all plants and animals, and that there must be the possibility for term extension for delay in grant and/or regulatory approval. The use of compulsory licences was limited and the protection for pharmaceutical and agricultural chemical products was expanded, including a period of exclusivity for test data and trade secrets submitted for product approval.[140] There are also enhanced enforcement obligations.[141]

This overview of FTAs indicates several quite straightforward, but potentially underestimated, points. First, it shows that small market economies calibrate their international relationships according to what is realistic with the other party. They do not have the standard form or template FTAs which large economies, such as the United States and the European Union, and even now possibly China, seem to have.[142] The

[134] Intellectual Property, available at www.fta.gov.sg/ftas_ussfta_intellect_prop.asp.
[135] See Chapter 4.
[136] For a discussion and overview of the Singapore–US FTA, see T. Koh and L. L. Chang (eds.), *The United States–Singapore Free Trade Agreement: Highlights and Insights* (World Scientific Publication co. Pte. Ltd, Singapore, 2004).
[137] Singapore–United States Free Trade Agreement, above n 131, art 16.3.
[138] Singapore–United States Free Trade Agreement, above n 131, art 16.3.
[139] Singapore–United States Free Trade Agreement, above n 131, art 16.2.1.
[140] Singapore–United States Free Trade Agreement, above n 131, art 16.7.
[141] Singapore–United States Free Trade Agreement, above n 131, art 16.9.
[142] For a discussion of China's FTA strategy, see P. K. Yu, 'Sinic Trade Agreements and China's Global Intellectual Property Strategy', in Christoph Antons and Reto M. Hilty (eds.), *Intellectual Property and Free Trade Agreements in the Asia-Pacific Region* (Springer, Germany, 2015), 247–283.

intellectual property obligations in the FTAs of New Zealand and Singapore seem to reflect the level of development of the trading partner. This is a sample of the kinds of provisions in FTAs that exist globally. This kind of adjustment to the appropriate level of development ideally ought to be achievable through multilateral instruments, so as to avoid the problems of FTAs.

New Zealand in particular has stated a preference for multilateral agreements, but plays the FTA game because it considers it the second-best, but necessary, option.[143] The small market economies exemplify the FTA problem. The domestic law of Singapore, for example, reflects the highest standard it has agreed to. That will apply to anyone who seeks intellectual property protection in Singapore unless Singapore applies national treatment exceptions. The problem is that these standards will eventually be multilateralised without a multilateral negotiation. Small market economies should be careful, therefore, to consider whether the bargain they make is really with one party or if in effect it is more global. So, such countries should consider whether what they agree to via an FTA is in the longer term worthwhile for its own intellectual property interests.[144] This is reflective of the general problem with FTAs – that they defeat multilateralism in the name of supporting it. In the intellectual property context, this defeats the ability for appropriate levels of intellectual property law to match stages of development. This is likely to be less rather than more trade-enhancing overall.

Another factor that emerges from looking at this sample of FTAs is New Zealand's negotiation tactic of including the space to have digital exceptions and traditional knowledge protection. These are examples of New Zealand preserving what the second quote, from Professor Gervais, at the beginning of this chapter calls calibration.[145]

Calibrating interests, fragmentation and harmonisation

The problem with multiple FTAs is that obligations are fragmented rather than harmonised. The role of national policy makers in balancing commitments and calibrating laws to match the domestic level of development also means that exact harmonisation is not desirable. It is precisely because countries have different levels of development and different sectors involved in innovation that a one-size-fits-all intellectual property

143 For a discussion of this phenomenon regarding FTAs generally, see M. Lewis, 'The Free Trade Agreement Paradox', *NZ Universities Law Review*, 21(4) (2005), 554–574.
144 See Frankel et al., above n 24.
145 How it achieves that balance at the domestic level is discussed in the topic-specific chapters of this book.

model makes no sense. That does not mean minimum standards are not necessary, but rather that minimum standards need to be coupled with appropriate degrees of flexibility. The case for harmonisation necessarily depends on some kind of rationale that because strong rights are justified in one economy, on the basis of supporting innovation in the relevant sector in that economy, the same strong rights are appropriate everywhere. That is an extended notion of what drives innovation and is not logical. Such an approach, however, seems to reflect a view that the purpose of intellectual property is to control prices and access on a worldwide basis. This approach is fundamentally that of rent-seeking, which as a purpose is distinct from supporting innovation and creativity. To be clear, that does not mean that global protection is not necessary, but that protection must be balanced in a way that allows for calibration. Many aspects of the TRIPS Agreement and its incorporated agreements, the Berne Convention[146] and the Paris Convention,[147] do allow for calibration. Too many aspects of TRIPS-plus FTAs erode this.

While it could be said that large developed countries have high standards which now suit their level of development[148] and some developing countries do not need that standard in order to incentivise innovation,[149] the position of small market economies is not very clear. Surface-level purpose statements about innovation and creativity can be found in the law, but the detail of how those big-picture goals play out is opaque or more likely not well-known. It is this that Chapter 4 of this book addresses in more detail.

[146] Above n 36. [147] Above n 37.

[148] Although one might question the longevity of high standards if the location of innovation shifts.

[149] It might also be that too high standards disincentivise local innovation.

3 Interpretation of international intellectual property agreements

> The WTO Agreement is a treaty – the international equivalent of a contract. It is self-evident that in an exercise of their sovereignty, and in pursuit of their own respective national interests, the Members of the WTO have made a bargain. In exchange for the benefits they expect to derive as Members of the WTO, they have agreed to exercise their sovereignty according to the commitments they have made in the WTO Agreement.[1]

> The principles of interpretation ... are to be followed in a holistic fashion. The interpretative exercise is engaged so as to yield an interpretation that is harmonious and coherent and fits comfortably in the treaty as a whole so as to render the treaty provision legally effective. A word or term may have more than one meaning or shade of meaning but the identification of such meaning in isolation only commences the process of interpretation, it does not conclude it ... Instead, a treaty interpreter is required to have recourse to context and object and purpose to elucidate the relevant meaning of the word or term. This logical progression provides a framework for proper interpretative analysis. At the same time, it should be kept in mind that treaty interpretation is an integrated operation, where interpretative rules or principles must be understood and applied as connected and mutually reinforcing components of a holistic exercise.[2]

The process of interpretation of the TRIPS Agreement[3] and its incorporated treaties (the Berne[4] and Paris Conventions,[5] in particular) is a

[1] Appellate Body Report, *Japan – Taxes on Alcoholic Beverages*, 4 October 1996, AB–1996–2, WT/DS8/AB/R, WT/DS10/AB/R, WT/DS11/AB/R, at 13 (section F).

[2] Appellate Body Report, *United States – Continued Existence and Application of Zeroing Methodology*, 4 February 2009, WT/DS350/AB/R, at 268.

[3] Agreement on Trade-Related Aspects of Intellectual Property Rights, Marrakesh Agreement Establishing the World Trade Organization, Annex 1C, 1869 UNTS 299; 33 ILM 1197 (adopted on 15 April 1994, entered into force 1 January 1995) ('TRIPS Agreement').

[4] Berne Convention for the Protection of Literary and Artistic Works, 24 July 1971 (Paris text), 1161 UNTS 3 ('Berne Convention').

[5] Paris Convention for the Protection of Industrial Property, 828 UNTS 303 (adopted on 20 March 1883, entered into force 16 April 1970), as revised at Stockholm (14 July 1967) ('Paris Convention').

continuous process, which takes place against a backdrop of the policy space found between members' commitments to meeting internationally agreed standards and those members' need to act in their own interests, which sometimes align with the international interest and at other times may not. At a macro-level, national interests and international commitments are often compatible. That is why, as the first quote above suggests, a country enters into an international commitment. Thus, a country might see its overall membership of the TRIPS Agreement, and more broadly of the World Trade Organization (WTO), to be in its interests, but specific aspects of that Agreement may raise internal policy conflicts. The same could be said of free trade agreements (FTAs).[6] Such conflicts and any consequent attempts to balance competing interests provide fertile ground for robust policy making. It is important to emphasise that balance does not necessarily mean accommodating the new players with the incumbents in a way that favors the incumbents. Finding a balance may require looking at problems anew and reconciling competing interests (i.e. balancing them) in a new way. Resources, however, may constrain the amount and degree of analysis that can be invested in such a process.[7] A murky understanding of how to interpret international intellectual property law will not make the process of achieving a balance of competing interests and consequent calibration of national law to local needs any easier. Understanding interpretation of international treaties is important for all treaty members and especially critical for those who see balance as important. Broadly put, the central question that small market economies often ask in intellectual policy reform is how to balance or even reconcile competing interests. Effective treaty interpretation can help answer that question.

As discussed throughout this book, effective intellectual property laws often have to deal with competing interests and bring them into some kind of equilibrium. The equilibrium must not be static but must also be capable of change. As the second quote above indicates, interpretation is a holistic process. A holistic and teleological[8] approach to interpretation ought to recognise both that the law reflects competing interests and the need for some overall policy equilibrium. Of course, the law should only be interpreted consistently with what it was designed to do. Such an approach can be complex, but is an attractive mechanism in the field of intellectual property because it allows for national policy goals and

[6] See Chapter 2. [7] See discussion of evidence-based policy in Chapter 4.

[8] This includes giving full effect to object and purpose. For a general discussion of the different approaches to interpretation, see J. Pauwelyn and M. Elsig, 'The Politics of Treaty Interpretation: Variations and Explanations across International Tribunals' (3 October 2011), available at SSRN: ssrn.com/abstract=1938618.

competing interests to potentially[9] be part of the interpretation process. In other words, if properly followed, it is an approach to interpretation that can methodically deal with competing interests and the sometimes competing goals of intellectual property law.[10]

Some may consider, however, that a holistic and teleological approach lacks a sufficient degree of certainty. The remedy of such critics is to provide a kind of certainty through a less holistic and more formalistic interpretation, which focuses on the words of part of the agreement without a proper analysis of the context of the words and the object and purpose of the agreement. Such formalism may, however, with equal certainty lead to a questionable result. A holistic and teleological approach is not the equivalent of an uncertain approach. 'Holistic', as the above passage (at the beginning of the chapter) shows, is not a 'rules-free' approach. Rather, the meaning of a treaty term, its context and the object and purpose of the treaty are all to be assessed in the interpretation process. Giving full effect to context, and object and purpose, as part of interpreting the ordinary meaning is what a teleological approach ought to be.[11] Holistic, therefore, means taking all of these factors into account and not privileging any one of them to the exclusion of any of the others. Thus, a holistic approach can, if properly applied, bring sufficient certainty to the interpretation process.

The potential of holistic interpretation is attractive because less robust approaches in international intellectual property have tended to mean that domestic lawmakers treat the TRIPS Agreement as some kind of straitjacket and, consequently, interpret it very formalistically. This is problematic because it tends to curb the use of national flexibilities and exceptions. Put differently, some policy makers may find it difficult to implement intellectual property flexibilities and exceptions, and formalistic interpretation methods increase the difficulty.

9 I say potentially because to date that has not been the approach of the WTO to these matters.

10 For a discussion of the competing goals of intellectual property, see S. Frankel, 'The WTO's Application of "the Customary Rules of Interpretation of Public International Law" to Intellectual Property', *Virginia Journal of International Law*, 46 (2005), 365–428, at 393 ('WTO's Application of the Customary Rules'); and see R. C. Dreyfuss and A. F. Lowenfeld, 'Two Achievements of the Uruguay Round: Putting TRIPS and Dispute Settlement Together', *Virginia Journal International Law*, 37 (1997), 275–334, at 283.

11 One criticism of teleological interpretation is that it gives predominance to object and purpose. That does not need to be so and is not the approach if an interpretation is holistic. What I suggest is giving full effect to object and purpose as part of the ordinary meaning in context approach to interpretation. See also S. Frankel, 'The Path to Purpose-Driven TRIPS Interpretation: A Hermeneutic of International Intellectual Property' (2015, forthcoming).

Apart from the (perhaps largely superficial) appeal of certainty, formalistic interpretation has little to offer, particularly outside of the dispute in which it is used. In the longer term, formalistic approaches cause difficulties. The boundary between formalism and a holistic and more purpose-driven approach is not always a bright line. However, there are some straightforward 'red flags' of formalism, such as the absence of substantive policy discussion or discussion of the object and purpose of the agreement at issue.

The WTO's predominantly formalistic approach to the interpretation[12] of the TRIPS Agreement to date has yielded results that have not always made it easy for domestic policy makers and legislatures to be appropriately flexible in their interpretation of international obligations.[13] In addition, formalistic interpretation is not, in any event, the internationally agreed basis for treaty interpretation.[14]

The focus of this chapter is the rules of the interpretation process and the actors involved in it. The rules of interpretation apply to all international intellectual property agreements. This chapter discusses the TRIPS Agreement in particular. This process of interpretation is not unique to any one type of economy or indeed particularly to small market economies. Small market economies, however, seem particularly conscious of international compliance issues in their law reform processes. This chapter provides guidance to the interpretative questions addressed in other parts of this book (and beyond, I hope).

[12] Outside of the TRIPS Agreement, the formalistic approach to disputes can be found in other trades disputes, e.g. Appellate Body Report, *European Communities – Customs Classification of Frozen Boneless Chicken Cuts*, 12 September 2005, WT/DS269/AB/R, WT/DS286/AB/R; Appellate Body Report, *Japan – Taxes on Alcoholic Beverages*, 4 October 1996, AB-1996–2, WT/DS8/AB/R, WT/DS10/AB/R, WT/DS11/AB/R. The reasons for this approach appear to be that the WTO, as a new organisation, was establishing its legitimacy.

[13] This is exacerbated by claims that the correct interpretation of an international agreement is a country's law. This argument seems to arise when a country submits the wording in the negotiation process and seeks to rely on its own law, therefore, as the paradigm of international interpretation. An international agreement is self-evidently not the law of one country. It is an agreement among several countries. See, for example, *Eli Lily* v. *The Government of Canada*, Notice of Intention to Submit a Claim under NAFTA, available at http://italaw.com/sites/default/files/case-documents/italaw1172.pdf, where the statement is made that the correct interpretation of Article 27 of the TRIPS Agreement is US and EU law because they are the WTO members who proposed the provision in the draft. In addition to that incorrect approach to interpretation of the international agreement, EU and US laws are not the same.

[14] The customary rules of interpretation of international treaties are contained in the Vienna Convention on the Law of Treaties, 23 May 1969, 1115 UNTS 331 (entered into force 27 January 1980) ('VCLT'), arts 31–32.

As well as the rules of interpretation and the WTO's approach to interpretation to date, this chapter discusses the framework of the TRIPS Agreement and that framework's relationship to the Agreement's interpretation.

Minimum standards as a framework

The TRIPS Agreement sets out a series of minimum standards of intellectual property that its members must comply with.[15] There can often be many ways for a member to meet these minimum standards. The TRIPS Agreement and other international intellectual property treaties (such as the substantive parts of the Berne Convention and the Paris Convention, which are incorporated into TRIPS[16]) are not for the most part prescriptive, beyond the setting of minimum standards (although, as discussed in Chapter 2, some FTAs have elements of prescriptiveness). The TRIPS Agreement, for example, requires that members provide patents for inventions in all fields of technology, provided they are 'new, involve an inventive step and are capable of industrial application'.[17] TRIPS does not prescribe a single definition of 'invention', 'field of technology', 'inventive step' and many other terms. Consequently, provided the TRIPS Agreement is complied with, its members have autonomy over how to implement the minimum standards and they do have their own approaches to the substantive law that relates to these terms.[18] A prescriptive agreement would, in contrast, provide a definition of such terms that all members would have to apply in their domestic law and the method of application in domestic law might also be prescribed. By this, I do not suggest that there is not some common ground, for example, about what amounts to an invention or what is a registrable trade mark. The common ground is simply that there are minimum standards rather than identical laws or, in the parlance of internationalism, complete harmonisation.

As TRIPS and its incorporated treaties are not prescriptive they should not be interpreted that way. For the most part, the TRIPS standards are

[15] These minimum standards cover various areas of intellectual property listed in Part II of the TRIPS Agreement; above n 3, see chapter 2.

[16] TRIPS Agreement, above n 3, arts 2 and 9.1.

[17] TRIPS Agreement, above n 3, art 27.1. Such terms are open-textured in nature. In TRIPS there are broadly two sorts of open-textured terms. The first is where intellectual property law is relevant to interpretation, e.g. invention. The second may refer to an area outside the immediate ambit of intellectual property law such as 'public health'. The different contexts of such terms may lead to differences in the interpretative process.

[18] The terms must have some operative meaning, however. As discussed in Chapter 2, 'inventive step' must be given some meaning or patents will not be granted, which would be in violation of TRIPS.

not prescriptive beyond the requirement that there must be a minimum standard in the members' national laws, although some provisions of TRIPS are more prescriptive than others. Article 15, which provides for the subject matter of trade marks,[19] gives more detail than Article 27, which sets the minimum standard for the subject matter of patents, for example.[20]

Prescriptive interpretation is usually not holistic but can be overly literal and consequently formalistic. Any part of the TRIPS Agreement should be interpreted holistically, having regard to context and object and purpose. As noted, this is not always an easy exercise.[21] A holistic approach is important especially for giving full weight to object and purpose, which is the gateway to normative underpinnings and policy imperatives as part of the interpretation process.

Why interpretation matters

Treaty interpretation is both a powerful and a limited tool. It is powerful because an interpretation method can be used to reach a result that favors one disputant over another. It is limited because it is only a tool of interpretation and as such is merely a road map to an existing network of obligations. Interpretation cannot be used to create new obligations or to resolve a true conflict of treaty norms by choosing one norm over another. Interpretation can only be used to establish whether the treaty itself prefers one norm over another: in other words whether the parties have in fact agreed that one norm prevails over another and demonstrated this intention in the words of the treaty.[22]

Interpretation is very important not least of all because of the impact of wrong interpretation.[23] Unfortunately, bad interpretation methods do

[19] TRIPS Agreement, above n 3, art 15 states: 'Any sign, or any combination of signs, capable of distinguishing the goods or services of one undertaking from those of other undertakings, shall be capable of constituting a trademark. Such signs, in particular words including personal names, letters, numerals, figurative elements and combinations of colours as well as any combination of such signs, shall be eligible for registration as trademarks. Where signs are not inherently capable of distinguishing the relevant goods or services, Members may make registrability depend on distinctiveness acquired through use. Members may require, as a condition of registration, that signs be visually perceptible.'

[20] As far as subject matter (and patentability criteria) goes, TRIPS Agreement, above n 3, art 27, states, 'patents shall be available for any inventions, whether products or processes, in all fields of technology, provided that they are new, involve an inventive step and are capable of industrial application'.

[21] See discussion below.

[22] See Frankel, '*WTO's Application of the Customary Rules*', above n 10, at 368.

[23] See S. Frankel, 'Some Consequences of Misinterpreting the TRIPS Agreement', *The WIPO Journal*, 1 (2009), 35–42.

not usually easily confine themselves to one dispute. They can create difficulties for future disputes and for those who rely on reported outcomes to make domestic policy and laws.

For economies that are conscious of complying with international obligations – this tends to be the situation with small market economies – a robust approach to interpretation at an international level is important in order that equal robustness of interpretation can be utilised at the domestic level, when implementing obligations and creating intellectual property policy and law. A robust approach to interpretation does not necessarily in and of itself lead to the best policy from an intellectual property perspective. A country may, for example, not utilise flexibilities because it does not want to offend, or wants to strike a deal (such as strong intellectual property in exchange for market access for goods or services) with its trading partners, even though flexibilities are entirely legitimate under the international agreements. Parallel importing provides such an example. New Zealand law allows parallel imports of copyright and trade marked goods, but not patented goods.[24] From a purely legal perspective, there is no necessity to differentiate between intellectual property rights and related products in this way, but, from a political and trade relationship perspective, parallel importing of patented products has not been something that the United States, in particular, has looked at favourably.[25] Parallel importing, discussed in Chapter 8, has at various times seen Singapore, New Zealand and Israel placed on the Special 301 watch-list, a unilateral measure of the United States,[26] even though parallel importing is undeniably legitimate under the TRIPS Agreement.[27]

[24] See S. Frankel, *Intellectual Property in New Zealand*, 2nd edn (LexisNexis, Wellington, 2011), pp. 82–112.

[25] In trade negotiations, the United States has agreed in FTAs with some countries to curb parallel importing; see Chapter 8. In the United States, trade marked goods can be parallel imported. Until 2013, copyright works could not be parallel imported. This means that trade mark owners might rely on copyright to prevent parallel importing. See M. La France, 'Using Incidental Copyrights to Block Parallel Imports: A Comparative Perspective', *Intellectual Property Journal*, 25 (2013), 149–171. This has changed with the Supreme Court decision that has allowed parallel imports of copyright works and in particular second-hand textbooks from Thailand; see *Kirtsaeng* v. *John Wiley & Sons Inc.*, 11–697 US (2013).

[26] The Special 301 Report is prepared annually by the Office of the United States Trade Representative under Section 301 as amended of the Trade Act of 1974. See, generally, S. Flynn, 'Special 301 of the Trade Act of 1974 and Global Access to Medicine', *Journal of Generic Medicines*, 7 (2010), at 451–472.

[27] Singapore was removed from the watch-list in 2003 for 'improvements' to its intellectual property law generally; see U.S. International Trade Commission, *U.S.–Singapore Free Trade Agreement: Potential Economy wide and Selected Sectoral Effects*, Inv.

Understanding the process of interpretation of international agreements is important for all relevant actors in all types of economies, but the issue is more acute with policy makers and lawmakers, for whom compliance with the international agreements is important so as to avoid formal legal or informal trade retaliation (or perhaps even security-related risks). Very often small market economies only make decisions about intellectual property policy if they consider those policies to be compatible with international obligations.[28] Consequently, treaty interpretation is important not only for the international bodies that administer the treaties and, in the case of the TRIPS Agreement, those that rule on disputes about the Agreement, but it is also important in the domestic law-making realm. Policy makers will look at international obligations when devising policy and when giving advice to government about what that policy should be.

Domestic courts may also look at international treaties where they are relevant to the issues before them. The degree of attention that domestic courts give to international agreements varies depending on factors such as the local legal tradition about the relevance of such sources and even whether or not the international treaty has been used in the submissions of parties to the dispute. Courts in small market economies tend to refer to international obligations in the context of national decisions. They do this because of a culture of complying with international norms. For example, in a decision about whether second-use pharmaceutical patents were patentable in New Zealand and in a related decision about whether methods of medical treatment could be excluded from the scope of invention, both courts, although for entirely different reasons, discussed compliance with the TRIPS Agreement in some detail.[29]

Given the range of actors and differing policy drivers involved, consistently applied and recognised rules around interpretation are crucial

TA2104–6 (USITC Publication 360, 2003). New Zealand introduced parallel importing of copyright works in 1998 and was placed on the watch-list. After some amendments to its copyright law in 2003, see Chapter 8, New Zealand was removed from the USTR's Special 301 watch-list. Israel remains on the watch-list for matters generally relating to pharmaceuticals, although parallel importing was not expressly named in 2013, Office of the United States Trade Representative, 2013 Special 301 Report, available at www.ustr.gov/. TRIPS Agreement, above n 3, art 6. See also D. J. Gervais, *The TRIPS Agreement: Drafting History and Analysis*, 4th edn (Sweet & Maxwell, London, 2012), 2.90–2.103.

[28] See Chapter 2.

[29] See *Pfizer Inc* v. *Commissioner of Patents* [2005] 1 NZLR 362 (CA), at [64–77], and *Pharmaceutical Management Agency* v. *Commissioner of Patents* [2000] 2 NZLR 529 (CA), at [28].

so that policy makers and lawmakers are not inhibited by lack of clarity about the extent of and limitations of international obligations.

Interpreters and the institutions of interpretation

> The meaning of a treaty is not carved in stone at the moment of its conclusion ... instead, debates continue, albeit no longer on what words to use in the treaty, but how to give meaning to the words that are used. Whoever controls this process controls the meaning of the treaty, and therewith controls whether or not the obligations ... are bearable or onerous, and controls whether the acts of States are faithful implementations of a text, or amount to breaches of that same text.[30]

Treaty interpretation takes place at the WTO in the dispute settlement system. This consists of ad hoc panels that hear disputes at first instance and a standing Appellate Body. Both are served by a secretariat. Recommendations of the panels and Appellate Body are adopted by the Dispute Settlement Body (DSB), which is a function of the WTO Council of Ministers,[31] and when adopted the recommendations become rulings. The dispute settlement system's code of practice is the Dispute Settlement Understanding (DSU).[32]

The panel and Appellate Body reports about the interpretation of the TRIPS Agreement are growing in number but still are not many. Only three of the disputes have been to the Appellate Body, and those were some of the earlier disputes brought to the WTO about TRIPS.[33] That body of reports is central to, but it is not the only relevant source of, international intellectual property law. The treaties are of course the primary source. Other sources include disputes under other trade agreements, including bilateral FTAs, bilateral investment treaties (BITs), dispute before national courts and interpretations of policy makers. FTA and BIT disputes are not always reported and are comparatively few. Each of these and the advice of experts play a role in the process of interpretation.

[30] J. Klabbers, 'On Rationalism in Politics: Interpretation of Treaties and the World Trade Organization', *Nordic Journal of International Law*, 74 (2005), 405–428, at 406–407.

[31] This is made up of representatives from each member of the WTO.

[32] Understanding on Rules and Procedures Governing the Settlement of Disputes, 15 April 1994, Marrakesh Agreement Establishing the World Trade Organization, Annex 2 (1994) 1869 UNTS 401 ('DSU').

[33] These were: WTO Appellate Body Report, *United States – Section 211 Omnibus Appropriations Act of 1998*, 2 January 2002, WT/DS176/AB/R; WTO Appellate Body Report, *Canada – Term of Patent Protection*, WT/DS170/AB/R; and WTO Appellate Body Report, *India – Patent Protection for Pharmaceutical and Agricultural Chemical Products ('India – Patents for Pharmaceuticals')*, 16 January 1998, WT/DS50/AB/R.

National intellectual property laws must comply with the minimum standards of the international agreements. No national law, however, is decisive of the meaning of the related internationally agreed minimum standard, but national laws may have a role in the interpretation of the standard as the international norm is often derived from national norms.[34] Additionally, the object and purpose of the national law and the compatibility of that with the TRIPS Agreement ought to be relevant to dispute settlement, although not decisive of a dispute. This is discussed further below.

Depending on who (including institutions and individuals) is the interpreter, the approach to interpretation will differ. The nature of an institution, the goals of that institution and the degree of involvement in the interpretation exercise, i.e. as an active interpreter or as a recipient of interpretation, will influence the approach taken to interpretation. Legal interpreters tend to be more formalistic (although not always). Legal interpreters are also trained to see variables and may conclude, 'it depends . . . '. Policy makers may, where the treaty refers to legal rules (as does TRIPS), often seek a legal answer as to what a treaty article means. Such answers are not always easy to give. A question such as, 'would an exception for uses of works for education be compliant with TRIPS?' provides an example. The answer is, 'it depends' on whether the proposed exception meets the requirements of the three-step test.[35] Perhaps the better question, therefore, which may eventually have to be more narrowly tailored to address appropriate detail, is whether an exception which is predominantly for an educational purpose is TRIPS compliant; the answer to that is 'yes'.

As noted above, interpretation of the TRIPS Agreement takes place in a variety of forums including national courts. Individual national courts and transnational courts, such as the EU Court of Justice, do not necessarily have influence over each other and policy makers are not bound by legal rules of jurisdiction. In small market economies, policy makers may use the jurisprudence of many places as examples. It is not uncommon for national policy makers of small market economies to spend a considerable amount of time looking not only at what the international obligations are but also at what other jurisdictions do. This is both a present and a historic phenomenon.

[34] Additionally, application of the Vienna Convention, above n 14, art 31 (3)(b), discussed below, recognises that any 'subsequent practice in the application of the treaty which establishes the agreement of the parties regarding its interpretation' is relevant to interpretation as part of context.

[35] TRIPS Agreement, above n 3, art 13. See also discussion in Chapter 7.

Historically the copyright laws of Israel and Singapore, for example, are substantively based on British law and particularly its 1977 Act.[36] New Zealand law is also based on the British Act and states in several places that it is also based on Singapore law. Singapore's more recent approach to copyright exceptions and its utilisation of fair use in copyright is much more closely aligned with US law than British law. Israel has taken a similar course. One provision of New Zealand law incorporates US fair use factors as guidance for the interpretation of that provision.[37] So while Singapore and Israel have a British tradition to their laws, they have taken more of a US approach in relation to fair use of copyright works.[38]

In addition to borrowing the legislative drafting of other jurisdictions, the approach of courts, patent and trade mark offices and policy makers in other jurisdictions may be very influential, especially where those other jurisdictions are trading partners. What the actual international obligation is, is a different question from one jurisdiction's interpretation of that obligation. What the obligation is can, however, be a difficult question. The difficulty may arise because the international minimum standard that is the obligation may be rather thin on detail or give no guidance. While that indicates that a flexible implementation in domestic laws is possible, countries may not always have the technical capacity or necessary resources to implement flexibility and consequently will be likely to adopt policies and laws from those who do.[39]

One lesson learnt from the WTO *China – Enforcement* panel report[40] is that reading any detailed obligations beyond what is found in the TRIPS Agreement does not lead to a correct interpretation of the Agreement's minimum standards. In that dispute, the Chinese law had certain thresholds, of numbers of infringing copies that had to be met before criminal enforcement was relevant. The United States argued that these threshold requirements did not amount to effective criminal enforcement. The relevant TRIPS obligations do not specify the details of how criminal enforcement should be applied, just that it should be available.[41] One of

36 Singapore has also modelled parts of its statute on Australian law, which also has its origins in British law.

37 Copyright Act 1994, s43(4) (NZ).

38 These issues are discussed further in Chapter 7. Small market economies, in their free trade agreements, provide some technical assistance to other countries.

39 See, generally, C. Deere, *The Implementation Game: The TRIPS Agreement and the Global Politics of Intellectual Property Reform in Developing Countries* (Oxford University Press, 2008).

40 WTO Panel Report, *China – Measures Affecting the Protection and Enforcement of Intellectual Property Rights*, 26 January 2009, WT/DS362/R.

41 TRIPS Agreement, above n 3, art 41. For a discussion of the dispute, see R. Howse, 'China – Measures Affecting the Protection and Enforcement of Intellectual Property Rights', *World Trade Review*, 10(1) (2011), 87–93.

the reasons the US claim did not succeed was that criminal enforcement was available and that was really all the minimum standard, which did not prescribe the specifics of that availability, required. Treaty interpretation does not allow the treaty interpreter, at an international organisation, to fill the gaps where details have not been negotiated.[42]

National courts and legislatures, however, when interpreting domestic law, can and do fill the gaps. Consider, for example, one of the most contentious issues in patent law, the scope of the undefined terms 'new' and 'inventive step',[43] where no dispute on this has ever been before the WTO. The standards in the United States, the European Union, China and India, for example, all differ.[44] Yet this sort of dispute is before national courts frequently and those courts often determine the scope of newness (or novelty) and inventive step (or non-obviousness). As noted above, one national court's view on the meaning of the terms will not determine the TRIPS Agreement meaning. This is particularly so when there can be several methods of compliance with the TRIPS minimum standard. There is a complex relationship between national interpretations and the international interpretation. They do inform each other. While national law should comply with the international standard, national law alone is not the tool to interpret the scope of the international standard. This is important for jurisdictions with few cases, such as small market economies. As noted above, they will often consider the case law of larger developed economies.

Without proper interpretative guidance, grey areas of interpretation become problematic for domestic policy makers. That tends to mean that using flexibilities is often not easy and may appear to be fraught with risk. One possible approach is that – as the answer is not clear – a particular flexibility is likely legitimate, but small market economies (and others) may

[42] DSU, above n 32, arts 3(2) and 19(2) respectively state, 'The dispute settlement system of the WTO is a central element in providing security and predictability to the multilateral trading system. The Members recognize that it serves to preserve the rights and obligations of Members under the covered agreements, and to clarify the existing provisions of those agreements in accordance with customary rules of interpretation of public international law. Recommendations and rulings of the DSB cannot add to or diminish the rights and obligations provided in the covered agreements.' and, 'in their findings and recommendations, the panel and Appellate Body cannot add to or diminish the rights and obligations provided in the covered agreements'.

[43] TRIPS Agreement, above n 3, art 27.

[44] For a general discussion, see L. Xiang, D. Lingli, O. Shiwen and Z. Ningournal, 'A Comparative Analysis of the Inventive Step Standard in the EPO, SIPO and USPTO', *Journal of Intellectual Property Law & Practice*, 8(7) (2013), 539–45; S. Basheer and T. P. Reddy, 'The "Efficacy" of Indian Patent Law: Ironing Out the Creases in Section 3(d)', *SCRIPTed*, 5(2) (2008), 232, available at www.law.ed.ac.uk/ahrc/script-ed/vol5-2/basheer.asp.

not always want to take such policy risks, particularly if there is no immediate national interest in doing so. Often, however, the perceived grey area is not grey; what is needed is appropriate interpretation of the international standard to point towards the implementation options.

The chapter now discusses the rules of treaty interpretation and the WTO's approach to treaty interpretation.

The fundamentals of treaty interpretation

The WTO dispute settlement system is often described as one of the strongest international dispute settlement mechanisms. Reports of the panels and the Appellate Body are not binding rulings until the DSB, which is comprised of the Member States of the WTO, adopt the report. The report binds the parties to the dispute. WTO dispute settlement is bilateral. The reports are not binding on parties to future disputes, although the WTO recognises that they may be relied on.[45] These are important features of the WTO dispute settlement system, which arguably distinguish it from a court structure. Under the DSU, panels and the Appellate Body are required to apply the 'customary rules of interpretation of public international law'.[46] These customary rules are codified in the Vienna Convention on the Law of Treaties (VCLT).[47] Article 31.1 of the VCLT is the key interpretative rule, which provides the following:

> A treaty shall be interpreted in good faith in accordance with the ordinary meaning to be given to the terms of the treaty in their context and in the light of its object and purpose.

The remainder of Article 31 sets out the meaning of context and other matters to be taken into account in the interpretation process.[48] It has

[45] The Appellate Body has stated that panels should give 'cogent reasons' for departing from Appellate Body decisions; see Appellate Body Report, *United States – Final Anti-Dumping Measures on Stainless Steel from Mexico*, 30 April 2008, WT/DS344/AB/R, at 160.

[46] DSU, above n 32, art 3.2. [47] VCLT, above n 14.

[48] VCLT, above n 14, arts 31(2) and (3) provide: '2. The context for the purpose of the interpretation of a treaty shall comprise, in addition to the text, including its preamble and annexes:
(a) any agreement relating to the treaty which was made between all the parties in connexion with the conclusion of the treaty;
(b) any instrument which was made by one or more of the parties in connexion with the conclusion of the treaty and accepted by the other parties as an instrument related to the treaty.
3. There shall be taken into account, together with the context:
(a) any subsequent agreement between the parties regarding the interpretation of the treaty or the application of its provisions;

long been established that Article 31 is a 'logical progression' rather than a 'hierarchy of legal norms'.[49] The second quote at the beginning of this chapter takes that statement further and emphasises that the logical progression should be conducted holistically, not hierarchically.

It is always tempting when looking at a treaty and interpreting its articles to look to the drafting history to shed light on its meaning. Such information is important, but it is not the first step in interpretation and, if taken as a first step, can lead to the wrong result or a faulty interpretation. The WTO has confirmed the VCLT rule that supplementary material, such as *travaux preparatoires*, is not the first port of call to illuminate the context.[50] A proper approach to interpretation should only consider supplementary material in circumstances where Article 31 analysis leads to an ambiguity or absurd result.[51] The prime reason for this is that the treaty is a text reached after negotiation. The treaty is the embodiment of the intention of the parties. The negotiating history may be one party's proposed text or may have been substantially altered as the negotiations progress. In spite of this clear guidance, panels in TRIPS disputes have not always followed this rule. In *Canada Pharmaceuticals*, the Panel, when interpreting Article 30 of TRIPS (exceptions in patent law), noted Article 30's 'antecedents in Article 9(2) of the Berne Convention'.[52] After this discussion, the Panel then 'examined the documented negotiating history of TRIPS Article 30 with respect to the reasons why negotiators may have chosen to use the term "limited exceptions" in place of "in special circumstances"'.[53] At that stage, the panel had not completed the Article 31 interpretative

(b) any subsequent practice in the application of the treaty which establishes the agreement of the parties regarding its interpretation;
(c) any relevant rules of international law applicable in the relations between the parties.
4. A special meaning shall be given to a term if it is established that the parties so intended.'

49 See A. Aust, *Modern Treaty Law and Practice* (Cambridge University Press, 2000), at 187.

50 Appellate Body Report, *United States – Standards for Reformulated and Conventional Gasoline*, 29 April 1996, WT/DS2/AB/R, 29.

51 VCLT, above n 14, art 32(a) provides, 'Recourse may be had to supplementary means of interpretation, including the preparatory work of the treaty and the circumstances of its conclusion, in order to confirm the meaning resulting from the application of Article 31, or to determine the meaning when the interpretation according to Article 31: (a) leaves the meaning ambiguous or obscure; or (b) leads to a result which is manifestly absurd or unreasonable.'

52 WTO Panel Report, *Canada – Patent Protection of Pharmaceutical Products, Complaint by the European Communities and Their Member States*, 17 March 2000, WT/DS114/R.

53 P. Roffe and C. Spenneman, 'Canada – Patent Protection of Pharmaceutical Products', in C. Correa (ed.), *Research Handbook on the Interpretation and Enforcement of Intellectual Property Under WTO Rules* (Edward Elgar, Cheltenham, 2010), at 244.

exercise. It had not fully discussed context or object and purpose. There is much criticism of that report because of its failure to assess policy behind the law at issue and the object and purpose of TRIPS.

Although a holistic approach is necessary, it is widely acknowledged that in order to discuss the Article 31 steps effectively, each step should be addressed in turn, remembering that the order is not hierarchical.

A potential difficulty with using the VCLT rules of interpretation is that it can lead to a formalistic approach. Formalism, however, is not the inevitable consequence of following VCLT rules.[54] As a co-author and I have said,[55]

> Formalism may stem from the fact that WTO panels and the Appellate Body seem particularly conscious that their role is to interpret the agreements and not to add to them or to modify the substance of negotiated concessions. That is rightly so. However, . . . giving interpretative effect to the context of an article and to the treaty's object and purpose is not the same as adding to the TRIPS Agreement. Put differently, if context, object, and purpose are fully utilized then VCLT interpretation will potentially be less formalistic and can be more purposive without modifying or adding to negotiated WTO texts.

A summary of the steps of treaty interpretation

Any holistic VCLT analysis includes several different factors. The good faith requirement will be relevant throughout the interpretation process. The steps of the interpretation process are, in summary and in a non-hierarchical order, as follows:

- What the article at issue says and its ordinary meaning (care must be taken, however, because what it says and tools such as dictionaries are one aspect of ordinary meaning).
- What the treaty article means in its immediate context.
- What the treaty article means in the context of the TRIPS Agreement and the WTO Agreements (here incorporated treaties will also be relevant context).

[54] There are many approaches to interpretation even within the VCLT rules and there can be a tendency for a tribunal to emphasise one part of the rules over the others depending on the aims of the tribunal and the nature of the agreement before it. See, generally, J. Pauwelyn and M. Elsig, 'The Politics of Treaty Interpretation: Variations and Explanations across International Tribunals', SSRN Working Paper Series, 2011, available at ssrn.com/abstract=1938618.

[55] S. Frankel and D. Gervais, 'Plain Packaging and the Interpretation of the TRIPS Agreement', *Vanderbilt Journal of Transnational Law*, 46(5) (2013), 1149–1214 ('*Interpretation of TRIPS*'), at 1169.

- What the object and purpose of the TRIPS Agreement is and how that is relevant to the dispute (this can also include the object and purpose of both the specific provision and the TRIPS Agreement as a whole).

What is Article 31 good faith?

This is a substantive requirement even though the phrase, if read in isolation, has the air of 'diplomatic speak'. The substance of the good faith requirement is that the rules of interpretation should not be used to reach an unreasonable or absurd result.[56]

The first TRIPS Agreement dispute to consider Article 31 was *India – Patent Protection for Pharmaceutical and Agricultural Chemical Products.*[57] There the United States[58] successfully challenged India's patent system before the Panel, and the Appellate Body overall upheld that Panel's decision. The complaint was that India neither provided for protection of pharmaceutical and agricultural chemical products nor had an adequate mailbox system for applicants to file such applications, as it was required to under the TRIPS Agreement.[59] The Panel found that good faith requires the protection of the parties' 'legitimate expectations'.[60] The Appellate Body disagreed that good faith was a requirement of interpretation separate

[56] For a discussion of the good faith requirement in the context of the plain packaging of tobacco and interpretation of TRIPS, see Frankel and Gervais, *Interpretation of TRIPS*, above n 55, at 1167.

[57] WTO Appellate Body Report, *India – Patents for Pharmaceuticals*, above n 33.

[58] The EC was a third party to Appellate Body Report, *India-Patents for Pharmaceuticals*, above n 33, and the EC brought its own proceedings against India on the same facts with the same result; see WTO Panel Report, *India –Patent Protection for Pharmaceutical and Agricultural Chemical Product – Complaint by the European Communities*, 22 September 1998, WT/DS79/R.

[59] This called for interpretation of TRIPS Agreement, above n 3, arts 27 and 70:8 (the mailbox system was to accept patent applications made even though they could not be granted until the appropriate patent regimes had been instituted) and 70.9 of the TRIPS Agreement (India was also challenged for failing to grant exclusive marketing rights for such products).

[60] WTO Appellate Body Report, *India – Patents for Pharmaceuticals*, above n 33, at para 44. There is also discussion in the report about what is a legitimate expectation in the TRIPS context and how the GATT non-violation meaning of that phrase is not applicable to TRIPS as non-violation disputes are not available under TRIPS, see TRIPS Agreement, above n 3, art 64.2-3. See also S. Frankel, 'Challenging TRIPS-Plus Agreements: The Potential Utility of Non-Violation Disputes', *Journal of International Economic Law,* 12(1) (2009), 1023, at 1038–1039 discussing the inapplicability of non-violation complaints in TRIPS and T. Cottier and K. N. Schefer, 'Good Faith and the Protection of Legitimate Expectations in the WTO, in M. Bronckers and R. Quick (eds.), *New Directions in International Economic Law: Essays in Honor of John H. Jackson* (Kluwer, 2000) at 60, discussing that the Appellate Body has rejected the use of legitimate expectations other than in non-violation cases.

from analysis of the actual language of the treaty. The Appellate Body emphasised that VCLT interpretation means that the treaty must not be added to.[61] Good faith means that an interpretation of the ordinary meaning should not defy context or object and purpose. A good faith interpretation takes all of the Article 31:1 factors into account so that the result of interpretation would not be absurd or unreasonable.[62]

Ordinary meaning

WTO panels often look to dictionaries for ordinary meaning of words. The dictionary can be helpful as part of a process. It is, however, a small part of the interpretative process. A dictionary meaning may be a useful starting point for words that have a general meaning. An example of a word in TRIPS with a general meaning is 'encumbrance' in Article 20.[63] The dictionary is not so helpful for interpreting words which have an intellectual property-specific meaning, such as 'inventive step', or an established or well-analysed meaning in the WTO context, such as 'necessary'.[64] The dictionary only takes any interpretation process a little way. After all, Article 31 defines the ordinary meaning as discernible in light of context and the object and purpose of the concerned treaty.

Other phrases found in TRIPS may have meanings in other international agreements. 'Public health' is a prime example of this. In situations where the phrase used is drawn from concepts outside of intellectual property (or indeed the WTO), a source of ordinary meaning of those phrases may be those other international agreements. The WTO has been careful to use other international agreements as one source that contributes to analysis of ordinary meaning in context rather than determining the meaning of a treaty external to the WTO or having another treaty's meaning determine the meaning intended by the parties to the relevant WTO Agreement.[65]

[61] WTO Appellate Body Report, *India – Patents for Pharmaceuticals*, above n 33, at para 45.

[62] I. Sinclair, *The Vienna Convention on the Law of Treaties*, 2nd edn (Manchester University Press, 1984), at 120.

[63] See Frankel and Gervais, *Interpretation of TRIPS*, above n 55, at 1172–1174.

[64] 'Necessary' is found in TRIPS Agreement, above art 8; see discussion in Frankel and Gervais, *Interpretation of TRIPS*, above n 55, at 1204–1206.

[65] See WTO Appellate Body Report, *United States – Import Prohibition of Certain Shrimp and Shrimp Products*, 12 October 1998, WT/DS58/AB/R. As I have said elsewhere, 'In the *Shrimp Turtle* report, the Appellate Body considered other rules of international law to interpret the phrase "exhaustible natural resources" found in Article XX(g) of GATT. The interpretation was necessary to consider the legitimacy of the United States ban on the importation of shrimp that was fished in a way that "incidentally" killed sea turtles. In order to interpret the phrase, the Panel and the Appellate Body referred to the United Nations Convention on the Law of the Sea (UNCLOS) in support of the conclusion that natural resources included both living and non-living resources'; see Frankel, 'WTO's Application of the Customary Rules', above n 10, at 424; Frankel and Gervais,

Context and the object and purpose of the TRIPS Agreement

Interpretation of any article of the TRIPS Agreement should be in the context of the area of intellectual property (e.g. trade marks or copyright) and TRIPS as a whole. Context and object and purpose blend into each other. They can be separated in order to logically propel the interpretation exercise. However, there are overlaps, and therefore separation, in order to achieve logical progression, should not result in artificial divides and constraints between the two steps. This chapter adopts a holistic approach (as the WTO has mandated), by discussing context and object and purpose in tandem.

Where they have mentioned object and purpose, dispute settlement reports have not had a full discussion of what that means in relation to the TRIPS Agreement.[66] It is well settled that Article 31's use of 'its' means the object and purpose of the agreement as a whole. However, the object and purpose of individual provisions will be relevant to working out the object and purpose of the whole.[67] To date, TRIPS-related dispute settlement reports seem to have chosen one objective over another without full explanation. The *India – Pharmaceuticals* dispute report is illustrative. There the Appellate Body said,[68]

> The Panel's interpretation here is consistent also with the object and purpose of the TRIPS Agreement. The Agreement takes into account *inter alia*, 'the need to promote effective and adequate protection of intellectual property rights'.

The statement is not wholly wrong but it is incomplete because the other objectives and purposes of TRIPS are not discussed or balanced with this goal.

Balancing multiple purposes is complex. Perhaps the greatest difficulty with interpretation is pinpointing the object and purpose of the TRIPS Agreement and the various parts of it.[69] This is by no means a simple

Interpretation of TRIPS, above n 55, at 1206. VCLT, above n 15, art 31 (3) (c), which provides that together with context 'any relevant rules of international law applicable in the relations between the parties' may also be taken into account. For a discussion of the WTO's approach to VCLT art 31(3) (c), see R. Howse, 'The Use and Abuse of Other "Relevant Rules of International Law" in Treaty Interpretation: Insights from WTO Trade/Environment Litigation', International Law and Justice Working Paper 2007/1, available at http://iilj.org/publications/documents/2007–1.Howse.web.pdf.

66 Frankel, 'WTO's Application of the Customary Rules', above n 10.

67 WTO Appellate Body Report, *European Communities – Customs Classification of Frozen Boneless Chicken Cuts*, 12 September 2005, WT/DS269/AB/R, WT/DS286/AB/R, at 238–239.

68 WTO Appellate Body Report, *India – Patents for Pharmaceuticals*, above n 33, para 57.

69 The VCLT elucidates that the context of a treaty for interpretation purposes includes its preamble and annexes. Article 31(2)(a) and (b) then make it clear that the context includes agreements and instruments relating to the treaty. In the context of the TRIPS Agreement, this could include agreed understandings on certain articles.

question because the Agreement and its incorporated treaties include multiple objectives and purposes. These multiple objectives and purposes sometimes conflict and are in competition with each other. This is not a competition where one objective cancels the other out; rather, it is a reflection that intellectual property law is a balancing act between differing interests. Those different interests and the agreed balance among them, which, as noted above, will include minimum standards which are often not prescriptively detailed, are all objects and purposes of the TRIPS Agreement.

The object and purpose of the TRIPS Agreement is complex. Keeping in mind that the VCLT approach is holistic, the object and purpose includes:

- Articles 7 and 8; 'principles' and 'objectives'
- The preamble of TRIPS
- The object and purpose of the incorporated treaties and their relationship with TRIPS
- Aspects of the object and purpose of the rationales and justifications of intellectual property protection and how national laws reflect those rationales and justifications.

In addition to the above, an analysis of object and purpose should take into account the object and purpose of the national provisions at issue in any dispute. That will not be determinative, but could well be relevant where it is a reflection of a country balancing competing interests and consequently utilising a flexibility or exception that TRIPS allows for. Recognising the ability of countries to calibrate their laws, through a framework of minimum standards and flexibilities, is part of the object and purpose of the agreement.[70] Some details of the above are now discussed.

Articles 7 and 8: 'principles' and 'objectives'

These Articles are part of the structural features of the TRIPS Agreement.[71] Where better to find object and purpose than in the

[70] See Frankel, *Challenging TRIPS-Plus Agreements*, above n 60, 1023–1066 at 1034: 'Freedom for WTO members to choose the method of implementation of TRIPS Agreement standards is an important recognition of some flexibility of the Agreement and consequent national autonomy that article 1 allows. The combination of the ability to have greater levels of protection, and the freedom for all members to implement domestic laws in a manner appropriate to them, creates a likelihood of differing intellectual property laws at national level. Thus, minimum standards structure can create disharmony. However, the members of the TRIPS Agreement have agreed to the minimum standards and national autonomy over implementation of standards. That approach is a structural feature of the TRIPS Agreement which forms part of the overall object and purpose of the Agreement.'

[71] As noted in the quote at above n 70, other structural features include the minimum standards framework, national treatment and MFN.

Articles that bear the titles 'objectives' and 'principles'? They provide the following:

Article 7 – Objectives

The protection and enforcement of intellectual property rights should contribute to the promotion of technological innovation and to the transfer and dissemination of technology, to the mutual advantage of producers and users of technological knowledge and in a manner conducive to social and economic welfare, and to a balance of rights and obligations.

Article 8 – Principles

1. Members may, in formulating or amending their laws and regulations, adopt measures necessary to protect public health and nutrition, and to promote the public interest in sectors of vital importance to their socio-economic and technological development, provided that such measures are consistent with the provisions of this Agreement.
2. Appropriate measures, provided that they are consistent with the provisions of this Agreement, may be needed to prevent the abuse of intellectual property rights by right holders or the resort to practices, which unreasonably restrain trade or adversely affect the international transfer of technology.

It is immediately obvious that these Articles are multi-faceted and that they embrace competing objectives and principles as well as notions of balance between intellectual property and other aspects of the public interest. The Articles do not provide stand alone exceptions to the other provisions of TRIPS, but they do provide an important and strong 'policy statement with active force'.[72] They have not been used to full effect in reports. In *Canada Pharmaceuticals*, Canada argued that Articles 7 and 8 supported its argument that the regulatory review and stockpiling exceptions in Canada's patent law complied with Article 30 of TRIPS.[73] The EC disputed Canada's approach, suggesting that Canada was trying to rewrite the balance in the Agreement. The panel said that Articles 7 and 8 must be taken into account. It also agreed with the EC that the TRIPS Agreement could not be renegotiated or added to in the context of dispute-related interpretation.[74] That point is almost where the panel stopped as far as Articles 7 and 8 were concerned. It is not clear how, if at all, the panel took them into account in its analysis of the exceptions at issue.

[72] See Frankel and Gervais, *Interpretation of TRIPS*, above n 55, at 1203.
[73] *Canada Pharmaceuticals*, above n 52. [74] *Canada Pharmaceuticals*, above n 52.

The significance of the objectives and principles to the interpretation of the TRIPS Agreement was underscored in the WTO's Doha Ministerial Declaration (Doha), which stated,[75]

> In applying the customary rules of interpretation of public international law, each provision of the TRIPS Agreement shall be read in the light of the object and purpose of the Agreement as expressed, in particular, in its objectives and principles.

The preamble of TRIPS

The VCLT expressly provides that preambles are relevant to context for interpretation.[76] The preamble sets out three interrelated aspects of the trade-related goal of the TRIPS Agreement:

> Desiring to reduce distortions and impediments to international trade;
>
> Taking into account the need to promote effective and adequate protection of intellectual property rights; and
>
> To ensure that measures and procedures to enforce intellectual property rights do not themselves become barriers to legitimate trade.

Similar to Articles 7 and 8, the preamble records multiple and sometimes conflicting objectives. 'Desiring to reduce distortions and impediments to international trade' suggests allowing free movement of intellectual property products, but that may compete with some domestic policies which prevent parallel importation on the basis of 'effective and adequate' intellectual property laws. The key to balancing these first two goals arguably lies in the third limb of measures not becoming barriers to trade. Measures and procedures to enforce intellectual property rights become trade barriers when intellectual property rights become so strong that they in fact distort rather than promote trade and innovation.[77] In other words, the trade-enhancing goal of the TRIPS Agreement cannot be said to be exclusively about protecting intellectual property at the cost of other objectives. Conversely, the balancing of other objectives should not defeat the protections of the TRIPS Agreement. This does not mean that flexibilities and exceptions are not permissible. As discussed, flexibility can arise through different interpretations of minimum standards, which must be compliant with TRIPS. In the case of exceptions, the relevant minimum standards relating to the exceptions must be complied with. Such exceptions

[75] WTO Ministerial Conference, Fourth Session, Doha, 9–14 November 2001, *Declaration on the TRIPS Agreement and Public Heath*, WT/MIN(01)/Dec/2, para 5(a).

[76] VCLT, above n 15, art. 31(2)(a). [77] See also discussion in Chapter 2.

include the three-step tests[78] and other exceptions such as those for *ordre public*[79] or methods of medical treatment.[80]

The object and purpose of the incorporated treaties and their relationship with TRIPS

An important part of the TRIPS Agreement's setting is that it is part of the WTO and consequently part of a body of trade rules.[81] The WTO agreements each govern their own areas of trade, but should not be interpreted to be in conflict with one another. Strictly speaking, all of the WTO treaties are interrelated and ought to be interpreted harmoniously.[82] This might mean that where TRIPS uses language similar to that found in other WTO agreements, those agreements may be relevant to TRIPS interpretation.[83] That said, such discussions will not be determinative, as the importance of context and object and purpose means that common phrases can mean different things in different contexts and one should not be transposed to the other.[84]

The TRIPS Agreement incorporates several other intellectual property treaties that were in existence at the time that TRIPS was negotiated and came into force. The negotiators of TRIPS recognised that international intellectual property agreements over certain minimum standards were not wholly new. Also, that incorporation is arguably advantageous as a mechanism to limit fragmentation of international intellectual property law. In doing so, they brought into its coverage the existing regimes and the experience of some one hundred years or more of multilateral intellectual property standards. In addition, the TRIPS

[78] TRIPS Agreement, above n 3, arts 13, 17 and 30, for example.

[79] TRIPS Agreement, above n 3, art 27.2. [80] TRIPS Agreement, above n 3, art 27.3.

[81] It can be disputed whether intellectual property should be part of trade and this was certainly a key part of the Uruguay Round negotiations. Intellectual property is, however, part of the WTO. For a discussion of the linkages, see K. Maskus, *Private Rights and Public Problems: The Global Economics of Intellectual Property in the 21st Century* (Petersen Institute for International Economics, Washington, DC, 2012), chapter 2.

[82] There is a general presumption against conflict of rules of international law; see J. Pauwelyn, *Conflict of Norms in Public International Law* (Cambridge University Press, 2008), at 240–244 and 247.

[83] Examples include the phrase 'public health', which is found in the TRIPS Agreement, above n 3, and in many other WTO agreements, including the General Agreement on Tariffs and Trade (GATT), 30 October 1947, 55 UNTS, 194 and General Agreement on Trade in Services (GATS), WTO Agreement, 1869 UNTS 183; 33 ILM 1167 (signed 15 April 1994, entered into force 1 January 1995), Annex 1B.

[84] One commentator warns against interpretative boundary crossings that go against object and purpose, see J. E. Alvarez, 'Beware: Boundary Crossings', September 18, 2014, NYU School of Law, Public Law Research Paper No. 14-51. Available at SSRN: http://ssrn.com/abstract=2498182.

Agreement brought new dimensions to coverage and also to the terms of dispute settlement.

The two main treaties incorporated in TRIPS are the Berne Convention[85] and the Paris Convention.[86] A panel has already recognised that the Berne Convention *acquis* is relevant to the interpretation of TRIPS.[87] The Paris *acquis* will also be relevant where the subject matter requires it. According to the panel, this *acquis* includes understanding about those agreements.[88] An extension of that logic is arguably that the fuller ambit of the purposes of intellectual property protection and flexibilities is relevant. Professors Dinwoodie and Dreyfuss suggest that an international *acquis* should be developed.[89]

The role of the object and purpose of national laws

The subject matter of all TRIPS Agreement disputes is whether a national law of a member is, or is not, in compliance with the TRIPS Agreement minimum standards. The underlying policy or purpose of the national law as articulated in the legislation and the legislative process would, one might think, therefore be relevant to TRIPS disputes. However, the WTO has not taken that approach. In the *US-110(5)* case, for example, the panel did not consider the domestic trade-off policy behind the US law to be relevant.[90]

No one national law will determine the meaning of an international law provision. First, because that is not what the VCLT rules require. That is because a national law is potentially illustrative of a party's negotiating position. It is not necessarily illustrative of the end agreement between parties. However, international agreements are often negotiated and framed based on national experiences. In this way, the systems relate to each other. In dispute settlement, the understanding of intellectual property terminology by reference to national laws is utilised. As many terms are specialist intellectual property terms, this is sensible as a resource, but as noted, no one national law can be dispositive of the international meaning. As discussed in the patents chapter of this book, that sort of analysis informed the panel in *Canada Pharmaceuticals* about patent

[85] Berne Convention, above n 4. [86] Paris Convention, above n 5.

[87] WTO Panel Report, *United States – Section 110(5) of the US Copyright Act*, 27 July 2000, WT/DS160/R, paras 6.60–6.66.

[88] *Section 110(5) of the US Copyright Act*, above n 86, paras 6.60–6.66.

[89] G. B. Dinwoodie and R. Dreyfuss, *A Neofederalist Vision of TRIPS: The Resilience of the International Intellectual Property Regime* (Oxford University Press, 2012), chapter 7.

[90] See Dinwoodie and Dreyfuss, *A Neofederalist Vision of TRIPS*, above n 89, at 117–118.

exceptions around the world, but it did not find there was any norm to be discerned from looking at either US or EU practice.[91] Such an analysis is no doubt useful, but it is one element to be taken into account rather than indicative of the final result.

The creation of substantive legal standards in international intellectual property agreements has usually involved a negotiation to reach a compromise between competing national approaches. Behind those national approaches are broad justifications for intellectual property law, such as utilitarian reward and incentive theories[92] and natural rights.[93] Other than compliance with international agreements, domestic laws are often premised on the basis of underlying rationales and justifications. Those rationales and justifications, however, take modern-day interpretation only so far. To the extent that it is true, for example, that the utilitarian theory of intellectual property is a justification for such laws, this justification does not directly address how countries can calibrate the domestic law to suit their needs. Put differently, a justification for a particular sort of intellectual property protection might be to encourage creativity and innovation, but this differs from the overall objectives of the TRIPS Agreement. The TRIPS Agreement ought not be construed as having abandoned already existing justifications for intellectual property law, or even rejecting legitimate emerging ones, because the treaty reflects the need to accommodate effectively the rights of both creators and users of intellectual property across international borders. A balance of rights also lies at the core of the justifications behind intellectual property protection in national regimes. The preamble of the TRIPS Agreement explicitly recognises this, as it states,

> *Recognizing* the underlying public policy objectives of national systems for the protection of intellectual property, including developmental and technological objectives.

These are some of the reasons why interpretation of the TRIPS Agreement should not be divorced from considering the national law justifications of provisions when those provisions are the reason that TRIPS is being interpreted.

[91] See Chapter 5. The panel also considered several third parties' laws.

[92] See, generally, W. Fisher, 'Theories of Intellectual Property', in S. Munzer (ed.), *New Essays in the Legal and Political Theory of Property* (Cambridge University Press, 2001), pp. 168–201.

[93] The natural rights theory is usually in one way or another attributed to Locke; see J. Hughes, 'The Philosophy of Intellectual Property', *Georgetown Law Journal*, 77 (1988), 287–366. See also discussion in R. Merges, *Justifying Intellectual Property* (Harvard University Press, 2011), at 31–67.

Overview of interpretation

As the above discussion shows, there are multiple sources of intellectual property law to draw on and national and international laws are inter-related. The ability to employ the tools of interpretation is critical not only for the settlement of disputes but also for the implementation of TRIPS standards and TRIPS flexibilities. Other barriers to implementation include lack of resources and expertise. This is more so with developing countries than small market economies, although, as small market economies run full government on limited resources, prioritising such endeavours is not always easily achieved.

The VCLT process of interpretation is multifaceted and should be approached on a holistic basis. Each step should be undertaken, and ordinary meaning in light of context and object and purpose should be considered. In taking each step one-by-one as a procedure, it should be remembered that the steps are not hierarchical.

The process of interpretation should take into account that flexibilities around the implementation of obligations and the availability of exceptions are integral to the object and purpose of the TRIPS Agreement. They should not be hesitantly used but rather utilised as reasonable options. When the pros and cons of the options are weighed that process can take into account both compliance with international agreements and local needs as they are permitted within the framework of the TRIPS Agreement.

4 Intellectual property and the nexus with innovation and cultural policies

> While trade theory provides little basis for mandating uniform standards of intellectual property across all countries, intellectual property rights is an issue that is here to stay on the international trade agenda ... The Uruguay Round TRIPS Agreement while at the level of general principle promoting a uniform approach, in fact allows for a balance to be struck between countries, legitimate interests in limiting intellectual property rights for consumer welfare and economic and social development reasons, and the interests of trading partners sustaining adequate incentives for innovation.[1]

> Traditional IPRs based on concepts of discrete innovation, linear technical progress and exclusive distribution control seem increasingly out of touch with modern innovation networking and learning. The system remains rather wedded to these notions some of which need to be reconsidered.[2]

> Intellectual Property Rights are important, but the importance of IPR has been exaggerated, as they form only one part of our innovation system. IPR should be seen as part of a portfolio of instruments. We need to strengthen the other elements of this portfolio and redesign our intellectual property regime to increase its benefits and reduce its costs. Doing so will increase the efficiency of our economy – and most likely even increase the pace of innovation.[3]

In many countries, intellectual property law has predominantly been a bundle of statutes which collectively are called intellectual property, but are not necessarily coherent in their nexus either with innovation or with cultural policy.[4] Often different parts of government administer these

[1] M. Trebilcock, R. Howse and A. Eliason, *The Regulation of International Trade*, 3rd edn (Routledge, New York, 2013), at 565.

[2] K. Maskus, *Private Rights and Public Problems: The Global Economics of Intellectual Property in the 21st Century* (Petersen Institute for International Economics, Washington, DC, 2012), at 17.

[3] J. E. Steiglitz, 'Economic Foundations of Intellectual Property Rights', *Duke Law Journal*, 57 (2008), 1693, at 1724.

[4] Sherman and Bentley discuss when the term 'intellectual property' emerged; see B. Sherman and L. Bentley, *The Making of Modern Intellectual Property Law* (Cambridge University Press, 1999).

statutes and they are recognised, in varying degrees, as part of business, science and innovation, agricultural, heath and cultural policies.[5] How the relationship between intellectual property and broader policies, such as innovation, should be framed is an emerging issue in many countries.[6] The linkages are often not clearly articulated and the details, in particular, are not fully known or understood.

Despite the linkages not always being clear, it is widely recognised that intellectual property law is one aspect of innovation policy. Other factors relevant to innovation policy include that innovation is often found in clusters, in places with higher education and where capital is available to invest in innovation.[7] Some points of connection between intellectual property and innovation are often asserted. Patents are, for instance, often counted as indicators of certain types of research and development (R&D).[8] On the one hand, it is often said that patents are vital for innovation, particularly in the pharmaceutical sector. On the other hand, '[i]n much economic analysis work, patents are treated as an innovation output measure. This implies that more patents indicate more innovation, which is not necessarily true.'[9]

The relationship between innovation and intellectual property is precarious because too much intellectual property can curb innovation, whereas too little intellectual property may create barriers to innovation.[10] This debate has been conspicuous in patent law, where some pharmaceutical companies are very dependent on patents[11] and seek to expand the scope of what is patented through various means. In contrast, some innovators in the field of computer software, for example, have fought against patent law. In 2013, New Zealand enacted, in its patent law, an exclusion from patentability for the protection of computer programs 'as

[5] For a discussion of this phenomenon in the United States, see S. M. Benjamin and A. K. Rai, 'Fixing Innovation Policy: A Structural Perspective', *George Washington Law Review*, 77 (2008), 1–88.

[6] For a general discussion of the relationship between innovation and intellectual property, see Maskus, above n 2, at 42–45.

[7] See D. Gervais, 'Of Clusters and Assumptions: Innovation as Part of a Full TRIPS Implementation', *Fordham Law Review*, 77 (2009), 2353–2378.

[8] See WIPO, 'Patent Statistics', available at http://www.wipo.int/ipstats/en/statistics/patents/.

[9] I. Hargreaves, 'Digital Opportunity: A Review of Intellectual Property and Growth', May 2011, available at www.ipo.gov.uk/ipreview.htm at 2.5. See also D. Benoliel, 'The International Patent Propensity Divide', *North Carolina Journal of Law and Technology*, 15(1) (2013), 49–100, where he discusses patenting and economic growth theory.

[10] See discussion in D. J. Gervais, 'IP Calibration', in D. J. Gervais (ed.), *Intellectual Property, Trade and Development*, 2nd edn (Oxford University Press, 2014), 86–114.

[11] Generic pharmaceutical companies in contrast are dependent on patents expiring or being otherwise available to use.

such'.[12] This move arose as a consequence of lobbying from local computer software companies.[13]

If intellectual property is recognised as a tool to 'power growth and development',[14] as the quote from WIPO in the Introduction to this book suggests, then the proper role of intellectual property law (patents in particular) is as a tool for innovation, not as the key determinant of what innovation looks like.[15] To be sure, patents may shape innovation if the existence of a patent requires innovators to invent around the patent, but that is different from patent law dictating whether or not there can be innovation.

A similar point can be made in relation to copyright and culture. Copyright should support and respond to culture by encouraging the proliferation of creative works; it should not be the driving force that shapes culture by determining creative boundaries or by inhibiting creativity. One way of looking at intellectual property law is that its 'parameters . . . are essentially a cultural construct. The lawmakers choose which cultural values to protect and to balance them.'[16]

Additionally, intellectual property law is often called upon to take into account other goals, such as supporting health, and various interests which it impacts, such as those of consumers. These sorts of other goals and interests often involve multiple issues and stakeholders. That is hardly surprising because all of humanity might claim to have an interest in culture and innovation and their outputs. Most of these other interests are frequently about access and use of the products of innovation and

12 Patents Act 2013 (NZ), s 11(2).

13 See, for example, the submissions to the Commerce Committee on the Patents Bill 2008 made by Catalyst IT (27 August 2009), New Zealand Biotech 2003 (27 August 2009), New Zealand Open Source Society (27 August 2009), Egressive (20 August 2009), Affinity (30 July 2009), available at www.parliament.nz/en-nz/pb/sc/documents/evidence/?Criteria.Parliament=49&Criteria.Author=Commerce%20Committee&Criteria.PageNumber=51.

14 See Chapter 1, footnote 1.

15 An analogy can be made in copyright. As Francis Gurry has said, 'The purpose of copyright is not to influence technological possibilities for creative expression or the business models built on those technological possibilities. Nor is its purpose to preserve business models established under obsolete or moribund technologies. Its purpose is, I believe, to work with any and all technologies for the production and distribution of cultural works, and to extract some value from the cultural exchanges made possible by those technologies to return to creators and performers and the business associates engaged by them to facilitate the cultural exchanges through the use of the technologies. Copyright should be about promoting cultural dynamism, not preserving or promoting vested business interests.' Francis Gurry, 'The Future of Copyright' speech at Blue Skies Conference on Future Directions in Copyright Law, Sydney, February 2011, available at www.wipo.int/about-wipo/en/dgo/speeches/dg_blueskyconf_11.html.

16 S. Frankel, 'From Barbie to Renoir: Intellectual Property and Culture', *Victoria University of Wellington Law Review*, 41 (2010), 1–14.

creativity. Access and use need to be reconciled with creativity and innovation goals. In global markets, access issues include both affordability and availability. This is one of the reasons why, for instance, small market economies parallel import.[17]

The relationship between intellectual property policy goals and the law may alter if seen as a global rather than purely domestic issue. For example, a law created in the name of supporting innovation at a domestic level may do exactly the opposite in the international arena. It may be a suitable policy, for example, for a country to extend patent term for pharmaceutical patents and protect new uses of existing pharmaceutical compounds[18] when pharmaceutical companies in that country research, develop, manufacture and even control worldwide distribution of pharmaceuticals. The same rationales do not apply to countries that do not do these things.[19] Yet, in the field of intellectual property, some countries will adopt laws that are based on policies or evidence relating to the economic conditions of somewhere else.[20] While most often described as developed country policies being forced on developing countries, this phenomenon is all too evident in small market economies, which also sometimes adopt ill-fitting intellectual property laws. The reasons for this vary but in the case of New Zealand are predominantly to gain some other trade goal, such as agricultural market access, and in the case of Singapore seem to be more explicitly about attracting foreign direct investment.[21]

Foreign direct investment (FDI) can support local innovation. Much FDI relating to intellectual property industries seems, however, not to be

[17] See Chapter 8.

[18] A highly contentious area of intellectual property is whether new uses should be protected. In some jurisdictions, they are protected on the basis that there is some inventiveness in the new uses. In other jurisdictions, the new use may not be patentable because the compound is known and accordingly the new use is not seen as involving sufficient inventive step. For a discussion of a different approach to inventive step and compatibility with the TRIPS Agreement, see G. B. Dinwoodie and R. C. Dreyfuss, *A Neofederalist Vision of the TRIPS Agreement: The Resilience of the International Intellectual Property Regime* (Oxford University Press, 2012), at 51–58.

[19] This is discussed further in Chapter 5.

[20] This can be particularly problematic where consumers are affected, which is more frequently the case now in intellectual property law. For a discussion of the problems of importing consumer law more broadly, see K. Tokeley, 'Consumer Law and Paternalism: A Framework for Policy Decision Making', in S. Frankel and D. Ryder (eds.), *Recalibrating Behaviour: Smarter Regulation in a Global World* (LexisNexis, Wellington, 2013), pp. 265–304.

[21] Whether strong intellectual property laws do attract valuable investment is highly disputed. See, generally, K. E. Maskus, 'Intellectual Property Rights and Foreign Direct Investment', Centre for International Economic Studies Working Paper No. 22, May 2000, available at SSRN: ssrn.com/abstract=231122 or dx.doi.org/10.2139/ssrn.231122.

directly invested in innovation. Aspects of the Singapore experience are illustrative here. Singapore has attracted investment in its pharmaceutical industry, but that investment is not predominantly in R&D or local innovation; rather, the investment has been in using Singapore as a hub for the re-exportation of pharmaceuticals to the South East Asian market.[22]

> The volume of trade in pharmaceuticals flowing in and out of Singapore is disproportionately large compared with the size of the country, due to its status as a distribution centre. The country exports a large amount of pharmaceuticals, although the majority of this total is from re-exported goods. The balance of pharmaceutical trade remains positive.

In Israel, Singapore and New Zealand, a majority of patents are foreign owned. So when patent law standards are increased, through free trade agreements (FTAs) in particular, the prime beneficiaries are offshore. The stronger patent law becomes in order to protect foreign-owned patents, the harder it can be for local innovation in some fields to grow.[23] Those who argue for stronger patent laws (including the introduction of patent term extension discussed in Chapter 5), reasoning that it will attract additional investment, are at best speculating. New Zealand has had relatively strong patent laws for some time and there has been no evidence of any substantial investment in New Zealand-based patent industries and particularly no investment from pharmaceutical companies as a result of these laws.[24] Even if stronger patent laws attracted investment in the pharmaceutical sector, there is no evidence that

[22] Epsicom Business Reports, 'The Pharmaceutical Market in South East Asia to Reach US $80 Billion by 2017 at Retail Prices', available at www.prweb.com.

[23] The New Zealand Pharmaceutical Management Agency (PHARMAC) stated in its submission about the Patents Bill, 2008, now Patents Act 2013, that 'PHARMAC recognises the inherent value in the workings of an effective patent system – one which provides adequate incentives for innovation and technology transfer while ensuring that the interests of the public are protected. PHARMAC is also well aware of the costs to society where the balance between ensuring innovation while protecting the interests of the public is distorted. Where the exclusive rights granted to patentees are disproportionate to the inventive contribution then competition is stifled and society is forced to bear the resulting losses and the absence of new and useful inventions.'; PHARMAC, 'Bill Submission to the Commerce Committee on Patents Bill', available at www.parliament.nz/resource/0000114753.

[24] When I said this at a seminar in Auckland relating to the Trans-Pacific Partnership negotiations, a representative of Medicines New Zealand (an organisation that represents major international pharmaceutical companies) responded that there was investment in clinical trials in New Zealand. Clinical trials, while important, are not the kind of innovation that develops more innovation or will bring New Zealand business further along the global value chain. When I suggested that a cost–benefit analysis could be performed to see if this 'investment' was worth the increased levels of patent law, I was informed that this 'elided' the issues.

investment will necessarily generate further innovation and the Singapore example is evidence of this.

Innovation and creativity are dynamic concerns. Thus, intellectual property faces the continuous challenge of responding to developing science and technology, and appropriately moving norms and expectations of those involved in innovation and creativity both as producers and as users. Those seeking to expand the protections of intellectual property law have for some time claimed that it is necessary for a range of activities from creativity to innovation. While that is true to a degree, the same generalised claims about encouraging innovation seem to be made to expand protection, rather than new evidence being directed specifically to explain why and to support the claim that those expansions are also necessary to encourage innovation.

Framing the appropriate regulatory detail to achieve such dynamic and important goals of encouraging innovation and creativity is a challenge. This challenge has led to a variety of calls for evidence-based policy. What evidence amounts to good evidence and what metrics could be used to measure whether or not intellectual property law works is are complex. Another complexity is that what is reliable or good evidence at national level may not translate to good evidence for international norms.[25]

As discussed above, intellectual property is one of the many factors that go into supporting innovation and creativity. But there are also other ways to incentivise innovation. In the field of patents, prizes have been used and discussed as an alternative incentive mechanism.[26] In addition to intellectual property, countries might choose to support their creative industries through special measures. Where goods such as films, for example, are involved, there is a detailed history of screen quotas under the GATT.[27] Countries may also support innovation through funding or subsidising R&D. Subsidies can take different forms such as direct payment, grants or tax breaks. Some subsidies are legitimate under trade rules and others are not.

[25] See discussion of evidence-based policy below.

[26] See J. E. Stiglitz, 'Prizes, Not Patents', Project Syndicate, 6 March 2007, available at www.project-syndicate.org/commentary/prizes-not-patents and see discussion in D. J. Hemel and L. L. Ouellette, 'Beyond the Patents-Prizes Debate', *Texas Law Review*, 92 (2013), 303–382.

[27] This is not the focus of this chapter; see GATT Agreement (General Agreement on Tariffs and Trade, 30 October 1947, 55 UNTS, 194) Article IV: Special Provisions relating to Cinematograph Films. For a discussion of the trans-Atlantic disagreement on this topic, see J. M. Grant, '"Jurassic" Trade Dispute: The Exclusion of the Audiovisual Sector from the GATT', *Indiana Law Journal*, 70 (1995), 1333–1366.

This chapter discusses evidence-based policy and how the presence of evidence does not necessarily mean the evidence will be followed. Small market economies sometimes may, even in the face of evidence that suggests they should not do so, adopt ill-fitting intellectual property policies. The chapter then discusses the use of subsidies for R&D, and the relationship between subsidies and intellectual property rules at the World Trade Organization (WTO).

Evidence-based policy

> Government should ensure that development of the IP System is driven as far as possible by objective evidence. Policy should balance measurable economic objectives against social goals and potential benefits for rights holders against impacts on consumers and other interests. These concerns will be of particular importance in assessing future claims to extend rights or in determining desirable limits to rights.[28]

The evidence-based approach to policy is internationally recognised as a good practice in law making. Whatever the field of law, questions arise about what constitutes evidence and, once evidence is found, or more often generated for a purpose, how that evidence should be used and interpreted.[29] Different disciplines have different approaches and make different value judgements about the weight to be attributed to different types of evidence. In intellectual property law, much weight continues to be attributed to economic evidence. Economic evidence is not always, however, a trump card that determines policy direction. Even though the United Kingdom (UK) Hargreaves Report, which analysed the state of UK copyright, notes that the economic evidence points against copyright term extension,[30] for example, further suggestions of extension continue to be made from time to time. Similarly, term extension in the United States has not received universal acclaim there. Yet it is a policy that the United States exports by requiring its trading partners to implement term extension in free trade agreements.[31] Challenges at the domestic level to laws such as term extension suggest that the reasons

[28] Hargreaves Report, above n 9, at 98.

[29] In relation to copyright, see ESRC Festival of Social Science, 'What Constitutes Evidence for Copyright Policy?', CREATe Working Paper No. 1, 8 November, 2012, available online at www.copyrightevidence.org/create/esrc-evidence-symposium/media/PDF/esrc-evidence-proceedings.pdf.

[30] Hargreaves Report above n 9, at 96-97.

[31] See, for example, the Australia–United States Free Trade Agreement (signed 18 May 2004, entered into force 1 January 2005), at 17.4, and Korea–United States Free Trade Agreement (signed 30 June 2007, entered into force March 2012), at 18.4.

for these laws are not based on the best outcome for a country as a whole, but are more in the nature of rent-seeking rights for certain sectors of the economy. Problematically, based on faulty foundations, these 'benefits' are then seen as worthwhile protecting globally, primarily because they might, for a period, bring export gains. To continue with the copyright term example, New Zealand has the basic rule of copyright term of life of the author plus 50 years or 50 years from the making. There is now almost certainly pressure to extend this term as part of the Trans-Pacific Partnership.[32] The majority of quality and independent evidence from around the world supports not extending. In spite of this evidence political pressure suggests the outcome will be extension.

Evidence other than economic evidence will be relevant if intellectual property is looked at as a development tool. As noted above, the use of evidence in domestic processes may well be different from the use of evidence in international processes. If a law has been developed based on evidence of a local overall benefit for a country to adjust and calibrate their laws, then quite obviously that evidence will not automatically translate beyond the domestic sphere. That is exactly why international norms should not purport to be based on evidence if the evidence is not applicable internationally. Therefore, if international norms are based on evidence, that evidence needs to be generally applicable. It may be that a norm is appropriate if evidence supports it for most, even if not all, treaty members. Consequently, it is sometimes possible to agree to some minimum standards of protection.[33] This underlies why minimum standards may be preferable to detailed harmonisation of intellectual property law, which will not be a one-size-fits-all model. Harmonisation should be based on evidence of common benefit, rather than harmonisation for harmonisation's sake or harmonisation for the sake of incumbent beneficiaries.

Evidence-based policy may well be the way of the future as intellectual property evolves, but there are some difficulties. These difficulties include what type of evidence is relevant and that much existing intellectual property law is not based on detailed evidence. Evidence therefore is potentially relevant to recalibrating existing laws as well as to developing new laws, including increased rights, and new flexibilities and exceptions.

In many areas of regulation, such as consumer protection law, it is well recognised that law based on evidence from one country might not be

[32] Out of the developed countries in the negotiation, both New Zealand and Canada have the 50-year term, and the United States, Australia and Singapore have 70 years. Mexico seeks copyright for a period of 100 years.

[33] This is exactly what the major multilateral intellectual property treaties do; see Chapter 2.

good evidence in another country where consumer behaviour may well differ.[34] In intellectual property law, there is a growing recognition that the needs of one country's domestic industry simply cannot provide good evidence of the need for the same law in another country without the same industries.[35] That said, there are some common interests in protection and common interests in flexibilities. Lessons learned from evidence can be used in other countries to assess if the evidence is relevant to the decisions about that other country's policies and laws. Evidence-based policy will be relevant to those commonalities but it may also support differences.

Evidence-based policy may well be used to justify non-harmonisation and this is where in some instances small market economies have created policies that 'collide' with larger developed country interests. Large developed country interests have resulted in both the adoption of 'bad-fit' policies and the non-adoption of other policies because they are a bad fit in small market economies. Also, in some instances, the suggestion of 'bad-fit' laws has led to the development of laws which are a better fit.[36]

Small market economies and bad-fit intellectual property policies

The implementation of the Agreement on Trade-Related Aspects of Intellectual Property Rights (TRIPS)[37] has shown that some intellectual property policies are a good fit in some places but are a bad fit in others. This has given rise to a period of looking for some balance in TRIPS and how it is implemented in members' laws. This 'calibration phase'[38] should not be taken as suggesting that laws need to return to pre-TRIPS levels of difference.[39] The TRIPS minimum standards still exist,

[34] See Tokeley, *Consumer Law and Paternalism*, above n 20.

[35] See discussion regarding patents in Chapter 5.

[36] See, for example, discussion of the non-adoption of protection for some aspects of technological protection mechanisms if they prevent reasonable access in New Zealand, and the development of fair use in Israel and Singapore, in Chapter 6.

[37] Agreement on Trade-Related Aspects of Intellectual Property Rights, Marrakesh Agreement Establishing the World Trade Organization, Annex 1C, 1869 UNTS 299; 33 ILM 1197 (adopted on 15 April 1994, entered into force 1 January 1995) ('TRIPS Agreement').

[38] D. J. Gervais, 'IP Calibration', in D. J. Gervais (ed.), *Intellectual Property, Trade and Development*, 2nd edn (Oxford University Press, 2014).

[39] TRIPS levels may still be too high in some aspects for some developing countries. Least-developed countries do not yet have to comply with the TRIPS Agreement. This was part of the original agreement and has been extended until 2015; see Extension of the Transition Period under Article 66.1 for Least Developed Country Members, IP/C/64, 12 June 2013.

but the focus has turned to better utilisation of the exceptions and flexibilities found in TRIPS.

There are some intellectual property policies which are a good fit in one or two places, but are a bad fit elsewhere. Some aspects of intellectual property are arguably a bad fit in many economies, including small market economies. One could say that, therefore, these matters should not be harmonised internationally, but rather should be left to national autonomy. They may also represent a kind of 'tolerated compromise' and thus are nevertheless incorporated into the law. There may be some situations where bad-fit policies cannot, however, be tolerated because they inhibit either innovation or creativity too extremely, and because they have a detrimental effect on the availability of intellectual property by inhibiting technology transfer or making products not available for consumers, or the policy has a detrimental effect on prices.

The Singapore experience with parallel importing provides an example of a good-fit policy adjusted to a less-good-fit compromise. Exhaustion of rights is one of the most contentious issues in international intellectual property and so the TRIPS Agreement exempts any disagreements about exhaustion from being subject to dispute settlement.[40] Singapore allows for international exhaustion in relation to intellectual property.[41] In an agreement with the United States, Singapore agreed to curb its parallel importing in some areas.[42]

When an intellectual property rule or policy is demonstratively a cost to the local economy, it is a deadweight loss. Some kind of cost–benefit analysis may determine if a cost is worth bearing in exchange for some other gain.[43] In the intellectual property context, the supposed benefit is either some trade gain or simply being part of a trade agreement. Even if there is an overall benefit to carrying an intellectual property related deadweight loss, the reasons for having intellectual property rules in such circumstances have changed. The reasons for intellectual property rules are no longer related to innovation incentives, but to something else. Intellectual property becomes essentially the equivalent of a market-

[40] TRIPS Agreement, above n 37, art 6.

[41] See Wee Loon Ng-Loy, *Law of Intellectual Property in Singapore*, revised edn (Sweet & Maxwell, 2009) ('*Law of Intellectual Property in Singapore*'), pp. 418–425, section 34.3.

[42] See Chapter 8; also see Ng-Loy, *Law of Intellectual Property in Singapore*, above n 41 at 34.3.12–34.3.16 explaining the amendment to parallel importing after the Singapore–US FTA.

[43] See S. Frankel, M. Kolsky Lewis, C. Nixon and J. Yeabsley, 'The Web of Trade Agreements and Alliances and Impacts on Regulatory Autonomy', in S. Frankel and D. Ryder (eds.), *Recalibrating Behaviour: Smarter Regulation in a Global World* (LexisNexis, Wellington, 2013), pp. 17–62, for a discussion of costs and benefits in relation to patent term extension in New Zealand.

distorting subsidy, for an offshore interest, and that means it functions as a protectionist measure and its role is primarily rent-seeking in nature. This phenomenon can sometimes easily be spotted. The potential of New Zealand agreeing to patent term extension in the Trans-Pacific Partnership negotiations is one example. There is a calculated cost of several millions, which will be borne by a combination of consumers and the public health-care budget, without any directly calculated gains.[44]

In trade law, some subsidies are considered trade barriers, where they distort competition by unduly protecting domestic industry. Before turning to the use of subsidies to directly support R&D that might lead to the creation of intellectual property, it is useful to consider how intellectual property can act as a trade barrier.

Intellectual property as a trade barrier

Intellectual property rules give exclusive rights often in the form of property rights to owners. Those who are not owners of intellectual property, but who seek to use it, usually can do so only if their conduct fallens within some legally condoned flexibility or their conduct does not otherwise infringe the intellectual property right. This basic paradigm is premised on varying rationales and theories, many of which are frequently disputed.[45] Broadly, however, if intellectual property fulfils its goal, it operates as a subsidy of some kind, even if that subsidy is justified. This is because at its most basic level a subsidy is something that transfers wealth from one group to another.[46] Property rules are a way of transferring wealth to the beneficiary of the relevant rule. One could easily dispute whether intellectual property rights in fact transfer wealth; rather, they confer rights which potentially can bring wealth. If one takes an international perspective, then the TRIPS Agreement does transfer wealth from developing countries to developed countries.[47] But this international

[44] Patent term extension may cost New Zealand $85–153 million; see MED, 'Review of the Patents Act 1953 The Pharmaceutical Patent Term in New Zealand Discussion Paper' (June 2003), at [46]–[47], available at www.med.govt.nz/business/intellectual-property/pdf-docs-library/patents/review-of-patents-act/patents-act-1953-pharmaceutical-patent-terms-pdf. See also discussion in Chapter 5.

[45] For a discussion of the rationales of intellectual property law, see, for example, W. Fisher, 'Theories of Intellectual Property', in S. Munzer (ed.), *New Essays in the Legal and Political Theory of Property* (Cambridge University Press, 2001), pp. 168–201, and R. Merges, *Justifying Intellectual Property* (Harvard University Press, 2011).

[46] For a general explanation of subsidies, see World Trade Report 2006, available at www.wto.org/english/res_e/booksp_e/anrep_e/wtr06-2b_e.pdf.

[47] See K. E. Maskus, 'Intellectual Property Rights and Economic Development', *Case Western Reserve Journal of International Law*, 32 (2000), 471–506. See also World Bank, *Global Economic Prospects and the Developing Countries* (Washington, DC, 2002), p. 503.

subsidisation, as we see below, does not otherwise fall foul of WTO anti-subsidy rules. Among other reasons, it is not a typical subsidy in the form of a government payment to support a domestic industry.

Intellectual property rights remove the outputs of creativity and innovation from the public domain of free use. The TRIPS Agreement is not, in trade rules terms, a mechanism which permits subsidies. It is, however, a tolerated kind of trade barrier. The existence of intellectual property rights as territorial rights creates trade barriers and the absence of any internationally agreed rule of exhaustion of intellectual property rights allows intellectual property owners to divide markets and to prevent the free flow of intellectual property and intellectual property related goods and services. The WTO recognises that intellectual property is a trade barrier both in the preamble of TRIPS[48] and in GATT. GATT provides that intellectual property rights for 'the protection of patents, trade marks and copyrights, and the prevention of deceptive practices' are an exception to GATT obligations, provided certain criteria are fulfilled.[49]

A few words about parallel importing illuminate the trade barrier point. Intellectual property rights are used in many jurisdictions to stop the importation of parallel imported products. Parallel imports are not counterfeit products, but are genuine products made for one market, that are then imported into another.[50] Countries that prevent the parallel importation of goods usually justify this as a way of ensuring that products made for and priced according to local conditions are not used to undercut a different market where a higher price is charged for that product and sometimes for products of higher quality.[51] The main GATT objective that seems to be ignored, when parallel importing is prohibited, is liberalising the movement of goods.[52] As one commentator has said, 'protecting the profit margin of certain producers by stopping goods at the border is precisely the sort of activity that the GATT

[48] The preamble of the TRIPS Agreement, above n 37, begins, 'Desiring to reduce distortions and impediments to international trade, and taking into account the need to promote effective and adequate protection of intellectual property rights, and to ensure that measures and procedures to enforce intellectual property rights do not themselves become barriers to legitimate trade.'

[49] GATT, above n 27, art XX(d). [50] They are sometimes called grey market goods.

[51] See, for example, the prevention of imports of inferior-quality toothpaste from Brazil to the United Kingdom, *Colgate-Palmolive Ltd and Another* v. *Markwell Finance Limited and Another* [1989] 106 RPC 497 (EWCA).

[52] GATT, above n 27, art III. See also S. Frankel, 'The Applicability of GATT Jurisprudence to the Interpretation of the TRIPS Agreement', in C. M. Correa (ed.), *Research Handbook on Intellectual Property Law and the WTO* (Edward Elgar Publishing, Cheltenham, 2010), pp. 3–23.

was meant to discourage'.[53] Consequently, the assertion of an intellectual property right to prevent the importation of goods is a trade barrier, which the TRIPS Agreement allows.

There is an important distinction, however, between the recognition that intellectual property is a trade barrier that the WTO supports through the TRIPS Agreement and the creation of trade barriers to goods in the name of intellectual property. The GATT exception does not mean that all intellectual property measures would otherwise violate GATT. It also does not mean that all intellectual property related regulation falls under the GATT exception. The GATT exception requires that regulation 'necessary to secure compliance with laws or regulations which are not inconsistent with the provisions of this Agreement'.[54] The prevention of parallel importing would not necessarily fall under this exception. A country relying on it would have to prove that it is necessary. Also, as the TRIPS Agreement does not provide a rule on exhaustion of rights, it would not be the correct interpretation to determine the matter through the GATT Agreement.[55] Thus, it is possible to provide for intellectual property protection and to support the free movement of goods.[56]

Other WTO agreements, particularly both GATT and GATS,[57] are market access agreements because they prohibit certain types of restrictions on market access.[58] In contrast, the TRIPS Agreement requires countries to enact intellectual property laws which enable owners of intellectual property rights to control aspects of the market for intellectual property related products. In this way, intellectual property rights protect rather than liberalise market access. Put differently, the structure of the WTO is such that protecting intellectual property rights on a territorial basis is treated as a legitimate trade barrier. Legally actionable trade barriers, which may take the form of subsidies, are, however, a different matter.

[53] P. J. Heald, 'Trademarks and Geographical Indications Exploring the Contours of the TRIPS Agreement', *Vanderbilt Journal of Transnational Law*, 29 (1996), 635–660, at 658.

[54] In addition, there is the chapeau of GATT, above n 27, art XX, which requires that 'measures are not applied in a manner which would constitute a means of arbitrary or unjustifiable discrimination between countries where the same conditions prevail, or a disguised restriction on international trade'.

[55] The WTO would interpret its treaties consistently and also as a specialist agreement TRIPS would be the primary source of relevance. See also Chapter 3.

[56] See Chapter 8.

[57] General Agreement on Trade in Services (GATS), WTO Agreement, 1869 UNTS 183; 33 ILM 1167 (signed 15 April 1994, entered into force 1 January 1995).

[58] In the case of GATT, above n 27, the main way in which this is achieved is by converting non-tariff barriers to tariffs and then gradually negotiating the reduction of tariffs.

Subsidising the creation of intellectual property

The WTO has chosen the TRIPS Agreement as the mechanism to support R&D. WTO rules make intellectual property rights the primary vehicle to incentivise innovation and creativity, rather than through R&D subsidies. Whether intellectual property rights necessarily achieve this incentive is another question. R&D subsidies are, however, permissible in some circumstances, but not just because they are R&D subsidies in name. If they fall within the prohibited or actionable subsidy rules of the WTO, then the relationship to R&D is not on its face a normative basis on which the subsidy might be permissible.

The World Trade Organization (WTO) has an agreement, the Subsidies and Counterveiling Measure Agreement (SCM),[59] which makes certain subsidies prohibited and others actionable. In the early years of its existence, the SCM also had some permissible subsidies, known as green light subsidies.[60] These included subsidies for R&D. The SCM provided that 'assistance for research activities conducted by firms or by higher education or research establishments on a contract basis with firms' was not actionable. This was as long as 'the assistance cover[ed] not more than 75 per cent of the costs of industrial research or 50 per cent of the costs of pre-competitive development activity'.[61] This provision expired five years after the SCM came into force.[62] Thus, R&D subsidies lost their green light status and became actionable subsidies.

At the same time, TRIPS standards were on the increase in the name of R&D. Thus, the WTO has effectively preferred one model of supporting research and innovation, the intellectual property model, over the subsidy model. There may be good reasons for doing this if intellectual property is working well and in a balanced way. That would be the situation if, for the most part, intellectual property incentivised innovation and creativity and did not also unduly stifle such goals. Whether or not the existing model of intellectual property is effectively doing this is a subject of hot debate.[63] Before turning to why intellectual property rules are seen as preferable to subsidies, the next section discusses when a subsidy is a trade-rule violation.

59 WTO, Agreement on Subsidies and Countervailing Measures, WTO Agreement, 1869 UNTS 183; 33 ILM 1167 (signed 15 April 1994, entered into force 1 January 1995) ('SCM').

60 Prohibited subsidies are known as red light subsidies and actionable subsidies as amber light subsidies.

61 SCM, above n 59, art 8.2. 62 SCM, above n 59, art 21.3.

63 See, for example, K. J. Strandburg, 'Evolving Innovation Paradigms and the Global Intellectual Property Regime', *Connecticut Law Review*, 41 (2009), 861–920.

What makes a subsidy an SCM violation?

WTO disputes over R&D subsidies have predominantly involved the aircraft industry. This industry is frequently subsidised because it is not only very expensive but also seen as crucial.[64] Other sectors, which are probably of more direct relevance to intellectual property and for which some countries often use subsidies are biotechnology and information technology.[65]

Subsidies are hard to define. The SCM definition is not definitive of what subsidies mean in all circumstances. It is, however, the basis on which the WTO defines subsidies. To be caught under the SCM rules, something must fall within the definition of a subsidy, which requires a financial contribution and a benefit resulting from that contribution.[66] The benefit must be more favourable than those otherwise available in the market.[67] The WTO has interpreted this to mean that there must be some kind of comparison made between the position of the beneficiary of the subsidy before and after the financial contribution. The Appellate Body said,[68]

> This must be so, for there can be no 'benefit' to the recipient unless the 'financial contribution' makes the recipient 'better off' than it would otherwise have been, absent that contribution. In our view, the marketplace provides an appropriate basis for comparison in determining whether a 'benefit' has been 'conferred', because the trade-distorting potential of a 'financial contribution' can be identified by determining whether the recipient has received a 'financial contribution' on terms more favourable than those available to the recipient in the market.

The financial contribution can take different forms including as a direct or an indirect transfer of funds, forgoing of government revenue (including tax breaks), provision of goods or services, or price or income support of some kind.[69] Once a subsidy falls within the definition, it is either prohibited or actionable. Prohibited subsidies are broadly export subsidies or import substitution subsidies, which are not prevalent in intellectual property.[70] Actionable subsidies need to be both specific

[64] W. Shin and W. Lee, 'Legality of R&D Subsidies and its Policy Framework under the World Trading System: The Case of Civil Aircraft Disputes', *STI Policy Review*, 4(1) (2013), at 5, available online at papers.ssrn.com/sol3/papers.cfm?abstract_id=2277560.

[65] Shin and Lee, above n 64. [66] SCM, above n 59, art 1.1.

[67] SCM, above n 59, art 14.

[68] Appellate Body Report, *Canada – Measures Affecting the Export of Civilian Aircraft*, WT/DS70/AB/R, 2 August 1999, at para 157.

[69] SCM, above n 59, art 1.1.

[70] An example of prohibited subsidies were the US subsidies of cotton, which were found to be in violation of the SCM; see Report of the Appellate Body, *United States-Subsidies on Upland Cotton*, WT/DS267/AB/R, 3 March 2005.

and have adverse effects.[71] Specific means limited to certain enterprises[72] and adverse effects means injury to domestic industry, nullification of the benefit otherwise received from a tariff concession or some serious prejudice.[73]

The problem with characterising all R&D subsidies as having adverse effects is that whether they do or do not cannot be considered a general rule. Rather, whether there have been adverse effects is fact-specific, meaning that some R&D subsidies may have adverse effects and others will not. This might be because[74]

> [F]undamental research carried out within companies may be commercially profitable and, in addition, produce positive external effects for society at large. Government support to R&D can be justified on the ground of the existence of such positive externalities. Yet, it is difficult to identify the exact compensation that allows companies to internalize positive spillovers. Any assistance beyond that amount results in subsidization of R&D activities that would in any case be profitable.

The definition of subsidy

As discussed above, excess intellectual property rules may have effects which are analogous to subsidies. If a country failed to provide intellectual property rules, the result would be that domestic imitations could 'legiti mately' occur. At a global level, if a WTO member does this, it would violate the TRIPS Agreement. Part of the justification for intellectual property rules is to prevent some sorts of free-riding. Could a failure to regulate for intellectual property protection amount to a subsidy of the producers who therefore can free-ride on others' intellectual property?

A question that has arisen, in the context of climate change, is whether the failure to regulate carbon emissions is a subsidy. Some commentators have said the answer is no, because a failure to regulate does not fall foul of the SCM. As Howse and Eliason explain, renowned economist Stiglitz has stated that the failure to internalise 'climate change costs caused by carbon emissions from the production of products is a subsidy to the producers of such products'.[75] In addition, Howse and Eliason suggest

[71] For a general discussion of subsidies, see M. Trebilcock, R. Howse and A. Eliason, *The Regulation of International Trade*, 4th edn (Routledge, New York, 2013), at 364–410.

[72] SCM, above n 59, art 2.1 [73] SCM, above n 59, art 5.

[74] See World Trade Report 2006, above n 46, at 52.

[75] R. Howse and A. Eliason, 'Domestic and International Strategies to Address Climate Change: An Overview of the WTO Legal Issues', in T. Cottier, O. Nartova and S. Z. Bigdeli (eds.), *International Trade Regulation and the Mitigation of Climate Change* (Cambridge University Press, 2010), pp. 48–94 at 73.

that there is arguably an SCM violation in the situation of the failure to regulate carbon emissions.[76]

For intellectual property, a failure to regulate is addressed by enforcement of the TRIPS Agreement. The remaining intellectual property problem is not a failure to regulate but sometimes over-regulation. However, analogy to the climate change issue is potentially useful because it illustrates the spectrum of how regulation can have subsidising effects. It is not simply whether there is regulation or not, but the effect of the relevant regulation, that is key. It logically follows that preferring intellectual property rules over subsidy rules makes sense only to a point. That point should be where international intellectual property rules achieve their object and purpose of incentivising research, innovation and creativity. This approach is also in accordance with the Vienna Convention rules on interpretation and the requirement for treaty obligations to be interpreted in context and in accordance with the object and purpose of the treaty.[77]

The question of whether a patent is the equivalent of a subsidy arose in a complaint about alleged subsidising of the US aircraft industry.[78] The facts are complex and involve much more than patents, but the patent-relevant point was whether the allocation of patent rights, under contracts between government agencies and Boeing, amounted to a subsidy. Based on the submission of the parties, the panel assumed, for the sake of argument, that the allocation of patent rights to government-financed research could constitute a subsidy. In the particular case, there was no SCM violation because the alleged subsidy was not specific in accordance with Article 2.1 of the SCM.[79] The Appellate Body cast doubt on whether

[76] Howse and Eliason, above n 75, at 74–76.

[77] Vienna Convention on the Law of Treaties, 23 May 1969, 1115 UNTS. 331 (entered into force 27 January 1980), art 31. See also Chapter 3. The difficulty is that the TRIPS Agreement, above n 37, art 1, allows members to adopt more extensive protection (see also discussion in Chapter 2). When that more extensive protection does not support innovation or creativity or other rationales and objectives of intellectual property, those increased protections arguably undermine the object and purpose of the TRIPS Agreement and other international intellectual property agreements. This would not be actionable as a violation complaint and non-violation complaints are not available under the TRIPS Agreement. For further discussion of non-violation and TRIPS, see WTO, 'TRIPS: Non-violation Complaints (article 64.2) Background and the Current Situation', available at www.wto.org/english/tratop_e/trips_e/nonviolation_background_e.htm and S. Frankel, 'Challenging TRIPS-plus FTAs – the Potential Utility of Non-Violation Complaints', *Journal of International Economic Law*, 12(4) (2009), 1023–1065.

[78] WTO Appellate Body Report, *United States – Measures Affecting Trade in Large Civil Aircraft* (Second Complaint), WT/DS353/AB/R, 23 March 2012 ('*Measures Affecting Trade in Large Civil Aircraft*').

[79] *Measures Affecting Trade in Large Civil Aircraft*, above n 78, para 724.

the panel should have proceeded on the assumption about patents, but did not revisit the point.[80]

Specific and adverse effects of subsidies

To be an actionable subsidy, once the measure meets the definition, it must be both specific and have adverse effects.[81] Given that the SCM requires specificity in regard to sectors, a general subsidy for R&D rather than a sector-specific R&D would therefore seem to be acceptable. Such a general subsidy may fall foul of the SCM if it turned out, in fact, to be specific.

A subsidy is specific if access to it is 'explicitly limited to certain enterprises'.[82] Conversely, if there are 'objective criteria or conditions governing the eligibility for, and the amount of, a subsidy, specificity shall not exist, provided that the eligibility is automatic and that such criteria and conditions are strictly adhered to'.[83] The Boeing dispute is illustrative. There the patent allocations were found to be not specific because[84]

> [o]nce the legal framework for the allocation of patent rights under R&D contracts and agreements with the government is taken into account, it becomes clear that the eligibility to receive the alleged subsidy is not limited to the class of enterprises that conducts aerospace R&D.

The allocation of patents in this way was uniform under government R&D contracts.[85] Thus, it was not the kind of subsidy the SCM restricted. The Appellate Body said it could not see 'how the object and purpose of the SCM Agreement would be frustrated'.[86] In some circumstances, however, if the beneficiaries of the subsidy are 'enterprises located . . . within the jurisdiction of the granting authority', the subsidy is specific.[87]

Sector specificity under TRIPS

Intellectual property standards under the TRIPS Agreement do not distinguish between sectors. The same rules for rights and exceptions apply whatever the sector involved. Some suggest that protection should

80 *Measures Affecting Trade in Large Civil Aircraft*, above n 78, paras 726–729.
81 SCM, above n 59, arts 2 and 5. 82 SCM, above n 59, art 2.1(a).
83 SCM, above n 59, art 2.1(b).
84 *Measures Affecting Trade in Large Civil Aircraft*, above n 78, paras 781–782.
85 *Measures Affecting Trade in Large Civil Aircraft*, above n 78, para 788.
86 *Measures Affecting Trade in Large Civil Aircraft*, above n 78, para 788.
87 SCM, above n 59, art 2.2. See also GATT, above n 27, art. XVI, 'Subsidies in General', refers to the Member's own 'territory'.

perhaps be different for different sectors because the connection between protection and innovation or creativity is not the same across industries and businesses, let alone between intellectual property businesses and amateurs. As discussed above, for example, patents may be more appropriate in the pharmaceutical sector than in the computer software industry. The same is true of copyright, which does not distinguish between the level of protection given to a simple drawing and a work of fine art, for instance. Distinguishing between intellectual property related industries might help solve some of the problems of intellectual property. From an intellectual property perspective, such arguments have merit. But from a broader 'trade rules' perspective, there may be difficulties. If looked at globally, it might amount to favouring one country's innovation or creative industry over another country's sectors and thus unfairly altering comparative advantage.[88]

The issue of privileging one sector over another has arisen in a WTO dispute over exceptions to Canadian patent law.[89] The issue was whether Canada's regulatory review exception[90] was specific to the pharmaceutical industry and thus fell foul of the requirement that patents do not discriminate between fields of technology.[91] Although 'fields of technology' is not defined, it seems reasonable that it could equate to industry sectors and may even be applicable to fields within those sectors. The panel found that exceptions to patent law must be neither de jure nor de facto specific.[92] On the facts of the dispute, it was found that the exception was not necessarily specific to the pharmaceutical industry and thus was TRIPS compliant. The decision has been criticised for many reasons.[93] Of particular note is the apparent contradiction of the

88 Broadly, this would not be consistent with the rationales of the World Trade Organization, which is a regime designed to allow countries to maximise comparative advantage; see, generally, A. O. Sykes, 'Comparative Advantage and the Normative Economics of International Trade Policy', *Journal of International Economic Law*, 1 (1998), 49–82.

89 WTO Panel Report, *Canada – Patent Protection of Pharmaceutical Products*, WT/DS114/R, 17 March 2000 ('*Canada Pharmaceuticals*').

90 A regulatory review exception is where a third party is able, during the patent term, to make the patented product for the purposes of submitting samples and/or information to a medicines regulator for review before the patent has expired.

91 The dispute also concerned a stockpiling exception, but that exception did not make it past the first step in the three-step test of the TRIPS Agreement, above n 37, art 30 and so was not considered in the discussion about non-discrimination.

92 *Canada Pharmaceuticals*, above n 89.

93 See, for example, R. Howse, 'The Canadian Generic Medicines Panel: A Dangerous Precedent in Dangerous Times', *Journal of World Intellectual Property*, 3(3) (2000), 493–507, and G. B. Dinwoodie and R. C. Dreyfuss, 'TRIPS and the Dynamics of Intellectual Property Lawmaking', *Case Western Reserve Journal of International Law*, 36(1) (2004), 95–122, at 99, 104 and 112.

non-discrimination requirement between 'fields of technology' (this could equally be called a requirement not to be sector specific) and the need, when having patent flexibilities, to make sure that the exception is limited. The panel found that Article 27's requirement that there be no discrimination between fields of technology was applicable to interpretation of the first step of the patent exceptions test that the exception be limited.[94] Often the most effective way to limit an exception is to direct it to the particular sector of relevance. The panel therefore said,[95]

> [I]t is not true that being able to discriminate against particular patents will make it possible to meet Article 30's requirement that the exception be 'limited'. An Article 30 exception cannot be made 'limited' by limiting it to one field of technology, because the effects of each exception must be found to be 'limited' when measured against each affected patent. Beyond that, it is not true that Article 27 requires all Article 30 exceptions to be applied to all products. Article 27 prohibits only discrimination as to the place of invention, the field of technology, and whether products are imported or produced locally. Article 27 does not prohibit bona fide exceptions to deal with problems that may exist only in certain product areas.

The line of distinction here is fine. Countries ought to be able to play to their strengths and doing so will likely involve diversifying and having laws that support that diversification. Such diversification should be possible without amounting to discrimination that breaches the non-discrimination rules.[96] Thus, Professors Dinwoodie and Dreyfuss have argued that a country ought to be able to diversify without being found to be discriminatory.[97] Such diversification is consistent with the trade ideal of countries playing to their strengths or their comparative advantage.

The rationale for preferring intellectual property rules over subsidies

Intellectual property rules are arguably justified as preferable to subsidies because they are only awarded once the intellectual property is created, whereas subsidies are *ex ante* to research and creation and may or may not result in innovative outcomes.[98] Additionally, subsidies are a

94 The relevant test is TRIPS Agreement, above n 37, art 30.

95 *Canada Pharmaceuticals*, above n 89, para 7.92.

96 In the TRIPS Agreement, above n 9 these rules are national treatment, art 3, and most-favoured nation, art 4.

97 G. B. Dinwoodie and R. Dreyfuss, 'Diversifying Without Discriminating Complying with the Mandate of the TRIPS Agreement', *Michigan Telecommunications Technology Law Review*, 13 (2007), 445–456.

98 For discussion of *ex-ante* and *ex-post* rewards see Hemel and Ouellette, above n 26, at 333–344.

cost for government,[99] whereas much of the cost associated with intellectual property rights is borne by private parties (except of course where the government is the innovator). The direct costs the government bears in the intellectual property regime are administrative costs relating to the running of the patent, trade mark and, where they exist, copyright offices. This does not take account of indirect costs such as not enabling innovative and creative domestic entities to the fullest extent possible. The picture is not as simple as intellectual property being *ex post* and subsidies *ex ante*; however, part of the justification for the existence of copyright and patent rights is the incentive of a potential right, which is *ex ante* in nature.

Subsidies are generally prohibited under the SCM because they support protectionism.[100] SCM rules target domestic market subsidies, but a significant part of the subsidy problem is the effect on the ability to compete in foreign markets. If industry X is subsidised in country A, then the equivalent industry in country B is unlikely to be able to compete with the industry in country A (particularly if country B's industry is not subsidised), but it also cannot compete with country A in country C.

The nature of intellectual property creation is that R&D happens in one place (or possibly in more than one place), but products of that R&D are sold not only in the market where the product originates, but also in other places. Those other markets, where the R&D does not take place, sometimes pay higher rates for products. The price paid in those markets may not be necessary to recoup the cost of R&D as that might be achieved in the home market. International sales protected by intellectual property rights in a situation, where the costs are recouped in the original home market resemble in effect a subsidy, although that does not mean that intellectual property owners should not be entitled to protection in foreign markets.

In comparing intellectual property rules to subsidies, it is important to distinguish between the rules of intellectual property which are created in the name of supporting innovation and creativity, and are used to prevent undue imitation, unfair free-riding and counterfeiting, and rules that are designed to ensure a price. An intellectual property right per se does not guarantee that there will be a market for any product or that the intellectual property will be a financial success. Intellectual property rights provide protections and rights to exclude third parties in a variety

[99] Subsidies can come from local government or quasi-government agencies.
[100] See S. Lester, 'The Problem of Subsidies as a Means of Protectionism: Lessons from the WTO EC – Aircraft Case', *Melbourne Journal of International Law*, 12 (2011), 345–372.

of ways.[101] The owner of intellectual property rights can use the rights to affect price, but the grant of an intellectual property right is not a guarantee of market success. The ability to control price is also not a direct rationale or justification for granting intellectual property rights. It can be an incidence of their use.

Additionally, the use of intellectual property to control price is unlikely to involve the transfer of R&D opportunities. One response is that the increased protections in third-party markets are also necessary for innovation and creativity. The situation becomes more complex if intellectual property is not working well in the originating market to incentivise innovation or creativity, such as patents which create difficulties for innovation because they are too far upstream. If this is the case, then the rationale for other countries to support bad patents is entirely unclear and arguably unjustified.

The claim that increased protections in third-party markets are needed to support innovation in the home market is also questionable and particularly so from the point of view of small economies. Small economies usually do not seek increased protection and for large economies the payback for investment in intellectual property is often achieved in the home market. In addition, such claims should necessarily be supported by evidence, not by statements that all increases of intellectual property protection support innovation and creativity.[102] They plainly do not. If there is evidence to support increased protection then that evidence ought to be both market-specific and specific to the law at issue rather than an amorphous notion of the value of intellectual property in general. The need for innovation support in the home market is not evidence of innovation support in other markets. One might say that it ought to be if a global perspective is placed on intellectual property. At least at present that is not the case and, in any event, that would be conveniently selective use of the notion of globalism, rather than the reality of globalism.

One advantage of being able to segment markets, based on price, is the possibility that say, say, pharmaceuticals can be sold at cheaper rates in markets that cannot afford to pay 'full' rates, such as least-developed countries purchasing pharmaceuticals. This should not be discouraged and it may be that those 'cheaper' products should not be exported to

101 Most intellectual property rights are expressed as exclusive rights or rights to exclude. For a discussion of the significance of this terminology, see S. Frankel and D. J. Gervais, 'Plain Packaging and the Interpretation of the TRIPS Agreement', *Vanderbilt Journal of Transnational Law*, 46 (2013), 1149–1214, at 1184–1186.

102 While this is widely accepted in the literature, it does not appear to have been so accepted by trade negotiators.

third-party markets that can afford to pay.[103] Appropriate pricing does not seem to occur often enough.

The small market economy problem is a different problem. If small market economies have to pay high prices in order to ensure innovation in other countries that do the R&D on the basis of globalisation, then territoriality should not be re-erected to prevent cheaper access to legitimate intellectual property products, such as through parallel importation of those products.[104] Again, this points to the fact that optimal global intellectual property is not a one-size-fits-all model. Not all countries will be innovators or creators in all sectors. Equally so, other countries should not always have to pay higher prices. Small market economies have shown, and are likely to continue to show, that innovation can have a different place in the global value chain.[105]

The place of local innovation and the global value chain

As international intellectual property rules have primarily developed from negotiations based on national positions, much law reflects national norms.[106] Behind some of these national laws lie implicit assumptions about business models and trade. The law does not explicitly require that these business models continue, but it is often structured in a way that supports incumbent business models. New technologies, however, give rise to new business models. In copyright, for example, businesses have evolved from using fair use exceptions and even structuring themselves so that their activities fall through loopholes in the domestic implementation of exclusive rights.[107] Many of these businesses could not easily be globalised because what is non-infringing in one country is not necessarily so in another. This is not necessarily ideal although it may be the inevitable result of allowing flexibility and exceptions to calibrate intellectual property law appropriately to local needs.

[103] This is the case where pharmaceuticals are made under compulsory licence under the TRIPS Agreement, art. 31bis system. See also Chapter 1 footnote 25 and the associated text.

[104] See Chapter 8.

[105] The patent chapter in this volume discusses how this questions the overall structure of patent law.

[106] However, as discussed in Chapter 3, those national norms are relevant to the interpretation of the international obligations, but are not determinative of it.

[107] See discussion of businesses built on fair use in Chapter 6. The fitting-between-the-rights model is illustrated in *WNET* v. *Aereo Inc.*, 712 F.3d 676 (2d Cir. 2013), where the business model is premised on falling between the 'gaps' in the US public performance right. The 2nd Circuit ruling was overturned in the Supreme Court, see *Am. Broad. Cos., Inc.* v. *Aereo, Inc.* (Aereo III), 134 S. Ct. 2498, (2014).

Small market economies did not enter into the TRIPS Agreement reluctantly, in the way that is often said to be the case for developing countries.[108] The TRIPS Agreement was part of the WTO single package, which overall is very important for trade-dependent small market economies. These economies also, given their size and scale, do not expect to be overall leaders in innovation, although they may be leaders in some specific fields. As discussed above, small market economies sometimes adopt bad-fit intellectual property policies because they are seen as worth the overall trade-off. In addition, many innovators in small market economies often do not bother with patents.

Research has shown that this can happen for several reasons, including that they are too expensive or, perhaps more surprisingly, that the local enterprises do not want patents. Why would an innovator not want a patent? As discussed above, in some industries this is broadly the case in many countries. In small market economies, the lack of patenting can occur in industries that elsewhere are patent intensive, such as medical research and biotechnology. This occurs because they do not develop, manufacture or distribute, or even intend to do so, in their local market or in any market at all; rather, they find a different place in the global value chain. They may patent overseas or partner with a foreign business that does the patenting. This business model is discussed further in Chapter 5 as it affects patent law specifically.[109] Here the central point is that the choice of intellectual property rights over subsidies may be a bad choice where the intellectual property rights do not incentivise research in the local economy. In these situations, subsidies, which are legitimate because they are not specific and so do not violate the SCM, seem an excellent approach for research and possibly also development of that research in small market economies. This may well be a way to raise productivity. This may be something unique that small market economies can offer. International intellectual property rules should support this place of innovation in the global value chain. High intellectual property standards, particularly those created through TRIPS-plus FTAs coupled with no or minimal investment in R&D, do not support this business model in the long term. Rather, those factors seem to have placed, and are likely to continue to place, limits on the innovative opportunities in small market economies.

108 See discussion in the Introduction to this book.

109 As discussed in Chapter 5, there are new models of contributing to global innovation. This might involve geographical separation between aspects of R&D, production and distribution. That chapter discusses how those structures may mean that some underlying assumptions about patent law are no longer correct in the global market.

5 Flexing patent law

> In England, notwithstanding early and rare cases back in the fourteenth century, the first concession to an inventor was granted in 1561. *The criteria for granting a patent were that the invention would substitute to imported goods* and that it would make the good available for a lesser price than the imported one. It should also not substitute domestically produced goods. Hence the economic impact was the primary criterion for granting patents, that the invention should not hurt domestic industry but rather provide it with new opportunities.[1]

> A good example [of a law-making trade-off] is the 1984 extension of the term of U.S. patent protection on pharmaceuticals subject to regulatory review. In exchange for lengthening the term, congress enacted the 'bolar exemption', which permitted generic drug manufacturers to use patented pharmaceuticals for the purpose of generating the information needed for market clearance. The net result – the Drug Price Competition and Patent Term Restoration Act (commonly called the Hatch-Waxman Act) – was a package that added to the protection enjoyed by patent holders in the pharmaceutical industries while accelerating public access to low-cost medicines after patent termination.[2]

> A patent was not a government-backed guarantee of monopoly revenues for a full 20 years.[3]

> Since knowledge is cumulative, exclusive rights have always had the paradoxical effect of slowing progress in the name of promoting it. Second-comers must pay the costs associated with identifying and negotiating with the holders of rights in the advances they seek to build upon. In the Knowledge Economy, this difficulty is magnified. Patent

1 D. Guellec and B. van Pottelsberghe de la Potterie, *The Economics of the European Patent System: IP Policy for Innovation and Competition* (Oxford Scholarship Online, 2007) ('*The Economics of the European Patent System*'), at 17.

2 G. B. Dinwoodie and R. Dreyfuss, *A Neofederalist Vision of TRIPS: The Resilience of the International Intellectual Property Regime* (Oxford University Press, 2012) ('*A Neofederalist Vision of TRIPS*'), at 117.

3 WTO Panel Report, *Canada – Patent Protection of Pharmaceutical Products, Complaint by the European Communities and Their Member States*, WT/DS114/R 17 March 2000 ('*Canada Pharmaceuticals*'), at para 4.35.

> rights have moved upstream to cover fundamental building blocks of nature. These patents dominate such a broad swath of inventive opportunities that it is not clear whether right holders have the cognitive capacity to fully mine their claims. The product-to-right ratio has also changed. In earlier eras, products were typically associated with one intellectual property right; now, products (and the products with which they must interoperate) involve orders of magnitude more rights.[4]

As each of the above quotes suggests, patents are complex bargains with far-reaching effects on the knowledge economy, imports and the price of medicines and other products and processes which result from scientific advances. Achieving balance of interests and appropriate calibration in patent law that takes into account both local development needs and international concerns is complex. A guiding mechanism to this complexity is that the central justification for patents is that they provide some incentive for innovators to invent.[5] Thus, they are an important feature of the innovation system.[6] Governments and international agencies have used patents as a proxy for innovation, which is usually treated as a public good in its own right, and information about innovation has the additional role of indicating aspects of related economic growth.[7] They are also shown to not work as a proxy for innovation.[8] The pharmaceutical

[4] R. C. Dreyfuss, 'Does IP Need IP? Accommodating Intellectual Production Outside the Intellectual Property Paradigm', *Cardozo Law Review*, 31 (2010), 1437, at 1441–42 ('*Does IP Need IP?*').

[5] For a summary of the incentive utilitarian theory, see W. Cornish, D. Llewelyn and T. Aplin, *Intellectual Property: Patents, Copyright, Trade Marks and Allied Rights*, 7th edn (Sweet & Maxwell, London, 2010), at paras 3–36–3–51 and D. S. Chisum et al., *Principles of Patent Law* 2nd edn (Foundation Press, New York, 2001), at 6.

[6] P. A. David, 'Intellectual Property Institutions and the Panda's Thumb: Patents, Copyrights, and Trade Secrets in Economic Theory and History', in M. B. Wallerston, M. E. Mooge and R. A. Schoen (eds.), *Global Dimensions of Intellectual Property Rights in Science and Technology* (National Academy Press, Washington, DC, 1993), pp. 1–61, at 23 states: 'there is no settled body of economic theory on the subject that can be stated briefly without doing serious injustice to the sophisticated insights that have emerged over many decades of debate. Instead, the relevant economic literature is extensive, convoluted, and characterized by subtle points of inconclusive controversy'. See also R. Gilbert, 'Looking for Mr. Schumpeter: Where Are We in the Competition–Innovation Debate?', in A. B. Jaffe, J. Lerner and S. Stern (eds.), *Innovation Policy and the Economy* (NBER and MIT, Cambridge, MA, 2006), pp. 159–215.

[7] See D. Banoliel, 'The International Patent Propensity Divide', *North Carolina Journal of Law and Technology*, 15 (2013), 49–100, summarising the literature behind this proposition. Some argue that patents endanger innovation; see, for example, A. B. Jaffe and J. Lerner, *Innovation and Our Discontents: How Our Broken Patent System Is Endangering Innovation and Progress* (Princeton University Press, 2004).

[8] It is now widely agreed that patent filings alone are not a good measure of innovation; see, for example, G. Ferenstein, 'Patent Director: "Patent Filings Do Not Equal Innovation", U.S. Needs New Measure', available at www.fastcompany.com/1738089/patent-director-patent-filings-do-not-equal-innovation-us-needs-new-measure, stating ' "Patent filings do not equal innovation, by any stretch," says Kappos. While his solution to the problem may

sector is reliant on patents,[9] while other sectors, or at least parts of them, dispute the value of patents for them.[10]

The features of a country's patent law ought to reflect its stage of development and the role of innovation. The small market economies discussed in this book all have strong patent laws, presumably because they are developed countries. They also exhibit some particular flexibilities (exclusions and exceptions) that are most likely attributable to their status as net importers of patented products. This illustrates, as the Introduction to this book suggests, that these countries have one foot in the developed world and the other in the developing world. This mixed economic position is particularly evident when it comes to patent-related issues.

Subject matter

The subject matter of patents is broad. The TRIPS Agreement defines patentable subject matter as 'patents shall be available for any inventions, whether products or processes, in all fields of technology, provided that they are new, involve an inventive step and are capable of industrial application'.[11] That 'patents must be available in all fields of technology' is frequently subject to literal interpretation, whereby patent advocates conclude that everything is patentable (provided it meets the criteria of newness and inventive step and is capable of industrial application). Courts and policy makers do not necessarily follow this view, but in small market economies the default position, particularly in the late twentieth and early twenty-first century, was that everything was patentable unless there was a common law-recognised limitation such as

not completely satisfy those eager to see the United States move beyond the patent paradigm, Kappos is pressing experts and universities to come up with new measures of innovation, such as job creation and job growth that arise from a particular idea.'

9 W. M. Cohen, R. Nelson and J. P. Walsh, 'Protecting Their Intellectual Assets: Appropriability Conditions and Why US Manufacturing Firms Patent (or Not)', NBER Working Paper No. 7552, 2000.

10 This has been particularly apparent in open source software and other models of open innovation; for an overview, see Dreyfuss, *Does IP Need IP?*, above n 4.

11 WTO, Agreement on Trade-Related Aspects of Intellectual Property Rights, Marrakesh Agreement Establishing the World Trade Organization, Annex 1C, 1869 UNTS 299; 33 ILM 1197 (adopted on 15 April 1994, entered into force 1 January 1995) ('TRIPS Agreement'), art 27. Footnote 5 explains that in the TRIPS Agreement, 'the terms "inventive step" and "capable of industrial application" may be deemed by a Member to be synonymous with the terms "non-obvious" and "useful" respectively'. It does not deem 'new' to be synonymous with 'novel', but many countries use one or the other, or both, of these terms.

mathematical formula or mere discovery or an express exclusion in the law.[12] The wording of other parts of TRIPS[13] and Article 27 in particular, however, shows that what amounts to patentable subject matter is more complicated.

First, TRIPS mentions inventions, but it gives no 'global' definition. Invention has different definitions in national laws, but in many countries there must be an invention (rather than a discovery), which might require a separate analysis from other issues of patentability.[14] That approach is certainly TRIPS compliant because the Agreement's wording makes it clear that patents must be available for inventions. The weight that intellectual property offices and courts give to 'invention' as separate from the other TRIPS criteria, however, varies between jurisdictions.[15]

The approach to subject matter in the small market economies is very similar at a high level; however, there are differences in the detail. Israel, Singapore and New Zealand all ask if there is an invention, but not necessarily as an analysis separate from the patentability criteria.[16]

[12] This has played out in different ways in the three jurisdictions. In New Zealand, this default position was related to patent applications not being subject to full examination and the patentee being given the benefit of the doubt about patentability. Prior to the Patents Act 2013, the Intellectual Property Office of New Zealand applied the rule that a patent application should only be refused if it was not a new invention on any reasonable interpretation of the law. The patent applicant was given the benefit of the doubt, meaning that something should be patented unless it clearly was not permitted under the legislation. Patents were not examined for inventive step or industrial application. This approach has its origins in the United Kingdom; see *Swift & Co's Application* [1962] RPC 37 (EWHC). Exclusions were developed at common law, if at all. The main exclusion was that methods of medical treatment were not patentable; see *Pfizer Inc* v. *Commissioner of Patents* [2005] 1 NZLR 362 (CA); see also discussion in S. Frankel, *Intellectual Property in New Zealand*, 2nd edn (LexisNexis, Wellington, 2013), at 409–412. The Patents Act 2013, s 15–16 provides for express exclusions. In Singapore, a list of express exclusions was included in the legislation and then repealed in 1994. For the effect of this change, see W. L. Ng-Loy, *Law of Intellectual Property in Singapore*, revised edn (Sweet & Maxwell, 2009), at [30.1.20], suggesting 'the deletion of the list of excluded matters does not mean that there is no longer any concept of "invention" in our patent law'. In Israel, express exclusions are found in Section 7. The definition of invention in Section 3 provides 'an invention, whether a product or process in any technological field'. Debate over technological field means that certain matters are excluded from patentability as a subject matter question, such as business method patents; see E. Liss and D. Adin, *Intellectual Property Law and Practice in Israel* (Oxford University Press, 2013), at [2.2.2.4].

[13] Exceptions are permitted under the TRIPS Agreement, above n 11, arts 27.2, 27.3 and 30.

[14] See, for example, in the United Kingdom the discussion in *Kirin Amgen Inc* v. *Transkaryotic Therapies Inc* [2004] UKHL 46; see also S. Frankel, 'Lord Cooke and the Scope of Patents', *Victoria University of Wellington Law Review*, 39(2008), 73–98, at 84–85.

[15] See, for example, J. Pila, *The Requirement for an Invention in Patent Law* (Oxford University Press, 2010), analysing the UK and EU requirements of invention.

[16] What invention means is complex and is frequently discussed in relation to exclusions for methods of medical treatment; see Liss and Adin, *Intellectual Property Law and Practice in Israel*, above n 12, at [2.2.2.1]; Ng-Loy, *Law of Intellectual Property in*

This is in part because the statutory definition in each country's law refers to 'invention' and also because when forming their patent law they adopted the English Statute of Monopolies 1623 and followed subsequent jurisprudence, which provides some parameters of 'invention'.[17] Additionally, Israel, Singapore and New Zealand all have some kinds of express exclusions from patentability.[18]

In addition to the requirement of an invention, there are patentability criteria that the invention must be new, involve an inventive step (not be obvious) and be capable of industrial application (be useful).[19] There is much written about these criteria and how they are applied in different jurisdictions. None of the terms is expressly defined in the TRIPS Agreement and they therefore depend on national legislatures and courts for their meaning. Thus, there is a wide variation on how these terms are interpreted. For example, one of the most disputed issues in patent law is what amounts to the required level or height of inventive step. The lack of agreement over the appropriate level reflects the ways that countries calibrate their patent law to domestic needs. Consequently, some countries will have high thresholds for patentability and other countries low thresholds, which most likely reflect their state of development. Notably, however, even developed countries do not have the same approach to 'inventive step' (they do not even call it the same thing).[20] Arguably the varying interpretations of 'inventive step' all comply with the TRIPS Agreement.[21] As discussed in Chapter 3, one country's interpretation of an internationally agreed term is not determinative of the internationally

Singapore, above n 12, at [30.1.20]–[30.1.21]; S. Frankel, 'A Patentable Invention: Will Current Proposed Law Reform Clarify Patentable Subject Matter?', *NZ Business Law Quarterly* (2005), 350–365.

17 The High Court of Australia explained that invention is not so much rigidly defined in the Statute of Monopolies, but is a concept; see *National Research Development Corp* v. *Commissioner of Patents* [1959] 102 CLR 252 at 271, 'The purpose of s 6, it must be remembered, was to allow the use of the prerogative to encourage national development in a field which already, in 1623, was seen to be excitingly unpredictable. To attempt to place upon the idea the fetters of an exact verbal formula could never have been sound. It would be unsound to the point of folly to attempt to do so now, when science has made such advances that the concrete applications of the notion which were familiar in 1623 can be seen to provide only the more obvious, not to say the more primitive, illustrations of the broad sweep of the concept.' In *Pfizer Inc* v. *Commissioner of Patents* [2005] 1 NZLR 362 (CA), at [54], the New Zealand Court of Appeal confirmed that New Zealand law incorporated the full breadth of s 6 of the Statute of Monopolies, including the proviso that patents should not be granted in 'hurt of trade' or if 'generally inconvenient'. For a discussion of the history and modern application of the Statute of Monopolies, see L. Palombi, *Gene Cartels: Biotech Patents in the Age of Free Trade* (Edward Elgar, Cheltenham, 2008).

18 See above n 12. 19 See above n 11. 20 The United States uses 'nonobvious'.

21 TRIPS Agreement, above n 11, art 1.1 recognises that countries can comply with the agreement in different ways.

agreed meaning. This is particularly so when at the time of entering into the agreement the parties knew there were variations in each other's approach to terms such as 'inventive step'.[22] An important point about compliance with the TRIPS Agreement is that the terms cannot be interpreted so that they have no real meaning at national law.[23] That would be non-compliance.

Small market economies have adopted developed country tests relating to inventive step.[24] They tend to look at cases from the United States and the EU (also Australia and Canada) and decide which approach best suits interpretation of their law. To illustrate this point further, an example of a disputed subject matter and inventive step issue is useful. On the world stage, one of the most disputed issues has been whether second and further uses of pharmaceuticals can be patented.[25] Developed countries patent these and some developing countries do not.[26] The small market economies discussed in this book all allow patents on second uses of pharmaceuticals. In this way, their patent policy is aligned with the developed world.

22 See Chapter 3.

23 In relation to inventive step, the meaning can vary. As Professors Dreyfuss and Reichman explain, 'Consider, for example, the eligibility requirement of an inventive step (non-obviousness). The standard of inventiveness is intimately tied to a nation's economic goals, and especially to its citizens' technological potential and to the types of creativity it can hope to foster. Even within one nation, determining the right standard can be difficult. In the United States, for example, the threshold of nonobviousness has varied widely at different periods, and it remains a contentious issue. Perhaps for these reasons, TRIPS leaves the height of the inventive step to national law. Presumably, deep harmonization requires convergence on a single standard. Yet finding one that would suit countries at different levels of technological sophistication and for all kinds of intellectual advances could easily prove impossible'; see J. H. Reichman and R. C. Dreyfuss, 'Harmonization without Consensus: Critical Reflections on Drafting a Substantive Patent Law Treaty', *Duke Law Journal*, 57 (2007), 85–130, at 98–99.

24 Decisions often refer to US and EU jurisprudence or Australian jurisprudence, which also refers to US and EU cases.

25 These are broadly new uses of known pharmaceutical compounds.

26 India and Brazil, for example, reject the patenting of second use pharmaceuticals because they judge them too incremental or not involving enough of an inventive step. In 2005, India amended its Patent Act 1970, adding s 3(d), which excludes patents for 'the mere discovery of a new form of a known substance which does not result in the enhancement of the known efficacy of that substance'; see S. Basheer, 'India's Tryst with TRIPS: The Patents Amendment Act 2005', *India Journal of Law and Technology*, 22 (2005), 15–46; F. A. Khander and S. Ragavan, 'Proof of Progress: The Role of Inventive Step/Non-Obviousness Standard in the Indian Patent Office', in R. Okediji and M. Bagley (eds.), *Patent Law in Global Perspective* (Oxford University Press, 2014), pp. 541–570. For Brazil, see C. Schulz, 'The TRIPS Agreement and Intellectual Property in Brazil', *American Society of International Law Proceedings*, 98 (2004), 100–106. See also R. Okediji, 'Legal Innovation in International Intellectual Property Relations: Revisiting Twenty Years of the TRIPS Agreement', *University of Pennsylvania Journal of International Law*, 36(1) (2014), 191–268.

In varying degrees, patents registered in Israel, Singapore and New Zealand are predominantly foreign-owned rather than locally owned. These countries also rely heavily on imports of patent products.[27] In this way, they have more in common with some parts of the developing world than with larger developed countries.

Patents are registered intellectual property rights and another reflection of small market economies having one foot in the developed world and one in the developing world is their innovative regulatory approach to registration and how to resource a patent office. A problem that all patent offices face is one of workload and how to examine applications in a thorough and timely way. The patent offices in the small market economies, both formally and informally, utilise other office examination processes. In the case of New Zealand, examination is, as a result of the 2013 Act, formally shared with Australia, although registration remains separate in each country and some of the legal tests are different.[28] Australia also examines for Singapore. Singapore utilises examination from many other patent offices.[29] Israel will grant a patent without substantive examination if there has been full examination of an parallel patent in the United States, Britain, the European Patent Office or another established patent office.[30]

The above is the background to the focus of this chapter. In sum, small market economies exhibit some common features. They are developed

[27] See WIPO, 'Statistics on Patents', available at www.wipo.int/ipstats/en/statistics/patents/, showing for 2012–2013 total patent applications divided by resident (R) and non-resident (NR): applications from Israel (R) 1319 (NR) 5473; New Zealand (R) 1425 (NR) 5674; and Singapore (R) 1081 (NR) 8604.

[28] For an explanation of the trans-Tasman single economic market proposed patent regime, see S. Frankel and M. Richardson, 'Trans-Tasman Intellectual Property Coordination', in S. Frankel (ed.), *Learning from the Past, Adapting for the Future: Regulatory Reform in New Zealand* (Lexis Nexis, Wellington, 2011), pp. 527–553, at 549 and S. Frankel, C. Nixon, M. Richardson and J. Yeabsley, 'The Challenges of Trans-Tasman Intellectual Property Coordination', in S. Frankel and D. Ryder (eds.), *Recalibrating Behaviour: Smarter Regulation in a Global World* (LexisNexis, Wellington, 2013), pp. 101–138, at 115–119.

[29] See Singapore IP Office, 'Applicant Requests for Search & Examination', at www.ipos.gov.sg/AboutIP/TypesofIPWhatisIntellectualProperty/Whatisapatent/Applyingforapatent/ApplyingforapatentinSingapore.aspx, discussing the 'all foreign' examination approach and that local examination can also be requested. Singapore is also a member of the ASEAN Patent Examination Co-operation, a regional patent work-sharing programme of ASEAN Member States Patent Offices of Brunei Darussalam, Cambodia, Indonesia, Lao PDR, Malaysia, the Philippines, Singapore, Thailand, and Vietnam. The programme was launched on 15 June 2009, aiming to coordinate patent registrations.

[30] Patent Law 5727–1967 (Israel), s 17(3). Also a favourable International Preliminary Examination Report under the Patent Co-operation Treaty is accepted as equivalent to an allowed application.

economies that are net importers of patents. In addition, they are places with world-class higher education and also have local, often niche, research and development (R&D). This combination has created a unique and evolving role in the patent-related global value chains and networks.[31] A value chain represents the different stages of innovation, R&D, manufacture and distribution.[32] Value may be added by various entities at any part of the chain. A global value chain is where these stages, or links in the chain, are in more than one country.

That unique and evolving role in global value chains seems not to be very well reflected in each country's patent law. And in turn that suggests that international patent law is not very well constructed to take account of global value chains. The next part of this chapter examines this idea through two lenses. The first is the structure of patent law, which is fundamentally territorial, and how that relates to the structure of patent-related global value chains. The second lens is how small market economies sometimes balance legal rules, in particular the relationship between patent exceptions (regulatory review and experiment use) and the term of patents including rules for patent term extension.[33]

Global value chains and patent law

The dominant model used to be large companies innovating in-house. Now, under pressure from competition and financial markets, companies are increasingly specialized. They don't have all the technology and competences they need in-house; they have to obtain it from others, through purchase and alliances. Such contractual relationships take inventions out of the company and put them on the market place. It requires all parties to protect their intellectual property to delineate clearly what they want to share or not and under which conditions. *A related trend is the growing importance of small, high tech start-up companies. They do not have control of, or even access to, distribution channels, they do not have brand names, and*

31 I use global value chain broadly to indicate chains or networks that link stages of research, development, manufacture and distribution as a global phenomenon. For a discussion of the growing importance of global value chains generally, see O. Cattaneo, G. Gereffi and C. Staritz (eds.), *Global Value Chains in a Postcrisis World: A Development Perspective* (The World Bank, Washington, DC, 2010).

32 One definition is 'The value chain describes the full range of activities that firms and workers do to bring a product from its conception to its end use and beyond. This includes activities such as design, production, marketing, distribution and support to the final consumer. The activities that comprise a value chain can be contained within a single firm or divided among different firms. Value chain activities can produce goods or services, and can be contained within a single geographical location or spread over wider areas.' See 'Global Value Chains', at http://www.globalvaluechains.org/concepts.html.

33 These rules have all been discussed in disputes at the World Trade Organization (WTO); see discussion below.

they do not have large manufacturing facilities. They have one thing: their technology, and they have, in general, no other way of protecting this technology than by filing patents.[34]

The above quote illustrates change within one economic territory or zone.[35] It refers to small high-tech start-up companies. Many of these become medium-sized or small enterprises. Small market economies are largely composed of small and medium enterprises. As commentators have noted, 'how to protect cumulative and sequential innovation as distinct from path-breaking innovation becomes an ever more pressing problem as more small- and medium-sized firms acquire a taste and capacity for such innovation'.[36] Additionally, these enterprises do not have control of international distribution chains. Sometimes small and medium enterprises do not even control local distribution. It is not in their business model to do so, because they enter agreements for development, manufacture and worldwide distribution with larger entities that do those things.[37] This business model seems to be relatively new. In such a situation, the idea conveyed in the last sentence of the above quote, that patents are needed, is both questionable and does not convey the full picture.

There is much written about innovation taking place without patents.[38] Open innovation seems particularly suited to some types of research. However, in fields which have been typically less open, such as pharmaceuticals and biotechnology, there are some research entities and businesses that function without local patents. These research interests do not patent locally but patent internationally because it is the international market that counts for licensing their patented research to manufacturers and distributors. For these entities, the cost of the local patent may not be worth incurring if there is no local manufacturer who will supply the market anyway and no foreign distributor who can supply the market until they license the foreign patents. In these situations, the local patent system is not supporting local innovation; rather, it operates regardless of local innovation.

It is known that different entities might undertake research, development to market, manufacturing and distribution in relation to the same product. What is new, however, is where those parts of the chain are in

34 Guellec et al., *The Economics of the European Patent System*, above n 1, 9 –10 [emphasis added].
35 The EU is a regional system and thus has elements of the national and the international.
36 Reichman and Dreyfuss, *Harmonization without Consensus*, above n 23, at 118–120.
37 The examples of this were found in a survey of New Zealand business uses of intellectual property in New Zealand, which I conducted with G. McLay. The details of participants in that survey are confidential in accordance with the Victoria University of Wellington Ethics Committee approval for the survey.
38 For an overview, see Dreyfuss, *Does IP Need IP?*, above n 4.

separate countries. Manufacturing may have moved 'offshore' for several countries some time ago, but that is only one part of the global intellectual property story. The business model of creating intellectual property, but partnering with entities in other countries for aspects of R&D (particularly development) and all of manufacturing and distribution, is a variation from outsourcing manufacturing. Outsourcing manufacturing is usually about getting something made for a cheaper price, whereas outsourcing the other steps in the global value chain is a way for the small businesses to address problems of scale. This enables small market economies to be places of research, not just recipients of it. But as noted above, this gives rise to the phenomenon of businesses in what are usually thought to be fields where patents are important not patenting locally. This is not something that the framework of international patent law has taken into account or that its designers seem even to have contemplated. Such businesses' incentive is to innovate, but they are not directly driven by local patents. If patents have an incentive role for such researchers, global patents provide a more direct patent incentive. One might say that does not matter because these entities are getting the benefit of patents somewhere. That is so, but it does not answer the question as to what the shape of the domestic patent law should be in order to effectively support that innovation. How this affects patent legal rules, in for example small market economies, seems little investigated or understood. It suggests that high patenting standards are only a small part of the picture. It may still be appropriate to protect many foreign interests, but equally, if not more so, it suggests that in such places research exemptions should be robust in order to support local innovation.[39]

The solution may differ for large developing economies because, like large developed economies, they often seek to control multiple parts of the value chain including R&D, manufacture and distribution. Almost all commentaries about the needs and justifications for patents say or imply that the patent system was designed for the innovation, manufacture[40] and distribution to occur in the same jurisdiction that the patent was granted.[41]

[39] See discussion below. See also generally, A. Stack, *International Patent Law: Cooperation, Harmonization and an Institutional Analysis of WIPO and the WTO* (Edward Elgar, Cheltenham, 2011).

[40] Even where manufacture takes place offshore, it is done on an agency model and shipped back to the source for distribution.

[41] This one-place model is implicit in many descriptions of the role of patent law. See, for example, R. D. Blair and T. F. Cotter, *Intellectual Property: Economic and Legal Dimensions of Rights and Remedies* (Cambridge University Press, 2005), at 16 where the authors say 'some inventions that would benefit society would not be invented or would not be optimally disclosed or commercialized. The patent system is premised on the

This one-country phenomenon is also seen in disputes over whether it is legitimate in patent law to have a local working requirement. Local working requirements are predominantly found in developing countries and are premised on the need for local development and local innovation opportunities, which would not happen but for local working.[42] The trade argument against local working requirements is that countries should play to their comparative advantage and import what they are not advantaged at producing.[43] The arguments in favour of local working requirements are that it can stimulate local innovation, provide local jobs and training and lead to collaborations, and that locally made products are potentially cheaper.[44] Leaving aside whether or not local working requirements are permissible under TRIPS,[45] what local working requirements in some instances can show is that patent systems alone do not stimulate innovation.

The small market economy problem is different. Such nations do not want to locally work something where they do not have a comparative advantage. They are happy to import. But the patent system does not adequately take account of this position. Put differently, patents are supposed to support innovation but the structure of patent law does not take into account the multiple contributors to innovation that exist in some global value chains. The system does not support all countries to make effective use of their place in the global value chain. Therefore, the structure of global patent law is a mismatch to the realities of global innovation.

Advocates for more harmonised standards of patent law[46] do not seem to have taken into account the global value chain. Rather, they position

reasonable assumption that the public will enjoy additional benefits when the government takes additional steps to encourage the creation, commercialization, and disclosure o[f] new inventions.' See also F. Scott Kieff, 'Property Rights and Property Rules for Commercializing Inventions', *Minnesota Law Review*, 85 (2000), 697–754, at 707–708, where he discusses that a major patent incentive is the commercialisation of an invention, not just the R&D before commercialisation and profits after.

42 The United States lodged a complaint against Brazil at the WTO. The dispute was settled. For a discussion of the dispute, see P. Champ and A. Attaran, 'Patent Right and Local Working under the WTO TRIPS Agreement: An Analysis of the U.S.–Brazil Patent Dispute', *Yale Journal of International Law*, 27 (2002), 365–393.

43 See B. M. Hoekman, *Trade Laws and Institutions: Good Practices and the World Trade Organization* (The World Bank, Washington, DC, 1995), at 36, arguing that TRIPS allows for working but not local working.

44 See, for example, G. B. Reddy, 'Local Working of Patents – Law and Implementation in India', *Journal of Intellectual Property Rights*, 18 (2013), 15–27.

45 See T. Cottier, S. Lalan and M. Temmerman, 'Use It or Lose It? Assessing the Compatibility of the Working Requirement in the Paris Convention and TRIPS', *Journal of International Economic Law*, 17 (2014), 437–471.

46 For a discussion of the problems of harmonising patent law even further than the TRIPS Agreement standards, see Reichman and Dreyfuss, *Harmonization without Consensus*, above n 23.

some countries as patent producers and others as buyers rather than recognising that buyers should also be able to innovate. Additionally, there have been unproven suggestions that higher levels of intellectual property laws always aid innovation, in spite of the many instances where higher levels of patenting seem to have impeded innovation.

Does the global chain matter for the structure of patent law? It certainly would matter if the structure of the patent law in fact makes it hard for such innovators to exist. This may be occurring because, for example, effective research exemptions are not available and therefore cannot be effectively used. Of course, patents are not the only issue; education, investment and other factors come to bear. But while these factors are absent or limited in developing economies that is not so in small market economies.

The structure of patent law does not take account of the many roles that different entities can play in the global value chain. A broad consideration of the justifications for patents may provide some insight into this proposition. Patents are primarily designed to intervene downstream and allow many players to create more upstream inventions. As the Supreme Court of the United States has said, citing Professor Dreyfuss,[47]

> [I]t is useful to conceptualize knowledge as a pyramid: the big ideas are on top; specific applications are at the bottom. The higher up a patent is on the pyramid, the greater the social cost and the greater the hindrance to further innovation.

Patents not only play the role of encouraging research but may also be more directed at enabling commercialisation of research. 'The patent system is essentially an attempt by government to create conditions for the market mechanism to work for the production and diffusion of technology.'[48] In situations where the research is taking place in a jurisdiction separate from the stages of commercialisation, the patent system arguably is intervening too far upstream in small market economies. Empirical work would likely be useful to test these propositions. Because of trading relationships, strong patent standards are chosen in small market economies, but it is not clear that those standards assist local innovation. The solution to that is not necessarily the same as the approach, found in developing countries, of having higher standards of inventive step and other criteria (although that is one possibility). The better fit is more likely to be to ensure that there are strong flexibilities in the system which are appropriate to local research needs. Such flexibility can also address local pricing issues.[49]

[47] *Bilski* v. *Kappos* 561 US (2010), at 41 citing R. Dreyfuss, 'Are Business Methods Patents Bad for Business?' *Santa Clara Computer & High Technology Law Journal*, 16 (2000), 263–280, at 275.

[48] Guellec et al, *The Economics of the European Patent System*, above n 1, at 63.

[49] See discussion below in relation to patent term extension and regulatory review.

The global nature of some patent-related industries is in part reflected in arguments that were made at the WTO in connection with Canada's patent flexibilities, which are discussed further below. As part of its overall argument, Canada pointed out,[50]

> Both the brand name and generic pharmaceutical industries were global in nature.
> Very few countries had fully integrated brand name or generic drug industries within their borders. Even in large countries, generic producers frequently had to obtain ingredients such as fine chemicals from producers in other countries. Many countries had no generic industries at all and had to obtain generic (as well as brand name) products from other countries. Smaller countries that did have generic industries did not have domestic markets sufficiently large to enable those industries to operate on an economic scale. Those industries had to export in order to be able to manufacture in sufficient quantities to achieve economies of scale, so that domestic consumers could receive the benefits of cost-effective generic products.
> The United States agreed that a 'pre-expiration testing' exception was a reasonable exception to the exclusive rights conferred under the TRIPS Agreement. However, the market in the United States was large enough for generic producers to manufacture on an economic scale. Very few countries were in that position. 'Pre-expiration testing' exceptions that had the effect of confining all activities to a single country were of little use to countries that, unlike the United States, depended on international trade to obtain generic products.

How research is undertaken and how it is commercialised have changed, but the structure of patent law has not changed accordingly. The above discussion is related to how science and technology research entities might find an innovation-related slot in the global value chain. Another angle for considering this issue is to recognise that climbing the value chain is part of the intellectual property game and should therefore ideally be part of innovation strategy.[51] An underlying premise of innovation is that value is added to commodities in the form of applied knowledge or intellectual property. New Zealand, for example, is a commodity-producing country, in the field of dairy. It exports a large quantity of milk products, which other companies turn into higher value products such as infant formula.[52] Some of these products are patented or involve patented processes. New Zealand companies may very well ask why they do not climb the value chain by improving their ratio of value-added products to producing the commodity. That is a question for disciplines other than law. It does, however, call into question the role of patent law

50 WTO Panel Report, *Canada Pharmaceuticals*, above n 3, at para 4.38.
51 See Chapter 4.
52 For analysis of New Zealand and infant formula in the global production chain, see NZPECC, 'Infant Formula Value Chain', available at http://nzpecc.org.nz.

in such an economy, which is somewhat different from its role in large developed countries, or developing countries (both large and small).

The role of patent law also seems to differ in Singapore. As discussed in Chapter 2, a considerable portion of the foreign direct investment that Singapore gained has not been investment in R&D; rather, it has been investment in Singapore for its role of a distributor.[53] Israeli patent policy is different again, particularly with regard to pharmaceutical patents. Of the three small market economies that are the subject of this book, Israel has, by a considerable margin, the strongest generic pharmaceutical industry. Commentators have said,

> On the one hand, the local pharmaceutical industry is led by well-established generic companies, which are quite dominant and involved in lobbying relating to any proposed amendments relating to Israeli patent laws. On the other hand, there are the large international ethical[54] companies, which are represented in Israel by the Israeli branch of the 'Pharma' organization. The ethical industry has contended that the Israeli legislature favours the local generic industry. Therefore, Pharma is also heavily engaged in patent-related lobbying activities.[55]

While similar contests are found in New Zealand and Singapore, the strength of the locally based generic industry in Israel has led to a different approach to some patent flexibilities, to which this chapter now turns.

Patent term extension and its relationship with regulatory review

Under the TRIPS Agreement, the minimum term of a patent is 20 years.[56] When TRIPS was negotiated, many of its future members' laws, including several developed countries, had a shorter term for patents. Part of the rationale for the 20-year term was the problem of delays in granting and obtaining regulatory approval for patented pharmaceuticals. Some considered that these delays compromised the so-called 'effective patent term'. Drafts of the TRIPS Agreement show that some parties tried to negotiate for a 15-year term for all other patents and 20 years for pharmaceutical patents.[57] In the end, however, a 20-year term for all patents was

[53] See Chapter 2.

[54] This is a term used to define pharmaceutical companies which routinely undertake R&D. The term 'innovative' is also used.

[55] Liss and Adin, *Intellectual Property Law and Practice in Israel*, above n 12, at 579, noting that this includes adding Israel to the US Special 301 blacklist.

[56] TRIPS Agreement, above n 11, art 33.

[57] D. J. Gervais, *The TRIPS Agreement: Drafting History and Analysis*, 4th edn (Sweet & Maxwell, London, 2012), at 508, setting out the draft with bracketed text showing negotiation positions in July 1990. A term of 20 years for all patents was agreed to in the Brussels draft.

agreed upon as the minimum standard.[58] This history of negotiation is revealing because it explains why in some countries patent term extension is not available beyond 20 years. From some viewpoints, 20 years incorporated the need for any extensions. That was the position in New Zealand, which is discussed further below. Importantly, the TRIPS Agreement does not mandate any patent term extension but allows it because parties to the Agreement may provide for more extensive protection.[59]

The applicability of the 20-year term to patents that were issued before the TRIPS Agreement came into force was the subject of one of the earliest TRIPS disputes.[60] The result in that dispute was that the 20-year term must be retroactive and applied to all patents in force at the time the TRIPS Agreement came into force.[61]

As the second quote at the beginning of this chapter shows, the US law of patent term extension is linked to regulatory review.[62] Some see the extension and the exception as balancing each other.[63] Under US law, extensions to pharmaceutical patents can be granted to compensate for delay in the patent being granted and for the patent coming to market because of delays in regulatory approval.[64] There are some balancing

58 TRIPS Agreement, above n 11, art 33. 59 TRIPS Agreement, above n 11, art. 1.1.

60 WTO Appellate Body Report, *Canada – Term of Patent Protection*, WT/DS170/AB/R, 18 September 2000.

61 See also discussion in Gervais above n 57, paras [2.435]–[2.437].

62 The Federal Circuit summarised this linkage in *Teletronics Pacing Systems Inc* v. *Ventritex Inc* 982 F.2d 1520 at 1525 (Fed Cir 1992), stating: 'The approval process was taking an average of seven to ten years from the time the patent was issued . . . The product thus could be unmarketable for a substantial part of the life of the patent. To avoid this unintended distortion of the purposes of the Patent Act, Congress provided for extending the patent term of patents related to certain products that could not be marketed before undergoing a lengthy regulatory approval process.'

63 Nevertheless, Canada argued in WTO Panel Report, *Canada Pharmaceuticals*, above n 3, at 92, 'The absence of a nexus between a regulatory review exception and patent term extension was illustrated by the situation in the United States. The "Bolar exemption" in the US Patent Act (35 U.S.C. § 271(e)) made no reference to the provision of the Act creating patent term extensions (35 U.S.C. § 156). The question of whether a particular patent could be extended, and for what term, was unrelated to whether anyone had taken advantage of the "Bolar exemption" with respect to that patent. Moreover, there were many other provisions of the US statute which advantaged either an innovator or a generic manufacturer. The scheme was very complex, and it was quite clear that Congress had not considered the matter to be a simple one of combining patent term extension with the "Bolar exemption". That was one reason why the US Statement of Administrative Action for the Uruguay Round Agreements Act referred to the "Bolar exemption" alone when it spoke of permissible limited exceptions under the TRIPS Agreement. Further, it is significant that the United States did not, in its oral statement in these proceedings, suggest that there was any connection between its "Bolar exemption" and patent term extension.'

64 35 USC s 156(a) provides that products, methods of using products, or methods of manufacturing products can be extended. S 156(f) gives a definition of product. See for

mechanisms within the US system, such as that the patentee must have acted with due diligence during the regulatory review period of the product.[65] The 'effective patent term including the restoration period may not exceed 14 years following FDA [regulatory] approval of the new drug'.[66] Also, extension can only be granted to either the product or an approved use or method of manufacture of that product, which has received regulatory approval.[67]

Thus, if one has three patents relating to drug X, one for the product per se and describing its use in the treatment of disease Y, a second for an improved means of producing drug X and a third for use of drug X in the treatment of disease Z, and one submits two applications to the FDA for approval of drug X, one for its treatment of disease Y and the other for its treatment of disease Z only two of the three patents may be extended, one for each of the two review periods.[68]

When generic pharmaceutical companies wish to bring their products to market, they, like the patent owner, must have regulatory approval before their product can be sold. This led to a regulatory review exception, known in the United States as the Bolar exception, which allows uses of the patent in order that generic pharmaceutical manufacturers can gain regulatory approval before the patent expires.[69] US policy is that term extension balances the effect of the Bolar exception. That balance may well be appropriate in a country that has both generic and innovative pharmaceutical manufacturers within its borders; however, as noted above,[70] very few countries are in that position and so the balance they choose to strike can justifiably be different.

The EU also allows patent term extension, which it calls a supplementary protection certificate (SPC). An SPC can only be granted for the pharmaceutical product that has regulatory approval.[71] Under the EU system, SPCs can be obtained for more than one product even if based on

an explanation, www.gpo.gov/fdsys/pkg/USCODE-2011-title35/html/USCODE-2011-title35-partII-chap14-sec156.htm.

65 35 USC s 156(c)(1). Due diligence is defined in s 156(d)(3) as the 'degree of attention, continuous directed effort, and timeliness as may reasonably be expected from, and are ordinarily exercised by, a person during a regulatory review period'.

66 *Merck & Co* v. *Kessler* 80 F.3d 1543 (1996). 67 35 USC § 156(b).

68 See Ladas & Parry LLP, 'Patent Term Extension', available at www.ladas.com/.

69 *Roche Products Inc.* v. *Bolar Pharmaceuticals Co. Inc*, 469 US 856 (1984) had held that a generic manufacturer's use of a patented invention to test and apply for marketing authorisation of its medicine did not fall under the common law 'experimental use' defence. That defence only covered experimentation for scientific, not commercial, purposes. This led to the amendment of Section 271(e) of the Patent Act (35 U.S.C. s.271(e)).

70 See above n 50 and the related text.

71 P. W. Grubb and P. R. Thomsen, *Patents for Chemicals, Pharmaceuticals and Biotechnology: Fundamentals of Global Law, Practice and Strategy*, 5th edn (Oxford

the same patent. SPCs can also be granted for second use patent claims where there is a new therapeutic use.[72] The EU challenged Canada's regulatory review exception at the WTO when the equivalent was not found in EU law. After losing the dispute, the EU introduced a kind of regulatory review exception.[73]

Canada's regulatory review exception was the subject of the dispute that the EU brought to the World Trade Organization (WTO).[74] In that dispute as well as regulatory review, the EU challenged another patent exception that allowed stockpiling of the product.[75] The panel, in its report of the dispute, found that the regulatory review exception was TRIPS compliant and that the stockpiling exception was not.[76] As part of the argument, the EU claimed that regulatory review exception should be balanced with patent term extension.[77] The panel said,

University Press, New York, 2010), at 173. EC Regulation 1768/92 governs patent term extension for pharmaceutical products and EC Regulation 1610/96 for plants.

[72] *Neurim Pharmaceuticals Ltd* v. *Comptroller-General of Patents* [2011] ECJ C-130/11. The history of the EU law reform is documented in *Canada Pharmaceuticals*, above n 3, at 43–45.

[73] Directive 2001/83/EC of the European Parliament and of the Council of 6 November 2001 on the community code relating to medicinal products for human use, Official Journal L – 311, 28 November 2004, pp. 67–128, Despite this being a directive, there are some different approaches, particularly where clinical trials are covered in the exemption; see Taylor Wessing, 'Not All Bolar Exemptions Are the Same', Background, September 2013, available at www.taylorwessing.com/synapse/september13.html.

[74] WTO Panel Report, *Canada Pharmaceuticals*, above n 3.

[75] Canada argued that 'While the European Communities and their member States were contending in the present proceeding that Canada was the only country with a stockpiling provision, subsection 55.2(2) of the Patent Act essentially paralleled a practice followed in the United States, where an FDA guideline required a generic manufacturer, as a precondition to marketing authorization, to make at least three full production runs on a full commercial scale: "The FDA will not approve an application if the manufacturing facility has not yet been 'scaled up' from the product development phase, during which only limited manufacturing capacity is required, to the commercial phase, where the company is ready to produce large quantities of product for immediate commercial distribution"', WTO Panel Report, *Canada Pharmaceuticals*, above n 3, 4.21 at 38.

[76] The reasons for this were that the stockpiling exception was not limited enough. TRIPS Agreement, above n 11, art 30, requires that exceptions be limited. For discussion of this case, see Chapter 3.

[77] The argument is summarised in *Canada Pharmaceuticals*, above n 3, at 7.78: 'The type of normative claim put forward by the EC has been affirmed by a number of governments that have enacted *de jure* extensions of the patent term, primarily in the case of pharmaceutical products, to compensate for the de facto diminution of the normal period of market exclusivity due to delays in obtaining marketing approval. According to the information submitted to the Panel, such extensions have been enacted by the European Communities, Switzerland, the United States, Japan, Australia and Israel. The EC and Switzerland have done so while at the same time allowing patent owners to continue to use their exclusionary rights to gain an additional, de facto extension of market exclusivity by preventing competitors from applying for regulatory approval during the term of the patent. The other countries that have enacted *de jure* patent term extensions have also, either by legislation or by judicial decision, created a

> This [extension of patent term] ... response to the claim for compensatory adjustment has not been universal, however. In addition to Canada, several countries have adopted, or are in the process of adopting, regulatory review exceptions ... thereby removing the de facto extension of market exclusivity, but these countries have not enacted, and are not planning to enact, any *de jure* extensions of the patent term for producers adversely affected by delayed marketing approval. When regulatory review exceptions are enacted in this manner, they represent a decision not to restore any of the period of market exclusivity due to lost delays in obtaining marketing approval. Taken as a whole, these government decisions may represent either disagreement with the normative claim made by the EC in this proceeding, or they may simply represent a conclusion that such claims are outweighed by other equally legitimate interests.[78]

The Panel concluded that the interest of patent owners in extension as a result of delays in marketing approval was 'neither so compelling nor so widely recognized that it could be regarded as a 'legitimate interest'.[79] The Panel finished its discussion of the issue by saying that a normative policy issue which was 'unresolved political debate' could not be resolved through adjudication.[80]

Singapore and Israel both have regulatory review exceptions, and patent term extension is available.[81] As mentioned above, there is a significant generic pharmaceutical industry in Israel and also the presence of non-generic pharmaceutical companies. This led to a debate about patent term extension and regulatory review, which resulted in a balance between domestic interests (these domestic interests also have international interests). In Singapore, this balance seems to have arisen through trade agreements even in the absence of a significant locally based pharmaceutical industry.[82] New Zealand, however, takes a different approach.[83] It has a

regulatory review exception similar to Section 55.2(1), thereby eliminating the possibility of an additional de facto extension of market exclusivity.'

78 WTO Panel Report, *Canada Pharmaceuticals*, above n 3, at 7.79.

79 WTO Panel Report, *Canada Pharmaceuticals*, above n 3, at 7.82.

80 WTO Panel Report, *Canada Pharmaceuticals*, above n 3, at 7.82.

81 Singapore Patents Act, s66(2)(h), see discussion in Ng-Loy, *Law of Intellectual Property in Singapore*, above n 12, at [34.2.1]–[34.2.4]; Israel Patents (Amendment No. 3) Law, 5758–1998, art1, s 54A, 'An experimental activity within the process of obtaining a licence for the marketing of a product after the expiry of a patent shall not be regarded as exploitation of an invention'.

82 See Singapore–United States Free Trade Agreement (signed 6 May 2003, entered into force 1 January 2004). As will be discussed in Chapter 8, Singapore also tightened its otherwise permissive parallel importation rules as regards pharmaceutical patents.

83 In the Canada and EU trade agreement negotiations, the EU claimed Canada is the only developed country without patent term extension; see J. Lexchin and M. Gagnon, Canada Europe Trans-Atlantic Dialogue, 'CETA and Intellectual Property: The Debate over Pharmaceuticals Patents', available at http://labs.carleton.ca/canadaeurope/wp-content/uploads/sites/9/CETD-Policy-Brief_CETA-and-pharmaceutical-patents_MG_JL.pdf. Perhaps the EU does not consider New Zealand developed because it is

regulatory review exception, but it does not provide for patent term extension.[84] This makes perfect sense for a country that imports most of its pharmaceuticals. New Zealand has assessed whether to have patent term extension in the post-TRIPS environment, and successive governments have chosen not to enact it because of the cost to health care. A review was undertaken and the government concluded as follows:[85]

If the patent term for pharmaceuticals is extended, then this would delay the entry of generic pharmaceuticals onto the New Zealand market. Generic pharmaceuticals are generally cheaper than the original patented pharmaceutical. This would have the effect of increasing the total amount that New Zealanders pay for patented pharmaceuticals.

The cost of this would be reflected through higher prices to consumers of the pharmaceuticals. For New Zealand, most of the cost would be incurred by the publicly funded health system. While the actual cost would depend on the design of an extension, the Government's agency for managing pharmaceutical expenditure, PHARMAC, has estimated that the cost of extending patents over the next four years could be from $85 to $135 million depending on PHARMAC's ability to renegotiate supply agreements. This will either reduce the availability of subsidised pharmaceuticals to New Zealanders or, to maintain the same level of access, require the government to increase health sector funding. There will also be increased costs to consumers for nonsubsidised pharmaceuticals.

Whether New Zealand will be able to sustain this approach through the Trans–Pacific Partnership negotiation remains to be seen.[86] In addition, Medicines New Zealand (the body that represents the large

small and far away or perhaps because New Zealand imports pharmaceuticals as a result of adjusting its industry to its comparative advantage. Perhaps the EU considers its highly subsidised and inefficient farms to be a symbol of development when compared with New Zealand's unsubsidised yet economically efficient agricultural industry. I also note that the Canadian authors of the document do not seem to be aware of New Zealand's law either.

[84] This is the post-TRIPS situation. Before the TRIPS Agreement, New Zealand had a patent term of 17 years and allowed for extension in some circumstances. The Patents Act 1953 (NZ), s 31(1) (repealed), provided, 'if upon application made by a patentee in accordance with this section the Court or Commissioner is satisfied that the patentee has not been adequately remunerated by the patent, the Court or Commissioner may by order extend the term of the patent, subject to such restrictions, conditions, and provisions, if any, as may be specified in the order, for such period (not exceeding 5 years or, in an exceptional case, 10 years) as may be so specified; and any such order may be made notwithstanding that the term of the patent has previously expired'.

[85] MED, 'Review of the Patents Act 1953 The Pharmaceutical Patent Term in New Zealand Discussion Paper' (June 2003), at [46]–[47], available at www.med.govt.nz/business/intellectual-property/pdf-docs-library/patents/review-of-patents-act/patents-act-1953-pharmaceutical-patent-terms-pdf.

[86] The leaked text of the Trans-Pacific Partnership negotiations (TPP), available at http://tppinfo.org/resources/leaked-texts-country-info/, shows that the United States is negotiating for patent term extension, but many parties oppose it, including some that have it such as Australia and Singapore; see QQ.E.14 and QQ.E.XX and see also QQ.E 13.

pharmaceutical industries) has suggested, without providing data, that the absence of patent term extension (and other matters relating to patent law and the set-up of New Zealand's purchasing system[87]) affects the availability of pharmaceuticals in New Zealand. This suggestion no doubt casts an influence on the trade negotiations.[88] It is true that in the system under which the Pharmaceutical Management Agency (known as PHARMAC) operates, some medicines are not publicly funded in New Zealand, but that is not as a result of regulatory review or the absence of term extension; rather, it is a result of PHARMAC's determination of the best value for its purchasing power.

The approach of all of the countries discussed above represents a bargain made in the domestic policy realm (that is so, even if the driver of the bargain is a trade agreement). As discussed in Chapter 3, this domestic policy bargain ought to be taken into account when interpreting the TRIPS Agreement.[89] Chapter 3, about interpretation of international agreements, discusses how balancing obligations with flexibilities, which are based on domestic policy preferences, is part of the framework of the TRIPS Agreement and thus should be part of an analysis of its object and purpose under the Vienna Convention rules.[90] Those rules are used to interpret the treaty and a member's compliance with it. If this approach is taken, then, as the report in *Canada Pharmaceuticals* shows, exceptions can be legitimate even if other countries do not have them and even if they represent different policies at the domestic level. That does not mean all exceptions and flexibilities will be unchallengeable just because they

[87] The Pharmaceutical Management Agency, which is known as PHARMAC, purchases pharmaceuticals for the New Zealand public health system. It operates various procedures, including bulk buying of pharmaceuticals through commercial arrangement with pharmaceutical companies. The negotiation and decision-making process involve many steps. For an explanation of PHARMAC's practices, see http://www.pharmac.health.nz/. Medicines New Zealand (the body that represents major international pharmaceutical companies in New Zealand) claims the system should be more transparent. The TTP negotiations, above n 86, reveal a leaked transparency chapter aimed at changing the system.

[88] See Researched Medicines Industry Memorandum (22 June 2010), www.medicinesnz.co.nz/assets/Uploads/Patents-Bill-the-position-in-brief.pdf. The New Zealand Law Foundation Regulatory Reform Project investigated this as far as was possible based on publicly available information and did not find it was supported. That project concluded, 'There are other factors that affect availability, such as the willingness of some sellers to supply a small market'; see S. Frankel, M. Lewis, C. Nixon and J. Yeabsley, 'The Web of Trade Agreements and Alliances and Impacts on Regulatory Autonomy', in S. Frankel and D. Ryder (eds.), *Recalibrating Behaviour: Smarter Regulation in a Global World* (LexisNexis, Wellington, 2013), pp 17–62, at 45–47.

[89] See Chapter 3.

[90] Vienna Convention on the Law of Treaties, arts 31–32, 23 May 1969, 1115 UNTS. 331 (entered into force 27 January 1980).

represent a domestic policy. There is still the matter of compliance with the TRIPS Agreement, such as compliance with Article 30.

In Israel and Singapore, the cost of patent extension has been seen as worthwhile to the local policy makers. The presence of patent term extension will almost certainly be a net cost to New Zealand. Even if extension becomes part of the law, there remains the question whether the law helps or hinders New Zealand innovation. Of course, other economies may continue to ask that question even when they have extension.

Experimental use exemptions and exceptions

Before the creation of the regulatory review exceptions, in several jurisdictions case law determined that the experimental use exception did not cover experimentation for purposes related to regulatory review. This was in fact the motivation for the US Bolar exception, where the case by that name had found that regulatory-related uses of the patent were not experimental.[91] The same ruling is found in the jurisprudence of Israel[92] and New Zealand.[93] Other types of experimental use and the need for exceptions have arisen more recently.[94] One commentator has concluded that the need for an experimental use defence has arisen due to three factors:[95]

> [T]he first has to do with the characteristics of modern science, especially biotechnology; the second, with transformations in the organization of science, again particularly in the biotech industry; and the third concerns broader changes in the political economy of information production.

Whether experimental use is called an exemption or an exception (or even an exclusion)[96] depends on whether the scope of experimental use is regarded as not covered by the exclusive rights of a patentee or whether it needs to be an exception to those rights. Arguments in favour of the former are broadly that the purpose of disclosure of a patent is not just so

[91] Above n 70. [92] *Eli Lily* v. *Teva Pharmaceuticals Industries Ltd*, CF 881/94.

[93] *Monsanto* v. *Stauffer* [1984] 1 NZIPR 518; *Smith Kline & French Laboratories Ltd* v. *Attorney-General* [1991] 2 NZLR 560.

[94] See R. S. Eisenberg, 'Patents and the Progress of Science: Exclusive Rights and Experimental Use', *University of Chicago Law Review*, 56 (1989), 1017, 1086 and discussion of why further exceptions may be needed.

[95] R. C. Dreyfuss, 'Protecting the Public Domain of Science: Has the Time for an Experimental Use Defense Arrived?', *Arizona Law Review*, 46 (2004), 457–472, at 463.

[96] WIPO Standing Committee on the Law of Patents Exclusions from Patentability and Exceptions and Limitations to Patentees' Rights, Study Report, SCP/15/3, Annex 1, p. 7, makes a distinction between exclusions and exceptions. It discusses the merits of both. In relation to experimental use, it treats these more as exceptions, although this is not an absolute category.

that the patent can be used after it has expired, but that disclosure should enable experimentation during the term of the patent.[97] This idea was also expressed in the WTO Panel report in *Canada Pharmaceuticals* (although the term 'exception' is used):[98]

> There was no internationally accepted definition of 'scientific/experimental use'. It could, however, be said that practically all Members of the WTO had such an exception albeit drafted in a great variety of ways. The practically universal existence of this exception was closely linked to the basic underlying deal between society and the patentee. The patentee agreed to disclose his invention and thus share with society the fruits of his inventive activities and investment at an early stage in order to avoid investment in multiple research and to make the invention available as the basis for further, more advanced research . . . [T]his exception was the corollary to the disclosure requirement, because otherwise researchers would only be allowed to read the description of the patented invention, without being able to experiment with the invention (e.g. to see if and how it worked).

Some commentators have suggested that having an exception tends to limit the common law rights.[99] Their view of whether experimental use is an exception suggests that experimental use is otherwise part of the patent owners' exclusive rights. That should not be so, given that a key purpose of disclosure is to enable others to use the disclosed information and its underlying ideas even during the patent term. If that was not so, the patent system would have kept the disclosure confidential until the end of the patent term.[100] Experimentation is something analogous to a user's right. Additionally, concern about limiting common law rights assumes a certain strength of the common law exceptions which does not necessarily exist and is not well adapted to the conditions of scientific research

97 K. J. Strandburg, 'What Does the Public Get? Experimental Use and the Patent Bargain', *Wisconsin Law Review*, 81 (2004), 81–155 ('*What Does the Public Get?*').

98 WTO Panel Report, *Canada Pharmaceuticals*, above n 4, at 55–56; see Strandburg, *What Does the Public Get*, above n 98, at 81.

99 A. Monotti, 'The Australian Experimental Use Exemption: A Current Overview', *Journal of World Intellectual Property*, 12 (2009), 422–445 and WIPO Standing Committee Report, above n 96, at 12–13 and 18.

100 See *Integra Lifesciences Inc. Ltd.* v. *Merck KGaA*, 331 F. 3d 860, at 875, where Judge Newman (in dissent) explains, 'The patent statute requires full disclosure of the invention, including details of enabling experiments and technical drawings and best modes and preferred embodiments, even commercial sources of special components. Such details would be idle and purposeless if this information cannot be used for 17–20 years. Indeed, there would be little value in the requirement of the patent law that patented information must be removed from secrecy in consideration of the patent right to exclude, if the information is then placed on ice and protected from further study and research investigation. To the contrary, the patent system both contemplates and facilitates research into patented subject matter, whether the purpose is scientific understanding or evaluation or comparison or improvement. Such activities are integral to the advance of technology.'

today.[101] In the end, an exception created for innovation in the twenty-first century may be more effective in achieving effective experimental use. In several jurisdictions common law experimental use, to the extent it exists, as a practical matter does not cover much or has been interpreted to apply only in very limited circumstances which are non-commercial or cannot lead to anything commercial. Also, in several jurisdictions courts have been unwilling to interpret exceptions to patent law that the legislature has not expressly provided for.[102]

There is a significant debate, particularly in the United States, about whether patent law should give greater scope for experimental use. The changing role of universities from places of fundamental research to more commercial research and patent-owning entities has significantly affected the debate.[103] Some are concerned that research tools should be free for experimentation.[104] One suggestion is that experimenting *on* an invention is a legitimate exception, but experimenting *with* the invention is not.[105] Because the distinction of experimenting on or with the invention tends to disallow any kind of experimentation that has even a hint of potential commercial use, another approach is to allow experimentation on the subject matter of the invention, but not experimentation which involves the use of a patented invention. This is the approach found in the EU and was also the approach recommended in Australia[106] and adopted with modifications in New Zealand. Until the passage of the Patents Act 2013, New Zealand had a very weak common law experimental use exception.[107] The 2013 Act has added that it is 'not an infringement of a patent for a person to do an act for experimental purposes relating to the subject matter of an invention'.[108] The following subsection sets out that this includes[109]

(a) determining how the invention works
(b) determining the scope of the invention

[101] S. Frankel, 'An Experimental Use Exception from Patent Infringement for New Zealand', *Journal of World Intellectual Property*, 12(2009), 446–466.

[102] See Frankel, *A Patentable Invention*, above note 16, discussing Canadian and New Zealand cases on this point. A similar approach has been taken in Australia; see *Bristol-Myers Squibb Company* v. *FH Faulding & Co. Ltd* [2000] 97 FCR 524.

[103] See Dreyfuss, *Protecting the Public Domain of Science*, above n 95.

[104] See UK Intellectual Property Office, *The Patent Research Exception: A Consultation Report* 2008, available at http://ipo.govt.uk/consult-patresearch.pdf, at 5; Janice M. Mueller, 'No "Dilettante Affair": Rethinking the Experimental Use Exception to Patent Infringement for Biomedical Research Tools', *Washington Law Review*, 76 (2001), 1, at 17.

[105] Strandburg, *What Does the Public Get?*, above n 97.

[106] See Monotti, *The Australian Experimental Use Exemption*, above n 99, at 426–527.

[107] Frankel, *An Experimental Use Exception*, above n 102, at 447–450.

[108] Patents Act 2013 (NZ), s 143(1). [109] Patents Act 2013 (NZ), s 143(2).

(c) determining the validity of the claims
(d) seeking an improvement of the invention (for example, determining new properties, or new uses, of the invention).

Given the newness of this exception, whether this is strong enough to allow for research in New Zealand that effectively supports local innovation remains to be seen.[110] In addition, other than the quote above suggesting that experimental use is found in many jurisdictions, such an exception has not been tested at the WTO.[111] In Israel there is a recognised exception allowing experimentation with patents as well as a regulatory review exception.[112] Singapore does not have an additional experimental use exception.

As suggested above, allowing for full experimental use could be the very place where patent laws could be made to better fit small market economies. Of course, the reasons that research might take place in a country have many factors other than patent law, such as higher education, investment and innovation clusters. The distance from markets and differing political situations will also have impact on matters in the global value chain such as manufacture and distribution. Distance is not necessarily a problem for research. It is irrelevant to the weightless online economy, and distance can also provide an advantage for experimentation. Distance is a good way to ensure good border control so that the products of experiments which can legitimately take place in one country do not necessarily leak back into other countries without authorisation.[113]

Conclusion

There is no 'one-size-fits-all' patent law. In a global market the suggestion of harmonised rules, such as all countries providing for patent term extension or even all countries having a regulatory review exception, is an example. One or the other of these, or both, will suit some countries and not others. The bargain that Israel has struck by allowing both reflects its attempt to balance the generic and other pharmaceutical industries. In contrast, New Zealand as a small market economy shows why it might be sensible to allow regulatory review but not patent term extension. Singapore's position seems to have been reached as part of a trade deal

[110] For critique of the similar exception proposed in Australia, see Monotti, above n 99.

[111] For discussion of what WTO compliance may require, see Dinwoodie and Dreyfuss, *A Neofederalist Vision of TRIPS*, above n 2, at 58–71.

[112] See *Transkaryotic Therapies Inc.* v *Genzyme Corporation* 19682/05 and discussion in Liss and Adin, *Intellectual Property Law and Practice in Israel*, above n 12, at 106.

[113] This is also an issue with parallel importing, which is discussed in Chapter 8.

and likely represents a trade-off. All of these countries and many other places in the world would likely benefit from proper research exceptions. Appropriate exceptions are not only an important part of patent law, but they also contribute to making better use of research capacity along the global value chain. This chapter has also suggested that the way in which global value chains work does not seem to be adequately reflected in international patent law, which is premised upon territoriality. Balancing patent law in light of global value chains includes flexibilities such as research exceptions.

6 Approaches to copyright

How do we measure the success of copyright and what metrics are used?

How do we ensure that everyone's voice is heard?

How is copyright working for individual artists?

How is copyright working for our nation's economy?[1]

New Zealand's intellectual property laws, including the Copyright Act, are an important element of our innovation framework. Copyright is the basis of the legal protection for the creative industries and is also vital in any industry that involves design or planning, the production of consumer goods or the expression of ideas or information.[2]

The results show that, prior to fair use amendments, the private copying industries in Singapore were in recession. After fair use amendments, this group experienced a rapid increase in growth rates and continued to exhibit strong growth over the five year period.[3]

The message being sent wasn't to do away with copyright – but to recognize that if the goal is to incentivize creativity such that the public benefits, you need to look at the whole market. That's why it still seems like a much more beneficial effort would have been one that had the kinds of representatives seen on both panels plus content creators plus people who make use of these various platforms in a variety of ways. Then you get a fuller picture of the ecosystem – and understand why a narrow focus on merely 'strengthening enforcement' or merely trying

[1] Statement of Judiciary Committee Chairman Bob Goodlatte; Subcommittee on Courts, Intellectual Property and the Internet; Hearing on 'A Case Study for Consensus Building: The Copyright Principles Project', 16 May 2013, available at http://judiciary.house.gov/_files/news/2013/05162013_4.html.

[2] Ministry of Economic Development Release of Position Paper – Digital Technology and the Copyright Act 1994 (11 December 2002), www.med.govt.nz/business/intellectual-property/pdf-docs-library/copyright/copyright-new-technologies-amendment-act-2008/position-paper-pdf, at p. 5.

[3] R. Ghafele and B. Gilbert, 'The Economic Value of Fair Use in Copyright Law. Counterfactual Impact Analysis of Fair Use Policy on Private Copying Technology and Copyright Markets in Singapore', October 2012, available at http://works.bepress.com/cgi/viewcontent.cgi?article=1021&context=roya_ghafele, at p.5.

> to 'stop infringement' will often miss the bigger picture, and make things more difficult and less beneficial for both creators and the wider public.[4]

The focus of the debate over what the scope of copyright law should or should not be, in what is often called the digital era, depends on who is the protagonist. Authors, for instance, may focus on how to make a living from creating copyright works.[5] Others would focus on how to enforce copyright (usually copyright owners, particularly businesses that have reaped considerable benefits from copyright).[6] Others still seek to overcome or, if possible, avoid, copyright issues (such as non-authorial distributors of copyright works, facilitators of the workings of the Internet, free Internet advocates and some users of other copyright works). The three positions (and their sub-groups) are neither mutually exclusive nor are they necessarily incompatible. Users, for example, can become authors and so sometimes adopt an author's view, such as 'don't copy my work'. Each category of protagonist may have an interest in copyright, but to date the focus on the needs and demands of the protagonists as competing concerns, rather than all being valid parts of a copyright 'ecosystem', has tended to result in no solutions internationally and sometimes piecemeal solutions at the national level.[7]

Changes to laws at the national level and negotiations at the international level (including bilateral, plurilateral and multilateral) have tended to focus on increasing rights, mandating or increasing flexibilities and strengthening enforcement regimes.[8] All of these have had a significant international presence and varying national implementation. There

[4] Techdirt, 'Two Key Points: Copyright Isn't the Only Business Model; And When Done Wrong Makes Other Models More Difficult', available at www.techdirt.com/articles/20130802/16454024049/two-key-points-copyright-isnt-only-business-model-when-done-wrong-makes-other-models-more-difficult.shtml.

[5] See J.C. Ginsburg, 'Exceptional Authorship: The Role of Copyright Exceptions in Promoting Creativity', in S. Frankel and D. Gervais (eds.), *Evolution and Equilibrium: Copyright in the Digital Age* (Cambridge University Press, 2014), pp. 15–28 ('*Evolution and Equilibrium*'). See also J.C. Ginsburg, 'The Author's Place in the Future of Copyright', *Williamette Law Review,* 45 (2009), 381–394 and J.C. Ginsburg, 'The Concept of Authorship in Comparative Copyright Law', *DePaul Law Review,* 52 (2003), 1063–1092. Others contest the centrality of the author; see, for example, O. Bracha, 'The Ideology of Authorship Revisited: Authors, Markets, and Liberal Values in Early American Copyright', *Yale Law Journal,* 118 (2008), 186–271, at 188. See also M. Woodmansee and P. Jaszi (eds.), *The Construction of Authorship: Textual Appropriation in Law and Literature* (Duke University Press, 1994).

[6] This focus has dominated the international agenda where free trade agreements (FTAs) have focused on increasing rights and enforcement; see Chapter 2.

[7] See S. Frankel and D. Gervais, 'Evolution and Equilibrium: An Introduction', in *Evolution and Equilibrium,* above n 5.

[8] See Chapter 2.

broadly remains, however, a lack of consensus over how, if at all, to balance the competing interests in copyright.

Maximising authorised and reasonably paid uses should arguably become the central focus of copyright rather than focusing on minimising infringing uses.[9] This is because if copyright works are available at a reasonable price and market demand is supplied, then some of the incentives for infringing uses will dissipate. There will always be those who do not pay (particularly commercial pirates), but those who use non-paying options because reasonable authorised options are unavailable are a different matter. Supplying those who are willing to pay has required business model solutions rather than legal rules, although presently there seems to be no clear divide between the two. Some of the new business models that arise are primarily driven not only by technological developments and progress, but also by finding loopholes in the law and creating a model to exploit those loopholes.[10]

There is no shortage of suggested solutions or remedies for aspects of the copyright debate, including strengthening rights and enforcement, strengthening flexibilities, creating mandatory exceptions,[11] converting copyright from property to liability,[12] requiring a registration process,[13] ensuring the centrality of the author for copyright protection,[14] recognising that users ought also to have rights[15] and protecting the interests of publishers and distributors of copyright works.[16]

[9] Statement of Professor Daniel Gervais, Vanderbilt University Law School before the Subcommittee on Courts, Intellectual Property and the Internet Committee on the Judiciary United States House of Representatives 113th Congress, 1st Session, 'A Case Study for Consensus Building: The Copyright Principles Project', 16 May 2013.

[10] See S. Frankel, 'The International Copyright Problem and Durable solutions', 18(2015) *Vanderbilt Journal of Entertainment & Technology Law*, (forthcoming).

[11] In 2013, WIPO created a treaty for the visually impaired; Marrakesh Treaty to Facilitate Access to Published Works for Persons Who Are Blind, Visually Impaired, or Otherwise Print Disabled, VIP/DC/8 REV (signed 28 June 2013). For a discussion of mandatory exceptions, see R. Okediji, 'The International Copyright System: Limitations, Exceptions and Public Interest Considerations for Developing Countries', UNCTAD, 2006, available at http://unctad.org/en/docs/iteipc200610_en.pdf.

[12] See discussion in Frankel, *The International Copyright Problem*, above n 10.

[13] C. Sprigman, 'Reform(aliz)ing Copyright', *Stanford Law Review*, 57 (2004), 485–568. For the opposing view see J. Ginsburg, '"With Untired Spirits and Formal Constancy": Berne-Compatibility of Formal Declaratory Measures to Enhance Title-Searching', *Berkeley Technology Law Journal*, 28 (2013), 1583.

[14] See above n 5.

[15] N. Elkin Koren, 'Affordances of Freedom: Theorizing the Rights of Users in the Digital Era', *Jerusalem Review of Legal Studies*, 6 (2012), 96–109.

[16] For example, the Copyright Principles project states: '6. Copyright law should support opportunities for innovation and competition in technologies for disseminating and experiencing creative works; it should also support rights holders' reasonable interests in effective protection of their rights in the face of technological change.

Aside from the self-interest claims of one group's rights over another group's (which may or may not be justifiable), broader approaches include directly addressing the policy and justifications behind the law. This includes applying the practice of utilising evidence-based policy[17] to frame copyright. This is sometimes expressed as only changing copyright law if the evidence supports it.[18] Requiring evidence-based policy for future changes to copyright may be a good idea, but the difficulty is that existing laws may not be based on very strong evidence. Another broad approach is stripping back copyright to examine its principles and to suggest where those principles and consequent details of the law might need adjustment.[19]

One significant aspect of the copyright debate is the role of copyright flexibilities and exceptions.[20] In the United Kingdom and Australia, there have been substantial reviews of copyright and both have focused their recommendations on increasing flexibilities.[21] The most significant group of such exceptions are variously known as fair use, fair dealing and permitted acts. These differences in nomenclature are not insignificant and reveal much about the policy behind them and their scope in practice. Fair use is an open-ended category which has certain guiding factors.[22] The most well known fair use system is that found in the United States. In addition to the broad fair use doctrine, US law has certain

6.1. Copyright law should recognize that new technologies may create new opportunities to infringe copyrights as well as new opportunities to transact over copyright rights and new opportunities to distribute and use copyrighted works. Some, but not all, of these opportunities should be subject to copyright owners' control.
6.2. Deciding whether a particular type of use should be within the scope of copyright's exclusive rights requires balancing the sometimes-competing interests of creators, *distributors*, consumers, and the public.' [emphasis added], P. Samuelsson, 'The Copyright Principles Project: Directions For Reform', *Berkeley Technology Law Journal*, 25 (2010), 1175–1245 at 1182.

17 See discussion of evidence-based policy in Chapter 4.

18 I. Hargreaves, 'Digital Opportunity: A Review of Intellectual Property and Growth', May 2011, available at www.gov.uk/government/uploads/system/uploads/attachment_data/file/32563/ipreview-finalreport.pdf.

19 See Samuelsson, *The Copyright Principles*, above n 16.

20 See, generally, S. Ricketson, 'WIPO Study on Limitations and Exceptions of Copyright and Related Rights in the Digital Environment', WIPO Doc SCCR/9/7, 5 April 2003.

21 Hargraeves Report, above n 18; Gowers Review of Intellectual Property, December 2006, available at www.gov.uk/government/uploads/system/uploads/attachment_data/file/228849/0118404830.pdf and 'Copyright and the Digital Economy', 13 February 2014, ALRC Report 122, available at www.alrc.gov.au/sites/default/files/pdfs/publications/final_report_alrc_122_2nd_december_2013.pdf.

22 There is an extensive literature on this topic. See, for example, N.W. Netanel, 'Making Sense of Fair Use', *Lewis and Clark Law Review*, 15 (2011), 715–771; J. Ginsburg and R. Gorman, *Copyright Law* (West Academic, 2012) 178–210; W. Patry, *Patry on Fair Use* (Thomson, Reuters, 2014); P. Samuelson, 'Unbundling Fair Uses', *Fordham Law Review*, 77 (2009), 2537–2621.

delineated exceptions which are akin to permitted acts.[23] Fair dealing exceptions (and permitted acts) tend to be drafted to target more specific purposes. Fair dealing provisions both in statutes and in case law sometimes utilise fair use-style guidelines to determine the scope of the fair dealing principle.[24] Case law determines the ambit of both, but fair use in particular requires more case law (and even then of course its ambit may not be clear). Multiple cases do not occur in small market economies, so the importance of other countries' jurisprudence or clear legislative guidance (which is not easy when technology evolves) should not be underestimated. Fair use and fair dealing disputes often become the forum in which competing interests in copyright do battle. The questions are often (even if indirectly expressed as such), is the use fair, or indeed unfair, and to whom and why?

Copyright always has competing interests, but the challenge for copyright lawmakers and policy makers is how to determine which competing interest prevails in any particular set of circumstances. This is not something which is static, but rather is the dynamic notion on which copyright is based.[25] The central question of copyright might, therefore, be somewhat broadly phrased as: which player in the copyright game should prevail based on the rules and why?

The answer may be different in a domestic context than in the international context. This is because justifications based on local needs or values are frequently not universal. Put differently, one domestic context will differ from another because of differing laws, differing national interpretations and different policy goals. One of the most fiercely contested domestic arenas about the scope of copyright law is in the United States, but this debate seems to have, at least to date, very little impact on US trade policy in copyright.[26] This seems to be because different

[23] In the United States, these are found in the Copyright Act of 1976, 17 U.S.C. § 107: 'In determining whether the use made of a work in any particular case is a fair use the factors to be considered shall include:

1. the purpose and character of the use, including whether such use is of a commercial nature or is for nonprofit educational purposes;
2. the nature of the copyrighted work;
3. the amount and substantiality of the portion used in relation to the copyrighted work as a whole; and
4. the effect of the use upon the potential market for or value of the copyrighted work.'

[24] See in Canada, *CCH Canadian Ltd* v. *Law Society of Upper Canada* [1999] 2 CPR (4th) 129. See below for discussion of Israel, New Zealand and Singapore.

[25] Interpreting dynamism can be difficult; see Chapter 3.

[26] In the United States, the Stop Online Piracy Act ('SOPA') and Preventing Real Online Threats to Economic Creativity and Theft of Intellectual Property Act ('PIPA') were defeated in the US Congress. Many of the principles in them seem to be pursued in FTAs; see Leaked Text of the TPP Chapter on Intellectual Property, available at http://wikileaks.org/tpp/static/pdf/Wikileaks-secret-TPP-treaty-IP-chapter.pdf, and see M. A. Carrier,

parts of government are responsible for trade policy than those that are responsible for domestic intellectual property policy.[27] The separation has resulted in those negotiating trade deals with the United States finding themselves referring to the United States' domestic debate as a way of contesting the US trade policy. In 2014, the US trade negotiators describe their approach in the trans-Pacific partnership negotiations[28] as a 'values-driven trade policy'; this is stated to include the values of the US Constitution in encouraging innovation and creativity.[29] However, problems are developing. While US trade policy aims to have greater control of copyright online, in the domestic arena analogous proposals were defeated.[30] This seems to arise because lobbyists for domestic industries may be successful in one arena but not in the other. Consequently, the resulting differences between trade and domestic policy may not be calculated to be a difference. In certain areas, however, trade and domestic policy have ended up, and will likely again end up, being different. Enforcement standards provide an example: the defeat of a higher standard in the domestic realm has not prevented those higher standard from being negotiated internationally in more than one forum. The differences will endure at least until the domestic law changes or other countries also decide not to follow the agreed trade policy. The latter is less likely in the case of small market economies; as discussed in this book, small market economies are by and large very compliant with their international obligations.

One might also ask whether it is legitimate for a country to have an approach to intellectual property standards in its domestic law that is different from that which it advocates internationally. Broadly, it is difficult to have a trade policy or international approach to copyright law which is different from a domestic approach, without an explicit, and potentially unjustifiable, acknowledgement that the trade policy

'SOPA, PIPA, ACTA, TPP: An Alphabet Soup of Innovation-Stifling Copyright Legislation and Agreements', *Northwestern Journal of Technology and Intellectual Property*, 11(2) (2013), 21–32.

[27] Kaminski suggests that the trade policy agencies are captured by lobby interests; see M. E. Kaminski, 'The Capture of International Intellectual Property Law through the U.S. Trade Regime', *Southern California Law Review,* 87 (2014), 977–1052.

[28] See Leaked Text of the TPP Chapter, above n 26, and S. M. Flynn, M. E. Kaminski, B. K. Baker and J. Koo, 'Public Interest Analysis of the US TPP Proposal for an IP Chapter', Northeastern University School of Law Research Paper No. 82–2012, 6 December 2011, available at http://ssrn.com/abstract=1980173.

[29] M. Froman, 'A Values-Driven Trade Policy', 18 February 2014, available at www.ustr.gov/about-us/press-office/press-releases/2014/February/A-Values-Driven-Trade-Policy_Remarks-by-USTR-Froman-at-Center-for-American-P.

[30] SOPA and PIPA, above n 26.

approach is about protecting domestic industries abroad. Such an approach is not anchored in what might be called copyright justifications, rationales or principles. Rather, it is protectionist and in trade terms may be equivalent to a kind of subsidy.[31] If the strong standards are also found in domestic law then the 'subsidising' effect is borne by domestic consumers. This approach may appear rational from the viewpoint of those seeking to increase revenue through exporting copyright, but some methods of subsidising industry are not consistent with the World Trade Organization (WTO) trade liberalisation approach, which includes removing domestic subsidies.[32] To protect one's own industries is understandable, but it is not always defensible to do so by heightening intellectual property protection if a global view of intellectual property is taken. After all, the TRIPS Agreement[33] is supposed to be a global regime.[34]

The international framework of copyright law

The framework of international copyright is made up of two key treaties: the TRIPS Agreement and the Berne Convention.[35] These treaties are structured around minimum standards, which allow for more extensive protection, and some voluntary flexibility. This means that countries are able to have different laws and different approaches to exclusive rights.[36] There is no internationally agreed definition of reproduction,[37] distribution rights vary[38] and so do communication rights.[39] As flexibilities and

[31] If the role of the international arena is primarily protectionist then this suggests a different role for copyright than the usual rationales of encouraging creativity, see discussion in Chapter 4.

[32] See Chapter 4 for further discussion of the relationship between intellectual property rules and subsidies.

[33] WTO, Agreement on Trade-Related Aspects of Intellectual Property Rights, Marrakesh Agreement Establishing the World Trade Organization, Annex 1C, 1869 UNTS 299; 33 ILM 1197 (adopted on 15 April 1994, entered into force 1 January 1995) ('TRIPS Agreement').

[34] In addition the TRIPS Agreement, above n 33, objectives and purposes are not just about protection, but include recognising national policy interests; see Chapter 3.

[35] Berne Convention for the Protection of Literary and Artistic Works (Paris text), 1161 UNTS 3, 24 July 1971 ('Berne Convention').

[36] See discussion in Chapter 3.

[37] No definition of reproduction is found in the Berne Convention, above n 35, and in the WIPO Copyright Treaty, 36 ILM 65 (1997) (adopted 20 December 1996, entered into force 6 March 2002) ('WCT'); in the negotiations, there was significant difficulty over agreeing on a definition of reproduction and so one is not included.

[38] Distribution in the WCT refers to the first sale or making available of the copyright work; see WCT above n 37, art 6.

[39] WCT, above n 37, art 8 provides that 'authors of literary and artistic works shall enjoy the exclusive right of authorizing any communication to the public of their works, by wire or

exceptions are voluntary, they will also vary, although many countries have flexibilities relating to education and research, for example.

The digital phenomenon was noticed by international law reformers in the last decade of the twentieth century and one of the first legal responses was to negotiate two treaties known as the WIPO Internet Treaties: the WIPO Copyright Treaty (WCT)[40] and the WIPO Performances and Phonograms Treaty (WPPT).[41]

There is no internationally mandated framework for fair use, fair dealing and permitted acts other than compliance with the rather complex three-step test.[42] That test has its genesis in the Berne Convention, which provides:[43]

> It shall be a matter for legislation in the countries of the union to permit the reproduction of such works in certain special cases, provided that such reproduction does not conflict with a normal exploitation of the work and does not unreasonably prejudice the legitimate interests of the author.

The test was incorporated into,[44] and also developed in, the TRIPS Agreement to apply to rights other than the reproduction right.[45] Article 13 of the TRIPS Agreement provides:

> Members shall confine limitations or exceptions to exclusive rights to certain special cases which do not conflict with a normal exploitation of the work and do not unreasonably prejudice the legitimate interests of the right holder.

A WTO dispute settlement panel[46] assessed a provision of US copyright law against the three-step test.[47] The complaint, which was brought by the European Communities, as it was then known, centred on s 110(5) of

wireless means, including the making available to the public of their works in such a way that members of the public may access these works from a place and at a time individually chosen by them.'

40 WCT, above n 37.

41 WIPO Performers and Producers of Phonograms Treaty, 36 ILM 76 (1997) (adopted 20 December 1996, entered into force 20 May 2002) ('WPPT').

42 For a general discussion of the three-step test, see M. Kennedy, 'The "Three-Step Test" and the Burden of Proof in Disputes under the TRIPS Agreement', *International Review of Intellectual Property and Competition Law,* 41(2014), 161–177 and C. Geiger, D. J. Gervais and M. Senftleben, 'The Three-Step-Test Revisited: How to Use the Test's Flexibility in National Copyright Law', *American University International Law review,* 29(2014), 581–626.

43 Berne Convention, above n 35, art 9(2). 44 TRIPS Agreement, above n 33, art 9.1.

45 TRIPS Agreement, above n 33, art 13 provides that 'Members shall confine limitations or exceptions to exclusive rights to certain special cases which do not conflict with a normal exploitation of the work and do not unreasonably prejudice the legitimate interests of the right holder.'

46 See Chapter 2 for an explanation of the WTO dispute settlement system.

47 WTO Panel Report, *United States – Section 110(5) of the US Copyright Act,* 27 July 2000, WT/DS160/R.

the US Copyright Act. That section incorporates two broad exemptions to a copyright owner's rights, known as the 'homestyle exemption' and the 'business exemption'. The homestyle exemption permitted the playing in public of radio or television by way of a single receiving apparatus of a kind commonly used in private homes. The business exemption permitted small shops and cafes to play non-dramatic musical works originated by licensed radio and television broadcasters. The panel found that the homestyle exemption complied with the TRIPS Agreement, but the business exemption did not. In sum, the panel's approach to the first step of the three step test was that 'special case' meant that an exception should be clearly defined and limited in its scope and reach. The panel took the view that the meaning of the second step, 'no conflict with normal exploitation', included empirical and normative considerations meaning that it applied not just to existing but also to plausible future revenue streams. The central issue in the third step, according to the panel, was whether prejudice to the legitimate interests of right holders reaches an unreasonable level if an exception or limitation causes, or has the potential to cause, an unreasonable loss of income to the copyright owner.

The three-step test has been subject to much discussion and criticism.[48] The panel's approach meant that the panel did not consider the reason for the exception. In the analysis of first step, it interpreted 'certain special cases' not with reference to purpose, such as for research. Rather, it looked at its 'scope and reach'. Arguably, these factors are more relevant to the second and third steps and certain special cases might be exactly the place to address the purpose of the exception, such as being for research or private study, criticism or review, parody, or even allowing small business to survive.

A variant on the three-step test is found in the WCT.[49] Different jurisdictions continue to impose differing standards of permitted acts, fair dealing, and fair use provisions in copyright law. This has led to various suggestions to 'harmonise' exceptions to copyright. This can

[48] Dinwoddie and Dreyfuss explain that 'the panel relied on an implausible reading of the statute' and did not take into account the United States' reasons and domestic policy bargain behind the exception; see G. B. Dinwoodie and R. Dreyfuss, *A Neofederalist Vision of TRIPS: The Resilience of the International Intellectual Property Regime* (Oxford University Press, 2012), 120–124. See also J. C. Ginsburg, 'Toward Supranational Copyright Law? The WTO Panel Decision and the "Three-Step Test" for Copyright Exceptions', *Revue Internationale du Droit d'Auteur* 187 (2001), 3–19; J. Oliver, 'Copyright in the WTO: The Panel Decision on the Three-Step Test', *Columbia Journal of Law & the Arts,* 25 (2002), 119–170; see also above n 42.

[49] WCT, above n 37, art 10 and Agreed Statements Concerning the WIPO Copyright Treaty (adopted 20 December 1996), concerning art 10.

include limiting the scope of exceptions in free trade agreements (FTAs) or defining them more precisely at multilateral level. An example of the latter is the WIPO treaty setting a uniform exception allowing for works to be reproduced for the benefit of the visually impaired and print disabled, which also includes the relevant three-step tests.[50] The result of all of these agreements is that there is no uniform three-step test. That is the international framework, as discussed in Chapter 2, provides little in terms of guidance for domestic policy makers, particularly about the scope of flexibilities and exceptions.

The scope and subsistence of copyright in small markets

What categories of work fall under the scope of copyright subject matter can vary within the framework of international agreements.[51] Small market economies tend to take a broad approach to copyright, using it to encompass not only those areas covered by the Berne Convention and the TRIPS Agreement, but also broadcasts, cable programmes and other communications. In European Union (EU) countries, broadcasts and cable programmes are treated as neighbouring rights. In the United States, broadcasts, cable programmes and other communications are not in themselves copyright works, although copyright works incorporated into communications are protected.

Industrial design

Small market economies use copyright extensively for industrial design protection.[52] The Berne Convention allows this option.[53] In such economies, many cases are about the design drawings and prototype models that lie behind mass-produced works.[54] The reason for

[50] Marrakesh Treaty to Facilitate Access to Published Works for Persons Who Are Blind, Visually Impaired, above n 11, art 11.

[51] The Berne Convention, above n 33, art 2, provides a definition of literary and artistic works, which includes music and dramatic work. The TRIPS Agreement above n 33, art 10, adds protection of databases and computer programs.

[52] New Zealand also has a registered design protection; see Designs Act 1953, but copyright is more often used.

[53] Berne Convention, above n 35, art 8.

[54] In New Zealand, for example, the leading case on infringement was about a Frisbee and related underlying copyright works; see *Wham-O MFG Co.* v. *Lincoln Industries Ltd* [1984] 1 NZLR 641. The only copyright case to have reached the newly established Supreme Court involved the layout of a glue packet; see *Henkel KGAA* v. *Holdfast New Zealand Limited* [2006] NZSC 102. In Singapore, cases have involved, for example, a fax modem's printed circuit board, *Real Electronics Industries Singapore (Pte) Ltd* v. *Nimrod*

including industrial design as part of copyright law is both long-standing as an inheritance from British law and practical in order to avoid both complication and cost.

In jurisdictions where design rights – both registered and unregistered – are separate from copyright, they seem to have become very complicated. The European Union is such an example.[55] In the United States, the rule is that if a work has utility, it can still attract copyright,[56] but commentators have said that 'the availability of copyright protection for the design of useful objects has evolved from the uncertain to the incoherent'.[57] A problem with including industrial design in copyright law is that doing so tends to lower the threshold of originality. The originality test is that what is original is that which is not copied, rather than requiring a spark of originality.[58]

A key, if not the main, reason to include industrial design in copyright is that it is usually thought to be cost-effective for small businesses because obtaining the right does not require the expenses of registration.[59] Such a view may be short-sighted because of the usually extensive costs of proving copyright in order to enforce it.[60] The cost of intellectual property is a significant barrier to its effective use by many types of businesses, especially small ones. While this is a worldwide phenomenon, from a small market economy perspective most businesses are small on a global scale.[61]

Engineering Pte Ltd [1996] 1 SLR 336 and drawings of a car exhaust pipe, *Remus Innovations Forschungs-Und Abgasanlagen-Produktionsgellschaft Mbh* v. *Hong Boon Siong* [1995] 2 SLR 148.

55 For a summary of the UK law, see E. Derclaye, 'A Decade of Registered and Unregistered Design Rights Decisions in the UK: What Conclusions Can We Draw for the Future of Both Types of Rights?', *IP Theory*, 3(2) (2013), 144–157.

56 *Bleistein* v. *Donaldson Lithographing Co.*, 188 U.S. 239, 23 SCt. 298 (1903).

57 R. A. Gorman and J. C. Ginsburg, *Copyright*, 7th edn (Foundation Press, Eagan, MN, 2006), at 221.

58 There is much written on this which shall not be repeated here, but see, for example, A. Rahmatian, 'Originality in UK Copyright Law: The Old "Skill and Labour" Doctrine under Pressure', *IIC*, 44 (2013), 4–34; J. C. Ginsburg, 'No "Sweat"? Copyright and Other Protection of Works of Information after Feist v. Rural Telephone', *Columbia Law Review*, 92 (1992), 338–388, at 339; D. Gervais, 'Feist Goes Global: A Comparative Analysis of the Notion of Originality in Copyright Law', *Journal of the Copyright Society of the USA*, 49 (2002), 949–982; and see S. Frankel, *Intellectual Property in New Zealand*, 2nd edn (Lexis Nexis, Wellington, 2011) at 233–242.

59 Ginsburg and Gorman make the point that obtaining a design patent in the United States may be 'expensive and in some cases prohibitively so ... An applicant with several new designs has no way of knowing which will be popular, but in most cases cannot afford to pay for design patents on all of them', Gorman and Ginsburg, above n 57, at 222.

60 As discussed in Chapter 7, trade marks may also be overused because they are an affordable method of registerable intellectual property.

61 There are some exceptions of course, such as New Zealand's Fonterra, which is one of the world's largest dairy companies.

Bringing down the cost of intellectual property is also a reason that lies behind not having formalities for copyright's substance.

Formalities

Copyright cannot be registered in many countries and the Berne Convention embodies the rule that copyright shall not have formalities for its subsistence.[62] Not all are happy with this situation and there is a growing view that the use of formalities could improve copyright.[63] Some formalities advocates suggest that not granting copyright unless there is registration can address not only the perceived problem of too much copyright but also issues such as orphan works.[64] It is true that some aspects of formalities, such as recording ownership, would in many instances be useful; however, some aspects may not be so.[65] Using formalities to create copyright would change the landscape of copyright and not necessarily for the better from the perspective of the small or medium-sized business or non-business copyright interests. If formalities were introduced (or reintroduced where they previously existed), a likely outcome would be that small or medium-sized players would form the bulk of those who lose their copyright through failure to register.[66] The

62 Berne Convention, above n 35, art 5(2) provides, 'The enjoyment and the exercise of these rights shall not be subject to any formality; such enjoyment and such exercise shall be independent of the existence of protection in the country of origin of the work.'

63 See, for example, Sprigman, above n 13, at 485.

64 The Center for Study of the Public Domain describes the orphan works problem as follows: orphan works 'probably comprise the majority of the record of 20th century culture. These works are still presumably under copyright (only works published before 1923 are conclusively in the public domain [in the U.S.]), but the copyright owner cannot be found. The default response of archivists, libraries, film restorers, artists, scholars, educators, publishers, and others is to drop copyrighted work unless it is clearly in the public domain. As a result, orphan works are not used in new creative efforts or made available to the public due to uncertainty over their copyright status, even when there is no longer anyone claiming copyright ownership, or the owner no longer has any objection to such use.' See http://web.law.duke.edu/cspd/orphanworks.html. To remedy the situation, see D. R. Hansen and others, 'Solving the Orphan Works Problem for the United States', *Columbia Journal of Law & the Arts*, 37 (2013), 1–56, where formalities are discussed as well as other options such as fair use and limitations on remedies.

65 See D. Gervais, 'The Future of United States Copyright Formalities: Why We Should Prioritise Recordation, and How to Do It', *Berkeley Technology Law Journal*, 28 (2013), 1459–1496 and Ginsburg, above n 13.

66 See N. Elkin-Koren, 'What Contracts Cannot Do: The Limits of Private Ordering in Facilitating a Creative Commons', *Fordham Law Review*, 74 (2005), 375–422, at 383 note 27, where she suggests that formalities 'could actually discriminate against individual creators who are unable to carry the burden of legal counselling and registration'. See also B. A. Greenberg, 'More Than Just a Formality: Instant Authorship and Copyright's Opt-Out Future in the Digital Age', *UCLA Law Review*, 59 (2012), 1028–1075, at 1048–1050.

introduction of formalities would make registration possible for large businesses that can afford such administrative costs, but not for smaller businesses.

Moving away from British law

The three small market economies discussed in this book (New Zealand, Singapore and Israel) all once adopted British copyright law. Each country has made substantive alterations to the law, particularly during the last decade, in response to digital technology.[67] As noted in the Introduction to this book, small market economies have interests in common with the developed world and with the developing world. Copyright law involves public goods relating to creativity, culture and economic benefits. Those benefits include private rights, which are an important function of copyright. Balancing these interests will not be the same in all countries because of economic diversity and because in different economies there will be varying numbers of players in various parts of the copyright regime. The optimal copyright law for a small market economy is a law that achieves a balance between the public goods in copyright and the private rights of copyright owners in a manner that is appropriate for a small market economy. The remainder of this chapter discusses small market economy approaches and legal innovations to aspects of copyright. First, subject matter and digital copyright in New Zealand are discussed and, second, the approach to copyright exceptions in Israel and Singapore.

Subject matter and digital copyright

The linkage between trade and intellectual property has been a major motivation for New Zealand to extend its copyright protection, particularly as it relates to the Internet, in order to achieve trade gains. Some types of digital copyright reform might be beneficial for economies with a much larger volume of copyright industries than found in New Zealand. The New Zealand government may very well be prepared to entertain high levels of copyright protection, even to the very extensive level as is found in the US FTA with Australia,[68] in order to obtain other gains particularly in relation to market access for agricultural

[67] The Copyright Act 1962 (NZ), for example, is much the same as the Copyright Act 1956 (UK).

[68] Department of Foreign Affairs and Trade, Australia–US FTA (signed 18 May 2004, entered into force on 1 January 2005), available at www.dfat.gov.au/trade/negotiations/us_fta/final-text, at chapter 21 ('AUSFTA').

products. So copyright law may not necessarily contribute to the growth and development of local copyright industries, but it might contribute indirectly to the growth and development of areas of importance to the New Zealand economy such as agriculture and tourism. This is the general policy statement that was included with the digital copyright reform when it was first read in Parliament:[69]

> The key principle that guides copyright reform in New Zealand is the enhancement of the public interest – copyright law must benefit New Zealand as a whole and contribute to overall growth and development.

I have noted elsewhere that the use of 'overall' to qualify growth and development seems to suggest that the relevant growth and development is not necessarily confined to copyright-related businesses and industries.[70] As copyright protection becomes more and more extensive, whether this trade-off is worth it becomes very questionable.[71] The short-term goal of striking a trade deal may not be worth the long-term consequences of paying much more to overseas interests for copyright works.

How copyright contributes to growth and development is paradoxically both obvious, because the products of creativity and culture are involved, and complex, because the contribution cannot be measured only by the earnings of cultural industries and businesses. Added to that complexity is the position of small market economies as net importers of copyright works. In reality, copyright law does not function to protect only locally created culture, but it also protects cultural products from all around the world. In view of this multifaceted role of copyright, two conclusions can be drawn. First, the optimal copyright law for one country will not be the same as in another country. This is not simply a question of size, although size and scale may lead to some commonalities and differences. Second, the economic and cultural outcomes that a country seeks from its copyright law will be important in ensuring that copyright law has a public interest role at the domestic level and is not simply an instrument of benefit to foreigners. Balancing such objectives needs careful analysis and legislative design. It should not be left to chance.

[69] Copyright (New Technologies and Performers' Rights) Amendment Bill (NZ), 102–1 (assented to 11 April 2008), at 2.

[70] See S. Frankel, 'Digital Copyright Reform in New Zealand: An Own Interest Approach for a Small Market Economy', in B. Fitzgerald and M. Perry (eds.), *Knowledge Policy for the 21st Century* (Irwin Law Inc. Publishing, Toronto, 2011), pp. 72–78.

[71] See S. Frankel, 'Intellectual Property in New Zealand and the TPPA', in Jane Kelsey (ed.), *No Ordinary Deal. Unmasking the Trans-Pacific Partnership Free Trade Agreement* (Bridget Williams Books, Wellington, 2010), pp. 163–175.

New Zealand legal innovations and experiments with digital copyright

New Zealand is not a member of the WCT.[72] The digital copyright reform process was intended to make New Zealand law compliant with that treaty and some of New Zealand's FTA commitments refer to having standards that meet that treaty.[73] The reform of New Zealand's law to address new technologies included a number of changes that provide more extensive copyright protection and new exceptions. In relation to both, there are some unique New Zealand legal innovations.

Communication and technological neutrality

Copyright owners have the exclusive right to communicate their copyright works to the public.[74] In addition to providing a right to communicate, the New Zealand law introduced a category of work called the 'communication work' and repealed the formerly specific categories and definitions of broadcast and cable programme.[75] A communication work includes all forms of communication: a broadcast, a cable programme and any combination of those two, as well as Internet communications.[76] The category of communication work, like the communication right, is designed to be technologically neutral.[77] This is advantageous where it avoids litigation based on technologically specific statutory detail rather than outcomes based on laws created to strike a balance between copyright's competing interests.[78]

[72] The Copyright Bill stated in its opening commentary that 'the bill takes into account international developments in copyright law, and incorporates many aspects of the two treaties negotiated by the members of the World Intellectual Property Organisation (WIPO) – the WIPO Copyright Treaty (WCT) and WIPO Performances and Phonograms Treaty', available at www.parliament.nz/resource/en-nz/00DBHOH_BILL7735_1/c3c6fb4dc0018a7c2fe45cd9b95b089777c4f80a.

[73] See, for example, the Trans-Pacific Strategic Economic Partnership ('P4') (signed 18 July 2005, entered into force 28 May 2006), art 10.3.4.

[74] Copyright Act 1994 (NZ), s 33.

[75] Copyright Act 1994 (NZ), s 4 (Meaning of cable programme service, and associated definitions); repealed in 2008 by the Copyright (New Technologies) Amendment Act 2008, s 6.

[76] Copyright Act 1994 (NZ), s 3.

[77] Like in the WCT, above n 37, the means of making the work available to the public is not technologically specified. 'Communicate' is defined as 'to transmit or make available by means of communication technology, including by means of a telecommunications system or electronic retrieval system'. Copyright Act 1994 (NZ), s 2. Also, like in the WCT, 'public' is not defined. See discussion in S. Ricketson and J. Ginsburg, *International Copyright and Neighbouring Rights: The Berne Convention and Beyond*, 2nd edn (Oxford University Press, New York, 2006), at 12.58.

[78] An example of this is *Telstra Corp Ltd* v. *Australasian Performing Right Association Ltd* (1997) 38 IPR 294 (HCA). There the issue was whether music played on the telephone

Fitting through the loopholes in copyright law in order to avoid infringement or claim a permitted or fair use is an expected response to a regulatory regime. Finding the loophole is both understandable and sometimes desirable. However, technology loopholes can be rather troublesome if they become the driver of the business model for creativity or distribution of creative works. There will always be a degree to which the framing of the law incentivises business behaviour but, in copyright, technological neutrality can minimise that to an appropriate rather than all-encompassing level. As Francis Gurry has said, technological neutrality should be a principle of copyright:[79]

> The purpose of copyright is not to influence technological possibilities for creative expression or the business models built on those technological possibilities. Nor is its purpose to preserve business models established under obsolete or moribund technologies. Its purpose is, I believe, to work with any and all technologies for the production and distribution of cultural works, and to extract some value from the cultural exchanges made possible by those technologies to return to creators and performers and the business associates engaged by them to facilitate the cultural exchanges through the use of the technologies. Copyright should be about promoting cultural dynamism, not preserving or promoting vested business interests.

Overall, it is preferable not to turn copyright law into the equivalent of tax avoidance, but into a system that allows various interests to effectively coexist.[80] The disadvantage of technological neutrality is that the rights are on the face of it very broad and, therefore, require carefully detailed exceptions. By this I do not suggest that authors should not have rights, but rather that authors (and owners) do not only need rights but also need users, consumers and distributors, all of whom also need authors.

In order to achieve a balance in this system, one of New Zealand's permitted uses is for transient reproductions of communication works.[81]

while on hold was a copyright infringement. The protection granted to copyright owners depended on whether their works were being transmitted to landline phones, where the communication was wire, or were being transmitted to mobile phones, where the communication was wireless. It should not matter what technology is used if the activity results in the exploitation of another's copyright work.

79 F. Gurry, 'The Future of Copyright', speech at Blue Skies Conference on Future Directions in Copyright Law, Sydney (February 2011), available at www.wipo.int/about wipo/en/dgo/speeches/dg_blueskyconf_11.html.

80 See S. Frankel, *The International Copyright Problem*, above n.10.

81 Copyright Act 1994 (NZ), s 43A provides, 'A reproduction of a work does not infringe copyright in the work if the reproduction – (a) is transient or incidental; and (b) is an integral and essential part of a technological process for – (i) making or receiving a communication that does not infringe copyright; or (ii) enabling the lawful use of, or lawful dealing in, the work; and (c) has no independent economic significance.'

Exceptions to the communication right include recording for the purposes of time shifting,[82] incidental recording for purposes of communication[83] and free public playing or showing of communication work.[84] It is not clear, as is the case around the world, whether these exceptions do in fact achieve balance, but certainly the extent of the exceptions is greater than those found where transient copying, for example, remains an infringement.

Technological protection mechanisms

The use of technological protection mechanisms (TPMs) as a means to protect copyright is controversial. TPMs are protected in their own right and not as copyright works. The use of TPMs can place severe restrictions on access to works.[85] TPMs can be used for both access restrictions and copyright restrictions. New Zealand's law protects TPMs for the purpose of preventing infringement,[86] but specifically excludes protection for TPMs based on access.[87] The New Zealand approach is designed to reflect that copyright is about protecting copying and encouraging access. Additionally, the approach is consistent with allowing parallel importing. If, for example, a DVD is parallel imported, then a TPM, such as regional coding, should not deny access in order to defeat that import.[88] Therefore, New Zealand copyright law has the effect of allowing access to copyright works whatever the region code. Some have suggested that the New

[82] Copyright Act 1994 (NZ), s 84. [83] Copyright Act 1994 (NZ), s 85.

[84] Copyright Act 1994 (NZ), s 87 and 87A.

[85] See, for example, K. R. Eschenfelder, 'Every Library's Nightmare? Digital Rights Management, Use Restrictions, and Licensed Scholarly Digital Resources', available at http://crl.acrl.org/content/69/3/205.full.pdf.

[86] Copyright Act 1994 (NZ), s 226A(1). Additionally, it is an infringement of copyright to sell a TPM circumvention device if the seller knows or has reasons to believe that it will be used to infringe copyright in a TPM-protected work. The provision makes it a prohibited act to 'make, import, sell, distribute, let for hire, offer or expose for sale or hire, or advertise for sale or hire' a TPM circumvention device; see Copyright Act 1994 (NZ), s 226A.

[87] Copyright Act 1994 (NZ), s 266 states 'TPM or technological protection measure –

(a) means any process, treatment, mechanism, device, or system that in the normal course of its operation prevents or inhibits the infringement of copyright in a TPM work; but

(b) for the avoidance of doubt, does not include a process, treatment, mechanism, device, or system to the extent that, in the normal course of operation, it only controls any access to a work for non-infringing purposes (for example, it does not include a process, treatment, mechanism, device, or system to the extent that it controls geographic market segmentation by preventing the playback in New Zealand of a non-infringing copy of a work).'

[88] See discussion in Chapter 8.

Zealand approach to TPMs is one of the more balanced in the world.[89]

The reasons that the legislature gave for protecting TPMs through the vehicle of copyright law are that they 'are necessary to manage the risk of piracy of copyrighted works in a digital environment, and that they strike the correct balance between the interests of copyright owners and those of copyright users'.[90] When TPMs are protected in their own right, the balance shifts in favour of owners and away from users of copyright works. The Bill that introduced digital copyright law reform in New Zealand contained a number of statements about government policy.[91] One of these was the objective of maintaining the balance among and between creators, owners and users in the digital world. Consequently, the New Zealand law includes a number of detailed permitted acts allowing circumvention of TPMs in limited circumstances.[92]

Repeat infringing online

One of the greatest challenges for authors and copyright owners in the online world is how to make a living from their works and how to enforce copyright. In addressing this issue, New Zealand decided not to adopt a notice and takedown process analogous to that found in the United States.[93] Instead, New Zealand instituted a form of regulated response to address repeat infringing online.[94] The Copyright Act sets out a procedure whereby an alleged infringer is sent a series of notices, beginning with a detection notice,[95] followed by a warning notice[96] and thirdly an enforcement notice.[97] Certain time frames and conditions apply to each type of notice. The notices are issued by the account holder's Internet Service Provider, known as Internet protocol address

[89] 'What Are the Best Examples of Laws on Technological Protection Measures with Exceptions for Lawful Uses?', available at http://infojustice.org/archives/30139.

[90] Copyright Bill, above n 72, commentary at 8.

[91] The Copyright (New Technologies) Amendment Bill, as reported from the Commerce Committee, available online at www.parliament.nz/en-NZ/PB/Legislation/Bills/b/2/a/00DBHOH_BILL7735_1-Copyright-New-Technologies-and-Performers-Rights.htm.

[92] Copyright Act 1994 (NZ), s 226E and Part III.

[93] Digital Millennium Copyright Act (US), 17 USC, s 512.

[94] Copyright Act 1994, s122B, gives an overview of the New Zealand system. For discussion and comparison of regulated response systems around the world, see R. Giblin, 'Beyond Graduated Response', in *Evolution and Equilibrium*, above n5, pp. 81–112.

[95] Copyright Act 1994 (NZ), s 122D. [96] Copyright Act 1994 (NZ), s 122E.

[97] Copyright Act 1994 (NZ), s 122F.

provider (IPAP)[98] under the legislation.[99] Notices are only issued at the request of the copyright owner. The IPAP is obliged not to reveal identifying information of the account holder to the copyright owner.[100] If the enforcement notice is not complied with, the copyright owner has the option to apply to the Copyright Tribunal for a monetary remedy against the alleged infringer.[101] The Copyright Tribunal has certain obligations under the legislation, including rules about evidentiary burdens and when a monetary award is appropriate.[102] The Copyright Tribunal is an independent quasi-judicial body.[103]

Fair use and fair dealing innovations within the international framework

Internationally the differences over what use of copyright works is permitted and what is not have been set in sharp relief in the digital age. This has led to extensive debate about the scope of rights and their relationship with flexibilities. There has been a considerable focus on how flexibilities and exceptions should work.[104] As discussed above, the international framework has been that exceptions are permitted within certain rules, but whether and how exceptions are utilised is a matter of national autonomy. The framework for exceptions to the reproduction right in the Berne Convention, for example, begins thus: 'It shall be a matter for legislation in the countries of the Union . . .'.[105]

98 IPAP 'means a person that operates a business that, other than as an incidental feature of its main business activities, –
(a) offers the transmission, routing, and providing of connections for digital online communications, between or among points specified by a user, of material of the user's choosing; and
(b) allocates IP addresses to its account holders; and
(c) charges its account holders for its services; and
(d) is not primarily operated to cater for transient users'; Copyright Act 1994 (NZ), s 122A.

99 Copyright Act 1994 (NZ), s 122C. 100 Copyright Act 1994 (NZ), s 122T(3).

101 Copyright Act 1994 (NZ), s 122I and J. At the time of writing I am the Chair of the New Zealand Copyright Tribunal.

102 See Copyright Act 1994 (NZ), s 122N and O and Copyright (Infringing File Sharing) Regulations 2011, s 12.

103 In addition to the jurisdiction relating to infringing file sharing, the copyright tribunal hears licensing disputes; see Copyright Act 1994 (NZ), Part VIII.

104 For a discussion from various US perspectives about fair use and common themes, see Samuelson, 'Unbundling Fair Uses', above n 22, 2537–2622; M. J. Madison, 'A Pattern-Oriented Approach to Fair Use', *William & Mary Law Review*, 45 (2004), 1525–1690; B. Beebe, 'An Empirical Study of U.S. Copyright Fair Use Opinions, 1978–2005', *University of Pennsylvania Law Review*, 156 (2008), 549–624; M. Sag, 'The Prehistory of Fair Use', *Brooklyn Law Review*, 76 (2011), 1371–1412.

105 Berne Convention, above n 35, art 9(2).

The TRIPS Agreement and Berne Convention framework provide rights in some detail and the three-step test as a framework for exceptions.[106] For some countries, this has meant that the exceptions are not easily enacted or that the form of the law is adapted from elsewhere rather than crafted as a matter of local policy. Some exceptions may have universal relevance, such as for research and private study. Other exceptions are likely to be more directly calibrated to local needs or local cultural norms.

The development of calibrated exceptions is frequently piecemeal. This is not surprising as the dynamic subject matter of copyright often means that the need for an exception is not known in advance. In the system of delineated permitted acts, the piecemeal approach is sometimes problematic. Unless an activity falls within an existing permitted act, it will not be permitted and legislative reform will have to address any new use even if copyright policy points to it being an act that ought to be permitted.[107] Delineated permitted acts systems do not have a general fair use principle,[108] as found in the United States, which can be adapted as new fair uses arise.

The sort of overarching principles which are found in fair use or fair dealing provisions could reflect the economic needs of a nation, such as its needs for supporting research.[109] Principles of this kind can also reflect the cultural policy of a nation, including its interest in supporting libraries, education and the arts and artists. If guiding principles include general aims, then those generalities have a flow-on effect for specific instances. Without such guiding principles, the policy of copyright law is potentially lost in the detail and less likely to be regarded as directly relevant in the litigation context where the scope of copyright exceptions is battled out and determined.

[106] TRIPS Agreement, above n 33, art 13 and Berne Convention, above n 35, art 9(2).

[107] This sort of legislative reform can be swift or slow. An example of a swift response to an adverse finding was the use of news clips in *TVNZ Ltd* v. *Newsmonitor Services Ltd* [1994] 2 NZLR 91 (HC), which was found not to be fair dealing for research or private study and which appears to have prompted the reform to add a section specifically to create a compulsory licensing scheme for news monitoring activity; see Copyright Act 1994 (NZ), s 91.

[108] For a discussion of the rigidity of this approach, see *Pro Sieben Media AG* v. *Carlton UK Television Ltd* [1998] FSR 43 per Laddie J, quoted by Robert Walker LJ in *Pro Sieben Media AG* v. *Carlton UK Television Ltd* [1999] 1 WLR 605 (EWCACiv), at 607–608.

[109] See W. F. Patry, *Patry on Copyright* (2008), § 10:4, which describes the development of the fair use doctrine in early American common law as a mechanism in which different social concepts were considered. See also W. F. Patry, *How to Fix Copyright* (Oxford University Press, New York, 2012).

Some are critical of the way in which the United States' fair use operates because it is, at least at present, not predictable.[110] Additionally, finding the parameters of fair use depends on an adequate number of cases before the courts in order to test the rules. Where cases are few, because the economy is small, or litigation is not a cultural norm, fair use may be less appropriate. The usual reason given for this conclusion is a lack of predictability or legal certainty.[111] Claims that legal certainty is achieved only through having rules that do not address the future are doubtful.[112] Appropriately framed discretion does not mean a lack of certainty; rather, it places the ability for a law that regulates a dynamic area to respond to that dynamism. The United States could be said to demonstrate that the presence of a considerable body of case law does not solve all issues, but equally so, neither does the absence of flexibility. The absence, however, of flexibility may mean that the law is so out of tune with social or business norms that it cannot achieve its underlying goals. Importantly, fair use is often combined with permitted acts. The fair use systems of Singapore and Israel discussed below, and the United States' law from which they have borrowed principles, sit alongside specific delineated permitted uses.

Some have suggested that there needs to be more coordination internationally over exceptions and this led to the treaty for exceptions for the benefit of the visually impaired.[113] The use of mandatory exceptions partially changes the framework of the international agreements, which have previously left exceptions to national autonomy.[114] Just as states are

[110] See, for example, G. Austin, 'The Two Faces of Fair Use', *New Zealand Universities Law Review*, 25 (2012), 285–317, where he argues that uses which do not transform an existing work into a work of new authorship but rather create a new market are not well grounded in purposes of fair use in US law.

[111] One commentator has said, for example, that the statutory language of US fair use provides 'very little guidance for predicting whether a particular use will be fair'; see M. Carroll, 'Fixing Fair Use', *North Carolina Law Review*, 85 (2007), 1087–1154. Decisions suggest that the courts see the rationales for fair use as broader than encouraging authorship. See also Samuelson, 'Unbundling Fair Uses', above n 22, at 2544; categorising transformative use in three groupings: transformative – creating new works that use pre-existing works, including parody and satire; productive – such as quotation; and orthogonal – using copyright material in ways different in purpose from the original.

[112] For a discussion of the relationship between certainty and discretion, see D. Kalderimis, C. Nixon and T. Smith, 'Certainty and Discretion in Regulation', in S. Frankel and J. Yeabsley (eds.), *Framing the Commons: Cross-cutting Issues in Regulation* (Victoria University Press, Wellington, 2014) pp. 112–141.

[113] Treaty to Facilitate Access to Published Works for Persons Who Are Blind, Visually Impaired, or Otherwise Print Disabled, above n 11.

[114] Berne Convention, above n 35, art 10 has a mandatory exception for quotation. Report of the ALAI ad hoc Committee on the Proposals to Introduce Mandatory Exceptions for the Visually Impaired, available at http://www.alai.org/en/assets/files/resolutions/report-mandatory-exceptions.pdf, states, 'If proposed exceptions are incompatible with

free to negotiate rights, they are also free to negotiate exceptions. Put differently, there is no rule of international law that means that countries cannot change or update the agreement between them. In fact international law anticipates this will happen.[115] Amending an existing treaty is complicated and so Protocols or other treaties are usually used in preference to amendment. Through such methods, parties to an existing treaty can agree to new practices which may differ from the existing regime and yet still be compatible with it. In any event, the visually impaired treaty has much discretion over implementation.[116] In fact, agreeing to the details is what makes negotiation so protracted and what has led to complex rules in order to enact such an exception.

Another way to look at the mandatory exception debate is as a pushback against the FTA process of strengthening rights and tightening exceptions, which undermines the multilateral system.[117] The mandatory exceptions discussion is arguably more legitimate[118] as it has taken place at the multilateral level and in the same forum as where the Berne Convention was created and is administered.

New Zealand copyright law adopts a permitted use framework and has no general guiding fair use principles on the face of the statute. The statute includes the guiding principles of US fair use[119] in the exception

the framework for exceptions and limitations set out at Berne art 9(2), TRIPs art 13, and WCT art 10, then Berne art 20 (incorporated in TRIPs via art 9(1), and in WCT via art 1(4)) would prohibit member States from enacting an international agreement mandating those exceptions. Article 20 bars Berne Member States from agreeing to provide a level of protection that is lower than that assured by the Convention's substantive minimum protections.' As the committee notes, Article 20 does not, however, bar exceptions that are compatible with the Conventions from being enacted at domestic law. Put differently, members of the Treaty can add to copyright law through subsequent treaties. That is exactly what the WCT does and arguably also the end result of the Treaty to Facilitate Access to Published Works for Persons Who Are Blind, Visually Impaired, or Otherwise Print Disabled, above n11.

115 Vienna Convention on the Law of Treaties, 23 May 1969, 1115 UNTS 331, 8 ILM 679 (adopted 22 May 1969, entered into force 17 January 1980), art 30.

116 Treaty to Facilitate Access to Published Works for Persons Who Are Blind, Visually Impaired, or Otherwise Print Disabled, above n 11, art 12.

117 See discussion in Chapter 2.

118 On the legitimacy and purposes, see generally, S. Frankel, 'The Legitimacy and Purpose of Intellectual Property Chapters in FTAs', in Ross Buckley, Vai Io Lo and Laurence Boulle (eds.), *Challenges to Multilateral Trade: The Impact of Bilateral, Preferential and Regional Agreements* (Wolters Kluwer, The Netherlands, 2008), pp. 185–199 and see Chapter 2.

119 17 USC, s 107 sets out four factors to be considered in determining whether or not a particular use is fair. These are: 1. The purpose and character of the use, including whether such use is of commercial nature or is for non-profit educational purposes; 2. The nature of the copyrighted work; 3. The amount and substantiality of the portion used in relation to the copyrighted work as a whole; and 4.The effect of the use upon the potential market for, or value of, the copyrighted work.

for research and private study, but the guidance is confined to that exception rather than applying to other permitted acts or a general fair use exception.[120] The kinds of exceptions which have been developed in other jurisdictions under a more expansive fair dealing or fair use approach have, however, been added to New Zealand law in increments through the Parliamentary process. As discussed above, some home-grown exceptions, particularly in relation to digital technology, have emerged. Although New Zealand has a delineated permitted acts model, the scope of coverage has evolved, but whether this piecemeal approach is the best method is questionable.

Singapore and Israel also have inherited a permitted acts approach. Both countries have, however, widened their approach to include something closer to fair use.[121] The quote at the beginning of this chapter suggests that this has been beneficial for Singapore.

Singapore and copyright exceptions

After the enactment of the Singapore–US FTA,[122] one reaction was to reform permitted acts and to introduce more flexibility close to the fair use model.[123] The author of a leading text on intellectual property in Singapore describes the fair dealing provisions in the Copyright Act as 'truly an indigenous species ... incorporat[ing] influences from the English and Australian concept of fair dealing and the American concept of fair use'.[124] One of the motivations for the change from permitted acts to a broader fair use seemed to have been to overcome the

120 Copyright Act 1994 (NZ), s 43:
(a) The purpose of the copying; and
(b) The nature of the work copied; and
(c) Whether the work could have been obtained within a reasonable time at an ordinary commercial price; and
(d) The effect of the copying on the potential market for, or value of, the work; and
(e) Where part of a work is copied, the amount and substantiality of the part copied taken in relation to the whole work.

121 A similar approach can be found in the law of Canada; see *CCH Canadian Ltd* v. *Law Society of Upper Canada* [2004] 1 SCR 339 (SCC) and see, for example, G. D'Agostino, 'Healing Fair Dealing? A Comparative Copyright Analysis of Canada's Fair Dealing to U.K. Fair Dealing and U.S. Fair Use', *McGill Law Journal*, 53 (2008), 309–366 and A. Katz, 'Fair Use 2.0: The Rebirth of Fair Dealing in Canada', in M. Geist (ed.), *The Copyright Pentalogy: How the Supreme Court of Canada Shook the Foundations of Canadian Copyright Law* (Ottawa University Press, 2013), 93–156.

122 Singapore-US FTA (signed 6 May 2003, entered into force 1 January 2004).

123 A similar post-FTA reaction can be seen in Australia, where shortly after the US FTA a parody exception was introduced and there has been a wholesale review of permitted acts in Australia; see ALRC Report above n 21.

124 W. L. Ng-Loy, *Law of Intellectual Property in Singapore,* revised edn (Sweet & Maxwell, 2009), at 11.3.2.

interpretation that resulted in some types of commercial research being excluded from the permitted act of research.[125] That particular issue was partially addressed by a 1998 amendment, but the overall dissatisfaction with the scope of permitted acts lingered, resulting in the 2005 reform. The reform essentially creates a general fair use defence. While activities which previously were permitted acts of research and study remain, the 'private' has been dropped from 'study', and research and study is an example rather than a specific purpose. The provision now reads,[126]

> Fair dealing [is permitted] . . . for any purposes other than the purpose referred to in s36 [criticism or review] or 37 [reporting of current events] which shall include research and study.

The drafting carve-out of criticism or review and reporting of current events have been done in a way that leaves some of the case law on those sections intact.[127]

The law provides factors relevant to whether or not a particular dealing is fair. These factors are identical to those in Australian law which have their origin in US-style fair use. They are:[128]

(a) the purpose and character of the dealing, including whether such dealing is of a commercial nature or is for non-profit educational purposes;
(b) the nature of the work;
(c) the amount and substantiality of the part copied taken in relation to the whole work;
(d) the effect of the dealing upon the potential market for, or value of the work; and
(e) the possibility of obtaining the work in a reasonable time at an ordinary commercial price.

The last factor is 'new' in Singapore law. The difficulty with the last factor may very well be that it provides an incentive to create collecting societies for which a payment needs to be made rather than a fair use for which no payment is made.[129]

125 See *Creative Technology Ltd* v. *Aztech Systems Pte Ltd* [1997] 1 SLR 621 (CA), and discussion in Ng-Loy, *Law of Intellectual Property in Singapore*, above n 124, at 11.3.7–11.3.8. The specific issues relating to decompilation of software have been addressed in New Zealand by a specific section; see Copyright Act 1994 (NZ), s 80A.

126 Copyright Act (revised) 2005 (Sing), s 35(1).

127 See Ng-Loy, *Law of Intellectual Property in Singapore*, above n 124, at 11.3.18.

128 See Copyright Act (Sing.), s 35(2) and Copyright Act (Cth.) 1968, s 40(2).

129 See Frankel, *Intellectual Property in New Zealand*, above n 58, at 362, where the same point is made in regard to that factor in New Zealand's Copyright Act, s 43, and the genesis of that approach in the *American Geophysical Union* v. *Texaco Inc* 60 F 3d 913 (1995). The relevance of licensing as fair dealing factor was rejected in Canada; see *CCH Canadian Ltd* v. *Law Society of Upper Canada* [2004] 1 SCR 339 (SCC), at [70], where the Chief Justice said, 'The availability of a licence is not relevant to deciding

It seems likely that overall the Singapore indigenous approach has been very successful. As the quote at the beginning of the chapter suggests, this has been beneficial for Singapore. The authors of a report on the economic value of fair use in Singapore concluded that the rise in private copying technology industries, which is in part because of the fair use exception, has not been problematic for copyright industries.[130]

Israel and fair use

In order to rid itself of the strictures of delineated permitted acts, Israel has adopted a fair use principle. The Supreme Court took the first step by adopting the United States' constitutional clause, to promote the progress of science and the useful arts,[131] as the objective of copyright in Israel.[132] There was subsequently statutory reform. It is worth noting that details of the statute differ from those described above in relation to Singapore, but are ostensibly intended to achieve the same goals. The law provides,[133]

> Fair use of a work is permitted for purposes such as self studying, research, criticism, review, newspaper summary providing excerpts, and use in the course of teaching or examination by an educational organisation.

This replaced the previously finite list[134] with an open-ended list. This is followed by four guiding factors similar to the US fair use and the Singapore factors, but not including the last factor relating to availability.[135]

whether a dealing has been fair. As discussed, fair dealing is an integral part of the scheme of copyright law in Canada. Any act falling within the fair dealing exception will not infringe copyright. If a copyright owner were allowed to license people to use its work and then point to a person's decision not to obtain a licence as proof that his or her dealings were not fair, this would extend the scope of the owner's monopoly over the use of his or her work in a manner that would not be consistent with the Copyright Act's balance between owner's rights and user's interests.'

130 Ghafele and Gilbert, above n 3. 131 US Constitution, art I, § 8, cl 8.

132 See *Interlego A/S* v. *Exin-Line Bros. SA*, Civil Appeal 513/89 48 PD (4), 133. For a discussion of goals and the education context in Israel, see A. Dotan, N. Elkin-Koren, O. Fischman-Afori and R. Haramati-Alpern, 'Fair Use Best Practices for Higher Education Institutions: The Israeli Experience', *Journal of the Copyright Society of the USA*, 57 (2010), 447–472.

133 Copyright Act 2007 (Israel), s 19(a). Translation is available at www.wipo.int/wipolex/en/text.jsp?file_id=132095.

134 See discussion in E. Liss and D. Adin, *Intellectual Property Law and Practice in Israel* (Oxford University Press, 2013), at 5.6.1. See also N. Elkin – Koren and O. Fischman Afori, 'Taking User's Rights to the Next Level : A Pragmatist Approach to Fair Use', 33 (2014), *Cardozo Arts & Entertainment Law Journal*, (forthcoming).

135 Copyright Act 2007 (Israel), s 19(b) the factors are: (1) The purpose and character of the use; (2) The character of the work used; (3) The scope of the use, quantitatively and qualitatively, in relation to the work as a whole; (4) The impact of the use on the value of the work and its potential market.

In order to address the point that case law is needed to delineate fair use, Israel has innovatively included the provision that the Minister of Justice can determine whether certain activities are fair use.[136] Fair use by its nature will never be finite. The laws that govern the regulation of creative activities ought not to be confined to a static view of creativity.

Conclusion

The small market economies all have utilised flexibilities and exceptions in copyright law, although that use is different among them and partial rather than in all areas of copyright law. These are, as the chapter title suggests, approaches to copyright law. The problems of calibrating copyright law are not exclusive to small market economies, but the small market economy approaches are examples of how innovative calibrations can take place.

[136] Copyright Act 2007 (Israel). According to Liss and Adin, above n 134, at 406, this power has not been used and they question the appropriateness of law not going through the proper legislative process, but note, 'In any event, the Minister has not yet used this power and it is doubtful whether he [or she] would ever use it.'

7 Trade mark law

> The power of attraction of trade-marks and other 'famous brand names' is now recognized as among the most valuable of business assets. However, whatever their commercial evolution, the legal purpose of trade-marks continues to be their use by the owner 'to distinguish wares or services manufactured, sold, leased, hired or performed by him from those manufactured, sold, leased, hired or performed by others' ... A mark is a guarantee of origin and inferentially, an assurance to the consumer that the quality will be what he or she has come to expect.[1]

> The purpose of [trade mark] registration is an integral aspect of interpreting the TRIPS Agreement's provisions about trademarks; ... the purpose and acquis of the TRIPS Agreement registration provisions and Paris Convention provisions incorporated into the TRIPS Agreement are to encourage the orderly use of trademarks in commerce; and ... the rights of trademark owners are limited, but they make little sense if seen as mere rights to exclude. Use of marks is, to use a WTO analogy, like free trade. There is no full explicit right to trade freely in any WTO document, and there are real limits to a member's ability to trade freely with other members.[2]

> If we accept that trade marks are typically applied for just before new or improved varieties of goods and services are introduced to market, then we can assess the value of innovation to firms by estimating the relationship of new trade mark applications to a firm's level of real net output, or value added.[3]

Trade marks are directly linked to the economic goals of intellectual property. They are protected when they are used in commerce. When

[1] *Mattel Inc.* v. *3894207 Canada Inc.* [2006] 1 S.C.R. 772.

[2] S. Frankel and D. Gervais, 'Plain Packaging and the Interpretation of the TRIPS Agreement', *Vanderbilt Journal of Transnational Law*, 46(5) (2013), 1149–1214, at 1181.

[3] C. Greenhalgh, M. Rogers, P. Schautschick and V. Sena, 'Trade Mark Incentives', Intellectual Property Office Research Report, UK, 2011/1, at 17, available at www.ipo.gov.uk/ipresearch-tmincentives-full-201107.pdf ('*Trade Mark Incentives*').

trade marks are used for other purposes, particularly those relating to freedom of expression (free speech), the law does not prevent those non-trade-mark-related uses.[4] Just how strong trade mark rights should be, and what it means (and does not mean) to call trade marks property[5] lies at the heart of many trade mark disputes both before national courts and at the international level. These are complex issues and this chapter discusses some aspects of those issues from the perspective of small market economies.

Commentators have suggested that trade marks can be used as a 'proxy for innovative effort such as the launch of a new or improved product' because when a firm introduces an innovation, it is often marketed with trade marks.[6] These commentators suggest that as patents are targeted at inventive aspects of products and processes[7] and smaller innovations do not meet the criteria, 'trade marks, which are used by more economic sectors than patents, can be a useful alternative indicator of innovation'.[8]

The suggestion that trade marks can be a proxy for innovative effort relies partly on the view that they contribute to motivating product

[4] This principle is embodied in the WTO, Agreement on Trade-Related Aspects of Intellectual Property Rights, Marrakesh Agreement Establishing the World Trade Organization, Annex 1C, 1869 UNTS 299; 33 ILM 1197 (adopted on 15 April 1994, entered into force 1 January 1995) ('TRIPS Agreement'), art 17, which provides: 'Members may provide limited exceptions to the rights conferred by a trademark, such as fair use of descriptive terms, provided that such exceptions take account of the legitimate interests of the owner of the trademark and of third parties.' With regard to what is meant by the legitimate interests of the trade mark owner, the WTO has said, 'every trademark owner has a legitimate interest in preserving the distinctiveness, or capacity to distinguish, of its trademark so that it can perform that function. This includes its interest in using its own trademark in connection with the relevant goods and services of its own and authorized undertakings. Taking account of that legitimate interest will also take account of the trademark owner's interest in the economic value of its mark arising from the reputation that it enjoys and the quality that it denotes', WTO Panel Report, United States – European Communities – *Protection of Trademarks and Geographical Indications for Agricultural Products and Foodstuffs*, WT/DS174/R, 15 March 2005, at para 7.664.

[5] Many national laws describe trade marks as property. In doing so, those laws do not suggest that trade mark rights are absolute, but that they have features of property, including exclusive rights, the ability for them to be assigned and licensed and so on. For a discussion of the development of trade marks as property, see L. Bentley, 'From Communication to Thing: Historical Aspects of the Conceptualisation of Trade Marks as Property', in G. B. Dinwoodie and M. D. Janis (eds.), *Trade Mark Law and Theory: A Handbook of Contemporary Research* (Edward Elgar Press, Cheltenham, 2007), pp. 3–41. ('*Trade Mark Law and Theory*').

[6] Greenhalgh et al., *Trade Mark Incentives*, above n 3, at 17.

[7] The TRIPS Agreement, above n 4, art 27.1, requires that its members provide patents for inventions that are products and processes, provided they meet certain criteria.

[8] Greenhalgh et al., *Trade Mark Incentives*, above n 3, at 10.

development and entry of new firms.[9] It is also the positive account of the negative phenomenon that trade mark infringement can affect innovation.[10] That trade marks can be a proxy for innovative effort is not the traditional rationale given for the legal protection of trade marks, which is that they operate as channels of communication between traders and consumers and therefore merit exclusivity in order to prevent uses that confuse or deceive consumers.

Rationales and functions of trade mark protection

Economic and legal literature explains trade mark law broadly in two ways. The first is that trade marks function as a badge of origin; that is, the trade mark serves to indicate the genuine source of the product. This information and signalling role of trade marks firmly underpins the exclusive rights of trade mark owners against third parties, which enable them to prevent consumer confusion.[11] The second function of trade marks relates to the building of a brand and quality associated with the trade mark. Landes and Posner conclude that this quality association creates efficiencies for consumers (that is, it reduces their search costs).[12] Trade marks often communicate more than just the origin and quality of the goods. They may have what Jessica Litman describes as 'atmospheric' qualities.[13] These qualities are more than information and may involve stories and social and lifestyle values and themes.[14] Whether these additional qualities should result in protection beyond preventing consumer confusion is debatable.

9 S. Mendonca, T. Pereira and M. Godinho, 'Trade Marks as an Indicator of Innovation and Industrial Change', *Research Policy*, 33 (2004), 1385–1404, cited in Trade Mark Incentives, above n 3, at 10.

10 See, for example, K. E. Maskus, S. M. Dougherty and A. Mertha, 'Intellectual Property Rights and Economic Development in China', in C. Fink and K. Maskus (eds.), *Intellectual Property and Development: Lessons from Recent Economic Research* (World Bank and Oxford University Press, USA, 2005), pp. 295–332, finding that the anecdotal information suggested that trade mark infringement negatively affected innovative Chinese enterprises.

11 As explained in *Villa Maria Wines* v. *Montana Wines Ltd* [1984] 2 NZLR 422 (CA) at 427 per Somers J, citing *Re Powells Trade Mark* [1893] 2 Ch 388 (CA). 'The function of a trade mark is to give an indication to the purchaser or possible purchaser as to the manufacture or quality of the goods – to give an indication to his eye of the trade source from which the goods come, or the trade hands through which they pass on their way to market.'

12 W. M. Landes and R. A. Posner, 'Trade Mark Law: An Economic Perspective', *Journal of Law and Economics*, 30(2) (1987), 265–309.

13 J. Litman, 'Breakfast with Batman: The Public Interest in the Advertising Age', *Yale Law Journal*, 108 (1999), 1717–1736.

14 See R. Dreyfuss, 'Recognizing Trademark Rights and Expressive Values', in *Trade Mark Law and Theory*, above n 5, pp. 261–293. ('*Trade Mark Law and Theory*').

There is controversy over whether trade marks also have additional functions, such as advertising and an investment function.[15] On the one hand, an issue arising from adherence to the 'badge of origin' and 'quality of source' rationales of the law is that those underpinnings do not recognise that trade marks, in addition to being valuable when applied to goods or services, can also have value as something distinct from and independent of the goods or services to which the trade mark relates.[16] On the other hand, this is also why trade mark law arguably should be anchored to its key rationales and should only allow for protection that is tied to preventing confusion or deception. Uses that do not cause confusion or deception may be fair competition, but in the online world the absence of traditional confusion and deception of consumers may still mean unfair competition in some circumstances. For example, when Google sells the use of trade marks as AdWords to third parties, courts do not readily find that this leads to confusion or deception of consumers, but questions arise as to whether the third-party use (or Google's use[17]) is fair.[18]

Framing the scope of trade mark protection is not straightforward. Thus, various jurisdictions approach trade mark protection in differing ways. When the United States, for example, introduced trade mark dilution protection (loss of value which can involve confusion, but not necessarily) it was described as a fundamental shift in the nature of trade mark protection.[19] This fundamental shift has given rise to a vigorous debate about the scope of trade mark protection. Similarly, in the European Union (EU), there has been considerable debate about the function and role of trade marks and unfair competition. There are a number of cases and arguably not a great deal of consistency.[20] The Court of Justice of the

[15] See, generally, N. Lee, G. Westcamp, A. Kur and A. Ohly (eds.), *Intellectual Property, Unfair Competition and Publicity Convergences and Development* (Edward Elgar, Cheltenham, 2014).

[16] *Levi Strauss & Co* v. *Kimbyr Investments Ltd* [1994] 1 NZLR 332 (HC), at 340.

[17] Some commentators have suggested that Google may be the beneficiary of unjust enrichment; see D. J. Gervais, M. L. Holmes, P. W. Kruse, G. Perdue and C. L. Roberts, 'Is Profiting from the Online Use of Another's Property Unjust? The Use of Brand Names as Paid Search Keywords', *IDEA: The IP Law Review*, 53 (2013), 131–172.

[18] See, for example, *Interflora* v. *Marks & Spencer* [2013] EWHC 273 (Ch), where Marks & Spencer's use of 'Interflora' in Google Ads was found to result in consumer confusion and deception. For a finding of no trade mark infringement, see *Rosetta Stone Ltd* v. *Google Inc.*, 676 F.3d 144 (4th Cir. 2012). See also discussion below.

[19] See, generally, C. Long, 'The Political Economy of Trademark Dilution', in *Trademark Law and Theory*, above n 5, pp. 132–147 and M. D. Janis and P. K. Yu, 'International and Comparative Aspects of Trademark Dilution', *Transnational Law and Contemporary Problems*, 17 (2008), pp. 603–610.

[20] See A. Kur, '*Trade Marks Function, Don't They? CJEU Jurisprudence and Unfair Competition Principles*', *International Review of Intellectual Property and Competition*, 45

European Union somewhat surprisingly stated that trade mark rationales 'include not only the essential function of the trade mark, which is to guarantee to consumers the origin of the goods or services, but also its other functions, in particular that of guaranteeing the quality of the goods or services in question and those of communication, investment or advertising'.[21]

This sort of expansive notion of the role of trade marks can be found in cases which consider the so-called merchandising function where trade marks are used to sell goods which are not the core business of the trade mark owner.[22] More recently, the boundaries of trade mark law continue to be tested in cases involving uses of trade marks in domain names and metadata (including google AdWords) on the Internet.[23] In these instances, a third party is making use of the trade mark for commercial gain, but not necessarily in a way that creates or is likely to create consumer confusion.[24] But it may be that a focus on trade mark function as a way to resolve these issues about what is fair and what is unfair competition is misplaced. As Annette Kur explains,[25]

> The CJEU fails to recognize that the key to these issues, where they become problematic, does not necessarily reside in the field of trade mark functions. Due to its genesis as a tool to sustain and limit the scope of trade mark protection in case of infringement, the functions discussion neither encompasses the way in which the trade mark was acquired, nor does it yield a basis for evaluating and actively preventing abusive behaviour by the trade mark proprietor.

(2014), 434–454, stating 'Few issues have raised as much controversy in trade mark law and policy as the case law of the Court of Justice of the European Union (CJEU) on trade mark functions', at 434. See also M. Senftleben, 'Trade Mark Protection – A Black Hole in the IP Galaxy', *International Review of Intellectual Property and Competition*, 42 (2013), 383–386.

21 1CJEU Case C-487/07, *L'Oréal* v. *Bellure*, [2009] I-05185, para 58. See also discussion in A. Kur, *Trade Marks Function*, above n 20.

22 See, generally, S. L. Doogan and M. Lemley, 'The Merchandising Right: Fragile Theory or Fait Accompli?', *Emory Law Review*, 54 (2005), 461–506, at 496–505.

23 Early cases were cybersquatting cases where a third party would obtain a domain name using a trade mark and seek to sell it to the trade mark owner, usually at an inflated price. See, for example, *British Telecom* v. *One in a Million* [1998] 4 All ER 476 (EWCA). In connection with Ad Words, see, for example, C–323/09 *Interflora Inc* v. *Marks & Spencer* (22 September 2011), *Intercity Group (NZ) Ltd* v. *Nakedbus NZ Ltd* [2014] NZHC 124, which discusses leading EU cases in the area and their applicability or otherwise in the New Zealand fact situation before the Court.

24 See, generally, G. B. Dinwoodie, 'Trademarks and Territory: Detaching Trademark Law Form the Nation State', *Houston Law Review*, 41 (2004), 885–974 and G. B. Dinwoodie and M. Janis, 'Confusion Over Use: Contextualism in Trademark Law', *Iowa Law Review*, 92 (2007), 1597–1668, arguing that trade mark use is a barrier to the appropriate development of trade mark law.

25 A. Kur, *Trade Marks Function*, above n 20, at 453.

The scope and function of trade marks in small market economies

As small market economies do not have an abundance of local patenting[26] but do have local innovation, the suggestion that trade marks can function as a proxy for innovative effort is potentially important. Without further empirical research in small market economies about the connection between trade marks and innovative effort, any conclusions about what the trade marks reveal about innovative effort is necessarily speculative. However, given the relative lack of local patenting when compared to local trade mark registration, and the presence of innovation in such economies, this seems a line of inquiry worth pursuing.

As small market economies rely heavily on imports, one would expect to find a lot of foreign-owned trade marks. However, one also finds many locally owned trade marks in such places. After all, trade marks are about preventing consumer confusion in local markets.[27]

Additionally, some small and medium-sized enterprises rely on trade marks as their main form of intellectual property protection.[28] Other chapters of this book have noted that small market economies are largely made up of small and medium-sized businesses. And as noted above, the type of innovation that small and medium-sized businesses undertake is not necessarily suitable for patents.[29] In addition, trade marks might be relied on because they are easier to obtain, even though they (theoretically) protect something different from patents (or copyright). Trade marks are often the cheapest form of intellectual property and therefore are more attractive for some businesses (of course there will be exceptions). A publicised example of this 'trade mark preferring' business behaviour involved a New Zealand company that made hockey helmets for export. A company representative stated that their trade mark name was enough protection even for the distinctive design and shape of their hockey helmet. The same representative also stated that everyone associated the name with the shape and quality of the helmet, so he believed

[26] As discussed in Chapter 6, a majority of patents are foreign owned.

[27] In both registered trade mark and passing off actions, the relevant consumers are those who are affected, which is usually where a claim is brought.

[28] For a discussion of small and medium enterprises and intellectual property in the UK, see M. Rogers and C. Greenhalgh, 'An Analysis of the Characteristics of Small and Medium Enterprises That Use Intellectual Property', Report for UK Intellectual Property Office, 2007.

[29] Although, as discussed in chapter 6 of this volume, this does not mean that small market economies do not undertake patentable research. Rather, they may work as part of a global group and others in that group may be the patent owners.

there was no way that a competitor could rip off the design or technology used, particularly in his view because the helmets were only of interest to a specialised market.[30] This is of course is only one story, but it raises questions about why companies would rely heavily on trade marks and not necessarily on other forms of intellectual property.

Using trade marks more than other types of IP

In addition to choosing trade marks over other forms of intellectual property, there is a growing trend for businesses whose patents, copyright or designs have expired to trade mark, in whole or in part, what was covered by those other rights. While businesses can and do own multiple intellectual property rights, issues arise if they are able to defeat the finite term of patents and copyright by using trade marks which do not have a finite term.[31] The issue of overlapping rights has not been resolved in many jurisdictions.[32] Part of the reason for this overlap is the expansive nature of trade mark subject matter.

The justifications for the protection of trade marks are frequently brought into question because of the expansion of trade marks through increased scope of subject matter (shapes, sounds and smells) and new types of infringement (well-known mark protection) and the pressure to expand trade mark law's reach even further.

To register a trade mark it must be distinctive in some way. This broadly means that it must not be descriptive of the nature, kind or quality of the goods.[33] The TRIPS Agreement recognises that in some countries trade marks that have acquired distinctiveness through use can be registered.[34] This is sometimes described as the trade mark having

[30] Obe Hockey TVNZ documentary Obo Hocky, TVNZ Documentry, 'Innovation Series' (S01,E12), http://tvnz.co.nz/the-learning-hub/innovation-stories-obo-4807198.

[31] TRIPS Agreement, above n 4, art 18, provides 'Initial registration, and each renewal of registration, of a trademark shall be for a term of no less than seven years. The registration of a trademark shall be renewable indefinitely.'

[32] See I. Calboli, 'Trademarking Creative Works: Trends and Negative Effects on the Copyright Equilibrium', in S. Frankel and D. Gervais (eds.), *The Evolution and Equilibrium of Copyright in the Digital Age* (Cambridge University Press, 2014), 52–78; N. Wilkof and S. Basheer (eds.), *Overlapping Intellectual Property Rights* (Oxford University Press, 2012).

[33] These principles are embedded and detailed in national law and case law. At international level they are found in the concept that 'Any sign, or any combination of signs, *capable of distinguishing the goods or services of one undertaking from those of other undertakings*, shall be capable of constituting a trademark'; see TRIPS Agreement, above n 4, 15.1.

[34] TRIPS Agreement, above n 4, art 15.1.

secondary meaning. As far as subject matter is concerned, the TRIPS Agreement requires that members' laws provide trade mark registration for words, 'personal names, letters, numerals, figurative elements and combinations of colours'.[35] Many countries, including the small market economies discussed in this book, also protect sounds, shapes, single colours and smells where they meet the requirements of registration, particularly of distinctiveness.[36] Also, trade marks have come to protect more and more expressive uses usually associated with copyright. Sentences and advertising jingles, for example, can be protected where they are distinctive of a trader's goods.[37]

Subject matter, expressive uses and functionality

Shape trade marks raise issues about protecting functional aspects of a product or the product itself rather than a mark applied to a product. In the United States, there is a doctrine against the protection of functional marks.[38] The doctrine is not the same in the EU[39] (and in England in particular). This is important because it is the English case law that has filtered through to the small market economies.[40] Broadly, the consequence of that is that merely because a trade mark is functional this does not prevent its protection. Where, however, the functionality amounts to the trade mark not being distinctive, or in some way it is the equivalent of being descriptive of the goods, then the trade mark will not be capable of being registered.

In England, shapes were not registrable as trade marks for a long time because that was thought to stretch the ambit of the law too far.[41] This was because a trade mark should be 'distinct from the thing marked'.[42]

35 TRIPS Agreement, above n 4, art 15.1.

36 See, for example, Trade Marks Act 2002 (NZ), s 5, which defines sign as including 'a brand, colour, device, heading, label, letter, name, numeral, shape, signature, smell, sound, taste, ticket, or word'.

37 Such matters may not necessarily be protected by copyright if they are deemed 'too trivial'.

38 For a discussion of the doctrine, see R. G. Bone, 'Trademark Functionality Revisited and Revised', University of Texas Law, Law and Econ Research Paper No. e554, 2014, available at SSRN: http://ssrn.com/abstract=2433179.

39 See A. Kur, 'Too Pretty to Protect? Trade Mark Law and the Enigma of Aesthetic Functionality', in J. Drexl, R. M. Hilty, L. Boy, C. Godt and B. Remiche (eds.), *Technology and Competition: Contributions in Honour of Hanns Ullrich* (Larcier, Bruxelles, 2009), 139–159, 2011 updated version available at SSRN: http://ssrn.com/abstract=1935289.

40 See discussion in the Introduction to this book.

41 *Re Coca Cola* [1986] 2 All ER 274 (HL), at 275.

42 *Re James Trade Mark* (1886) 33 Ch D 392 (CA).

Allowing the registration of shapes (and also packaging) as trade marks has modified this approach.[43]

New Zealand law provides that a trade mark may consist of 'the shape of goods or their packaging'.[44] This has proved problematic because the courts have interpreted such trade marks to be unaffected by the availability of other intellectual property rights (patents, copyright and designs).[45] For example, in the leading case, an application for the shape of a tie for grape vines (known as a Klipon tie) was found to distinguish the applicant's goods in the market. The applicant was able to convince the Court of Appeal that the shape of the vine tie, which had a swan head configuration, distinguished its goods because the product was recognised by its swan head shape.[46] This recognition (the distinctiveness) arose from the product being the only one on the market, which was possible because of other intellectual property rights (registered design and patent rights). Even though those other rights had prevented competitors in the market and were at the time of the trade mark application expired, the Court of Appeal held that the shape was registrable.[47] The Court reasoned that in order to obtain a registered design, the features of shape must have already been treated as not purely functional. Therefore, those features arguably were, in the trade mark sense, capable of distinguishing the goods of the applicant from those of other traders and consequently registrable as a trade mark. The facts did not support that, however, as there were no competitors in the market. The Court said it did not need to conclusively decide whether a functional mark could be a trade mark on the facts before it.[48] The Court noted, however, that trade marks may protect functional shapes, because trade marks do not give a monopoly over the functionality.[49] The decision did not adequately deal with functionality or with the issues relating to overlapping rights, which is an increasing problem globally.

Israel's trade mark law does not explicitly refer to shapes or packaging as the subject matter of trade marks, but refers to marks as registrable if

[43] For a history of the legislative amendment and how to strike the right balance, see S. Frankel, *Intellectual Property in New Zealand*, 2nd edn (Lexis Nexis, Wellington, 2011), at 538–539.

[44] Trade Marks Act 1994 (UK), s 1(1).

[45] For comparison with the law of the United Kingdom and of Australia, see Frankel, *Intellectual Property in New Zealand*, above n 43, at 538–541.

[46] The overlap with patents may present more difficulties.

[47] *Fredco Trading* v. *Miller* (2006) 11 TCLR 751 (NZCA).

[48] *Fredco Trading* v. *Miller* (2006) 11 TCLR 751 (NZCA), at [64]–[65].

[49] *Fredco Trading* v. *Miller* (2006) 11 TCLR 751 (NZCA), at [38].

they are in either two or three dimensions.[50] In a Supreme Court case about whether the shape of a confectionary product was capable of being a trade mark, the Court held that such shape marks could be protected in Israel.[51] It qualified this conclusion with the requirement that the distinctiveness must be acquired through use. Such shapes could not be what trade mark law calls inherently distinctive.[52] Importantly, the Court held that even when there had been use, and therefore arguably secondary meaning had been established, if the trade mark incorporated substantially functional or aesthetic elements it could not be registered. This approach was taken in order to maintain a difference between trade marks and registered designs.[53]

Singapore law also allows registration of some shape marks, but provides that shapes will not be registrable in some cases – where the shape mark exclusively results from the nature of the goods, the shape of the goods is necessary to obtain a technical result or the shape gives substantial value to the goods.[54] There is little local case law on this section and reliance is placed on UK and EU decisions because the wording of the section comes from the EU Directive and related English statute.[55]

Although functionality is conceptually straightforward, it is hard to apply in practice in most if not all jurisdictions. The practical difficulties of applying a no functionality rule, and having few cases in which to do so in small market economies, tend to suggest that trade marks (such as shapes) are less often challenged than in places where market size usually results in more competition and where there are more entities with a direct interest in challenging such trade marks. The position in Singapore, the few cases in Israel and the New Zealand decision described above, all perhaps illustrate two difficulties with small market economies. First, there is simply not enough case law locally (or not enough expertise) because of the scale of small market economies.[56] Issues about the need for specialist judges and courts, balanced with the problems of

[50] Trademark Ordinance (New Version), 5732-1972, (Israel), available in English at www.wipo.int/edocs/lexdocs/laws/en/il/il031en.pdf, Chpr 1. 1 definition of 'mark'.

[51] *August Strock KG* v. *Alfa Intuit* CA 1187/03.

[52] An inherently distinctive mark is one that is distinctive and it in no way describes the goods.

[53] For a discussion of the cases in the Trade Mark Office following the Supreme Court case, see E. Liss and D. Adin, *Intellectual Property Law and Practice in Israel* (Oxford University Press, 2013), pp. 176–179.

[54] This is based on the UK Trade Marks Act 1994. For history and lead-up to this provision, see W. L. Ng-Loy, *Law of Intellectual Property in Singapore*, revised edn (Sweet & Maxwell, 2009), at 21.2.1–21.2.12.

[55] See *Law of Intellectual Property in Singapore*, above n 54, at 21.1.1–21.4.15.

[56] This could of course be said in any area of intellectual property (or indeed other areas of law) and it frequently is in relation to fair use and copyright; see Chapter 5 in this volume.

over-specialisation, are raised frequently in large market economies.[57] These problems are exacerbated in small market economies.[58] A possible solution to such difficulties may be for small market economies to match their laws as closely as possible to larger economies where the laws are good fit.[59] This enables the case law of those larger economies to be relied on. Where trade marks and functionality are concerned, the differing approaches and experiences of Israel, Singapore and New Zealand seem to show that choosing the right law is difficult, and consequently important in controversial areas of the law.

The 'Patent' and 'Copyright' chapters (Chapters 5 and 6, respectively) of this book include discussion about when and how differences from other economies should result in different rather than replica laws.[60] In relation to functional trade marks, similar rules to other jurisdictions would be useful so as to prevent trade marks, which cannot be registered elsewhere, not being so easily registered in small market economies. This is particularly important because of the effects that allowing too expansive an approach to trade marks has on competition, which as noted earlier is harder to achieve in smaller markets.

Overcoming the disadvantages of being small may not be achieved if the issue remains unresolved internationally or national models are not necessarily a good fit. These difficulties are also apparent in relation to well-known marks.

Well-known marks

On the one hand, well-known mark owners say that people should not reap where they have not sown, that bad faith should be punished, that people who sidle up to their well-known marks are guilty of dishonest commercial practice. These vituperations lead nowhere. One might as well say that the well-known mark owner is reaping where it has not sown when it stops a trader in a geographic or market field remote from the owner's fields from using the same or a similar mark uncompetitively.[61]

[57] See, for example, R. C. Dreyfuss, 'The Federal Circuit: A Case Study in Specialized Courts', *New York University Law Review*, 64 (1989), 1–78.

[58] See, for example, S. Glazebrook, 'A Specialist Patent or Intellectual Property Court for New Zealand?', *Journal of World Intellectual Property*, Special Issue: Patent Law Reform: Getting it Right to Support and Drive Innovation, 12 (2009), 524–569.

[59] For discussion of this issue generally, see S. Frankel and J. Yeabsley, 'Features of the Uniqueness of New Zealand and Their Role in Regulation', in S. Frankel and J. Yeabsley (eds.), *Framing the Commons – Cross-Cutting Issues in Regulation* (Victoria University Press, Wellington, 2014), pp. 17–54.

[60] See Chapters 5 and 6.

[61] D. Vaver, 'Unconventional and Well-known Trade Marks', *Singapore Journal of Legal Studies*, (2005), 1–19, at 16.

Trade mark owners use their trade marks to build what are sometimes described as brands through advertising. When this happens, firms may use the trade mark for a range of products. This leads to greater expectations for protection of trade marks than merely preventing consumer confusion. While trade mark owners may see such expansion as necessary to protect their global markets, this can impact the development of local trade marks (and some kinds of innovative effort), particularly where the mark is in fact not used in the local market. As Greenhalgh explains, 'there is also a conundrum in global markets, where the need for successful domestic brands to engage in worldwide competition in order to retain profits and jobs in the economy has to be balanced against the promotion of new firms within the domestic economy'.[62]

The Paris Convention[63] and the TRIPS Agreement require that members protect well-known marks. These Agreements do not explain what a well-known mark is. The Paris Convention requires that a mark 'be well known ... as already a mark ... used for identical or similar goods'.[64] TRIPS extends the protection required to service marks and further provides,[65]

> In determining whether a trademark is well-known, Members shall take account of the knowledge of the trademark in the relevant sector of the public, including knowledge in the Member concerned which has been obtained as a result of the promotion of the trademark.

This guidance does not resolve whether a mark can amount to a well-known mark in a territory in which it is not used. The World Intellectual Property Organization (WIPO) Joint Recommendation Concerning the Provision on the Protection of Well-Known Marks[66] tries to fill this gap and others. It provides some factors which are relevant to assessing whether a mark is well known (other factors may also be relevant depending on the case) these include:[67]

62 Greenhalgh et al, *Trade Mark Incentives*, above n 3, at 10.

63 Paris Convention for the Protection of Industrial Property, 828 UNTS 303 (adopted on 20 March 1883, entered into force 16 April 1970), as revised at Stockholm (14 July 1967) ('Paris Convention'). The relevant provisions are incorporated into the TRIPS Agreement, above n 4, art. 2.1.

64 Paris Convention, above n 63, art 6bis.

65 TRIPS Agreement, above n 4, art 16.2.

66 Joint Recommendation Concerning the Provision on the Protection of Well-Known Marks (adopted by the Assembly of the Paris Union for the Protection of Industrial Property and the General Assembly of the World Intellectual Property Organization), 20–29 September 1999 ('Joint Recommendation').

67 Joint Recommendation, above n 66, art 2 (1) (B).

1. the degree of knowledge or recognition of the mark in the relevant sector of the public;
2. the duration, extent and geographical area of any use of the mark;
3. the duration, extent and geographical area of any promotion of the mark, including advertising or publicity and the presentation, at fairs or exhibitions, of the goods and/or services to which the mark applies;
4. the duration and geographical area of any registrations, and/or any applications for registration, of the mark, to the extent that they reflect use or recognition of the mark;
5. the record of successful enforcement of rights in the mark, in particular, the extent to which the mark was recognised as well known by competent authorities;
6. the value associated with the mark

'Relevant sector of the public' is then expansively defined so that it includes small segments of business sectors rather than a requirement for general public awareness.[68] The infringement parts of the Joint Recommendation require that trade mark owners have exclusive rights against most types of dilution-related infringements, including those that are not anchored in preventing confusion and deception (blurring, tarnishment and, more generally, free-riding).[69] This expansion causes difficulties for many countries and notably comes in the form of a recommendation rather than binding rules.[70] Although the Joint Recommendation is not a binding agreement, it is in some spheres more than a recommendation, as compliance with it is an obligation through free trade agreements (FTAs).[71] The US–Singapore FTA provides an example.[72]

Burton Ong has noted that not all FTAs with the United States include this enhanced trade mark protection. Against that background, he considers that such protection may be particularly advantageous for US businesses in countries like Singapore where the main language

[68] Joint Recommendation, above n 66, art 2(2).

[69] Joint Recommendation, above n 66, art 4.

[70] Dinwoodie and Dreyfuss note that the definition of 'well known' in the Joint Recommendation was adopted by consensus but the infringement dilution-related extensions were not; see G. B. Dinwoodie and R. Dreyfuss, *A Neofederalist Vision of TRIPS: The Resilience of the International Intellectual Property Regime* (Oxford University Press, 2012), at 165.

[71] See R. Dreyfuss and S. Frankel, 'From Incentive to Commodity to Asset: How International Law is Reconceptualizing Intellectual Property', *Michigan Journal of International Law*, 36 (2014), (forthcoming).

[72] Singapore–United States Free Trade Agreement (signed 6 May 2003, entered into force 1 January 2004).

of commerce is English.[73] Ong also notes that the Singapore approach is arguably narrower than the US approach and more 'stringent' in its requirement of actual dilution compared to the US approach of a likelihood of dilution because Singapore adopted the English statute.[74]

In small market economies, the definition of 'well known' and the increased level of trade mark protection are likely to create an imbalance between such economies and larger ones. Marks which are well known and originate from the large economies of the world are protected in small market economies, but the converse of well known in small economies and therefore protected in large economies is rarely likely to be true. A mark which is well known in New Zealand, Israel or Singapore may not be well known in large economies such as the United States and the EU. Thus, size and scale creates an imbalance which the Joint Recommendation serves to exacerbate. An example of a New Zealand trade mark, 'World Famous in New Zealand', is both illustrative and designed to evoke questions of what makes something famous. 'World Famous in New Zealand' is a trade mark applied to the New Zealand-made soft drink (soda) known as Lemon and Paeroa (L&P), perhaps ironically owned by the Coca-Cola Company.[75]

In Israel, the trade mark legislation provides that a mark can be well known in Israel even if it is not used in Israel.[76] In assessing if a mark is well known, the scope of recognition among the relevant public and the extent of recognition as a result of marketing are taken into account.[77] When this law was introduced, infringement rules were amended to include protection against dilution.[78] A central principle

[73] B. Ong, 'The Trade Mark Law Provisions of Bilateral Free Trade Agreements', in *Trade Mark Law and Theory*, above n 5, pp. 229–261, at 247.

[74] The Singapore statute provides that the use must 'cause dilution in an unfair manner to the "distinctive character of the proprietor's trademark"', Trademark Act 1998, s 8(4)(b)(ii)(A); compare to 'likely to cause dilution by blurring . . . or tarnishment of the famous mark', Lanham Act s 43(c), US. See Ong, *Trade Mark Law Provisions*, above n 73, 244.

[75] Trade Mark number 719220. This mark is owned by the Coca-Cola Amatil NZ Ltd.

[76] Trade Mark Ordinance (Israel), above n 50, Chpr 1.1, definition of 'well-known trade mark'.

[77] Trade Mark Ordinance (Israel), above n 50, Chpr 1.1, definition of 'well-known trade mark'.

[78] Infringement includes unauthorised use of of a well-known trade mark even if it is not registered, Trade Mark Ordinance (Israel), above n 50 Chpr 9, 57(a). Also '(a) The proprietor of a well known trade mark, even if it is not a registered trade mark, shall be entitled to the exclusive use of the mark in respect of the goods for which the mark is well known in Israel or in respect of goods of the same description. (b) The proprietor of a well known trade mark that is a registered trade mark shall also be entitled to the exclusive use of that mark in respect of goods which are not of the same description if use of that mark by a person other than the proprietor would be likely to indicate a connection between the said goods and the registered proprietor of the mark, and the

is that the mark must be well known (but not necessarily used) in Israel. The advent of the Internet and global trade make this more likely than ever.[79]

In New Zealand, the Trade Marks Act includes a dilution provision against use of a mark on dissimilar goods and services, which are identical with or similar to the registered trade mark, where the 'trade mark is well known in New Zealand and the use of the sign takes unfair advantage of, or is detrimental to, the distinctive character or the repute of the mark'.[80] Similarly to other jurisdictions, in New Zealand well known marks will also receive protection in passing off, but the passing off standard is different from the dilution standard.[81] The problem of the asymmetry of well known between the small and the large affects New Zealand also in its relationship with Australia. A single trade mark regime has been proposed between the two countries.[82] The details are not yet finalised, but if it goes ahead then marks known in either New Zealand or Australia will be registered in a way that covers both, but whether well known in one is sufficient for it to be well known in another is a different and as yet unresolved question.[83]

registered proprietor is likely to be damaged by such use', Trade Mark Ordinance (Israel), above n 50, Chpr 7, 46A.

[79] For a discussion giving examples of the Israel law, see Liss and Adin, above n 53, at pp. 193–198.

[80] Trade Marks Act 2002, s89(1)(d). The phrase 'well known' also appears in the Trade Marks Act as part of a ground for not registering a trade mark. Section 25(1)(c) provides that the Commissioner 'must not register a trade mark (trade mark A) if . . . it is, or an essential element of it is, identical or similar to, or a translation of, a trade mark that is well known in New Zealand (trade mark D), whether through advertising or otherwise, in respect of those goods or services or similar goods or services or any other goods or services if the use of trade mark A would be taken as indicating a connection in the course of trade between those other goods or services and the owner of trade mark D, and would be likely to prejudice the interests of the owner'.

[81] See, for example, *Wineworths Group Ltd* v. *Comité Interprofessionel du Vin de Champagne* [1992] 2 NZLR 327 (NZCA), where the New Zealand Court of Appeal found that 'champagne' is protectable under passing off in New Zealand. See also discussion in Frankel, *Intellectual Property in New Zealand*, above n 43, at 680–682, and 613–616, where it is discussed that the reputation required for passing off must have some local presence even if well known overseas. Also discussed is the different standard for reputation in opposing registration in trade marks.

[82] See, generally, 'Single Economic Market', at www.med.govt.nz.

[83] Further issues relating to the trans-Tasman proposal are discussed in S. Frankel and M. Richardson, 'Trans-Tasman Intellectual Property Coordination', in S. Frankel (ed.), *Learning from the Past, Adapting for the Future: Regulatory Reform in New Zealand* (Lexis Nexis, Wellington, 2011), pp. 527–553; and S. Frankel, M. Richardson, C. Nixon and J. Yeabsley, 'The Challenges of Trans-Tasman Intellectual Property Coordination', in S. Frankel and D. Ryder (eds.), *Recalibrating Behaviour: Smarter Regulation in a Global World* (LexisNexis, Wellington, 2013), pp. 101–138.

In Israel, the trade mark 'Carmel' relating to wines was held to be well known.[84] While this seems correct, interestingly the status is not just the modern use of Carmel, but the wine activities in that region have been well known for hundreds of years. For small market economies, well-known marks are often those related to geographical names and indications. Perhaps ironically all three small market economies are not supporters of expansive (EU-style) geographical indications but have at the international level supported the US approach of predominantly recognising geographical indications through certification marks.[85]

Conclusion

The obvious beneficiaries of well-known mark protection are global businesses which most likely have heavy investment in advertising. These trade mark goals, which are fundamentally different from the badge of origin rationale behind the protection of trade marks, form the backdrop which has promoted the well known mark aspect (and possibly other aspects) of the expansion of trade mark law. While trade mark law can benefit all businesses, expansive notions of trade mark law tend to primarily, if not only, benefit large businesses. This is where trade marks are becoming more and more contentious and the international issues are less and less easily resolved.[86]

As trade marks are identifiers of business and consumers are very much based in local markets, even if they buy imported products, local market conditions should not be overtaken by attempts to ensure extra protections for the famous who in most instances, if not all, will already have sufficient intellectual property protection at home and globally.

[84] *Infineon Technologies AG* v. *The Rishon Letzion Cooperative Wineries*, decision 120949–120950 (trade mark opposition).

[85] On the debate over geographical indications, see, generally, J. Hughes, 'Champagne, Feta, and Bourbon: The Spirited Debate about Geographical Indications', *Hastings Law Journal*, 58 (2006–2007), 299–386. See also D. J. Gervais, 'Cognac after Spanish Champagne? Geographical Indications as Certification Marks', in J. C. Ginsburg and R. Dreyfuss (eds.), *Intellectual Property at the Edge: The Contested Contours of IP* (Cambridge University Press, 2014), pp. 130–156.

[86] So far, global disputes in trade mark law at the World Trade Organization have covered trade marks's relationship with geographical indications, prevention of use of Cuban trade marks in the United States and at the time of writing the interference with trade marks through plain packaging of tobacco.

8 Why small market economies do and don't parallel import

Some of New Zealand's trading partners – particularly the United Kingdom, the United States, and Switzerland – have large and powerful pharmaceutical industries, and they expressed concern at any possible overriding [caused by parallel importing] of the intellectual property rights of their pharmaceutical companies.[1]

The Parties [to the Trans-Pacific Partnership Agreement] are encouraged to establish international exhaustion of rights,[2]

[R]emoving restrictions on parallel imports are generally thought to be welfare enhancing, certainly by economists. All studies point to the benefits of removing parallel importing restrictions. These are mainly in the form of price reductions and in some cases, a better quality service as competition increases.[3]

[1] Bill Sutton MP (23 May 1990) NZPD 1739. Sutton's statement made in Parliament continues: 'It was not the Government's intention to override such rights, and it has proved possible to provide for the original thrust of the Bill without breaching any of this country's international obligations.' In fact, had New Zealand parallel imported, it would not have been breaching any international obligations; see discussion below.

[2] Leaked negotiation text of the Trans-Pacific Partnership, available at https://wikileaks.org/tpp/static/pdf/Wikileaks-secret-TPP-treaty-IP-chapter.pdf, Art QQ.G.17: International Exhaustion of Rights. The quoted proposal is supported by the negotiating parties Singapore, New Zealand, Chile, Malaysia, Brunei, Vietnam, Peru and Mexico and opposed by the United States and Australia. Canada proposes: 'Nothing in this Chapter shall affect the freedom of the Parties to determine whether and under what conditions the exhaustion of copyright and related rights applies.' The US proposal is found in art QQ.G.3: Copyright and Related Rights, which proposes 'Each Party shall provide to authors, performers and producers of phonograms the right to authorize or prohibit the importation into that Party's territory of copies of the work made without authorization: or made outside that Party's territory with the authorization of the author, performer, or producer of the phonogram.' A negotiator's note at footnote [136] states 'Negotiator's Note: The US is considering the relationship between this provision and other proposals regarding the exhaustion of IP rights, as well as other TPP countries' legal regimes.' There is also a US proposal for a distribution right, Article QQ.G.4.

[3] S. Frankel, C. Nixon, M. Richardson and J. Yeabsley, 'The Challenges of Trans-Tasman Intellectual Property Coordination', in S. Frankel and D. Ryder (eds.), *Recalibrating Behaviour: Smarter Regulation in a Global World* (LexisNexis, Wellington, 2013), pp. 17–62, at 49.

> Parallel imports are one of the most iridescent and enigmatic phenomena of international trade. On the one hand, they strictly follow the laws of the market; yet on the other hand, the laws of the market are not the only ones that apply to this kind of activity. While industrial producers are pressing for general barriers in order to maintain price differences of goods among various countries, consumers find such differences puzzling in a world that is increasingly heading towards international trade and the removal of trade barriers.[4]

Parallel importing and related rules are a controversial area of intellectual property law. It is notable that the small market economies discussed in this book (Israel, New Zealand and Singapore) all allow parallel importing of some intellectual property products. They each, however, have different parallel importing regimes and have in different ways limited what they parallel import so as to make deals with their trading partners.

The short explanation of why small market economies parallel import is that they do so in order to ameliorate the limited competition that exists in small markets. Small market size will mean that there is not sufficient demand to create effective competition. Consequently, more effective competition is achieved through imports. Countries with high prices for consumer goods are ideal places for competition from parallel imports, which are usually lower-cost versions and genuine versions of the same or similar product. This chapter discusses parallel importing and the small market economy approaches of balancing the competing interests of increasing local competition and giving market exclusivity to certain intellectual property owners. First, the international framework is discussed.

Parallel importing and the international framework

The legal principle which is central to how parallel importing works is the rule of exhaustion that a country chooses to apply to intellectual property rights. Broadly, countries apply rules of national, regional or international exhaustion to either prevent or allow parallel importation. National exhaustion means that parallel importing is not permitted because the rights of the intellectual property owners are treated as having a wholly independent existence in each national market. This means that the placing on the market of products in one national territory does not exhaust the intellectual property related distribution right in another

[4] C. Heath, 'Parallel Imports and International Trade', available at www.wipo.int/edocs/mdocs/sme/en/atrip_gva_99/atrip_gva_99_6.pdf.

national territory. National exhaustion can be extended to a group of countries (typically a customs territory), in which case it becomes regional.[5] International exhaustion means that a product can be parallel imported because when placed on the market anywhere in the world, the right to control further distribution is exhausted.

Exhaustion, as it applies to parallel imports, is a concept distinct from (but sometimes related to) a domestic law first sale rule. A country can have a first sale rule so that once a product is sold domestically, the product can be on-sold domestically without 'interference' from the intellectual property rights owner. This is because it is the product, not the intellectual property, that is on-sold. A country can apply a first sale rule domestically and prevent parallel importing by applying national exhaustion to intellectual property rights or it can apply the first sale rule and allow for parallel imports on the basis of international exhaustion. International exhaustion could be described as a first sale rule where the first sale takes place anywhere in the world.

The contrast among national, regional and international exhaustion highlights the question of what is a distribution right or an importation right. These rights vary among the different areas of intellectual property. Distribution and importation rights relating to each of patents, copyright and trade marks are discussed below.

Disagreement about parallel importing and whether it should be permitted, or not, is found at both national and international levels. Internationally, no agreement has been reached on what is the appropriate rule globally for parallel importation.[6] And, there may well not be a one-size-fits-all rule that is appropriate. The lack of international agreement is reflected in Article 6 of the TRIPS Agreement,[7] which provides that nothing in the Agreement 'shall be used to address the issue of the exhaustion of intellectual property rights'. As one commentator notes, the inclusion of Article 6 indicates that parallel importing falls under the TRIPS Agreement. However, as there is no agreement on any minimum

[5] The EU regime, which is generally referred to as regional exhaustion, is complex. See, for example, in relation to trade marks, T. Hays, 'The Free Movement (or not) of Trademark Protected Goods in Europe', in G. Dinwoodie and M. Janis (eds.), *Trademark Law and Theory: A Handbook of Contemporary Research* (Edward Elgar, Cheltenham, 2008), pp. 204–227.

[6] See V. Chiappetta, 'The Desirability of Agreeing to Disagree: The WTO, TRIPS, International IPR Exhaustion and a Few Other Things', *Michigan Journal of International Law*, 21 (2000), 333–392.

[7] WTO, Agreement on Trade-Related Aspects of Intellectual Property Rights, Marrakesh Agreement Establishing the World Trade Organization, Annex 1C, 1869 UNTS 299; 33 ILM 1197 (adopted on 15 April 1994, entered into force 1 January 1995) ('TRIPS Agreement'), art 6.

standard relating to exhaustion of rights, the members of the TRIPS Agreement have agreed that World Trade Organization (WTO) dispute settlement is not appropriate.[8] In sum, parallel importing is relevant to the TRIPS Agreement, but TRIPS does not include determinative and enforceable rules on the subject.

Although some countries oppose international exhaustion, the wording and the object and purpose of the TRIPS Agreement do not support that as an inevitable conclusion.[9] The preamble of the TRIPS Agreement includes that intellectual property should not become a barrier to trade.[10] This reflects the broad role of the WTO to reduce tariffs and non-tariff barriers. Intellectual property is, to a degree, an acceptable trade barrier.[11] The TRIPS Agreement does not only require countries to provide intellectual property rights, but it also has objectives and principles which include that intellectual property should be for 'the mutual advantage of producers and users of technological knowledge in a manner conducive to social and economic welfare, and to a balance of rights and obligations'.[12] This objective arguably supports parallel importing.[13] Equally, one could not say that permitting parallel importing is required. The middle ground, and correct interpretation, is that a country will be TRIPS compliant if it applies either national or international exhaustion.

Copyright and parallel importation

National laws are able to prevent parallel importing by utilising the territorial nature of copyright combined with rules about distribution. Those against parallel importing sometimes suggest it encourages pirating because distinguishing between the genuine imports of more than one distributor and pirated goods is not always easy.[14] Copyright owners of

[8] D. Gervais, *The TRIPS Agreement: Drafting History and Analysis*, 4th edn (Sweet & Maxwell, London, 2012) at 2.99. In addition, the TRIPS Agreement, above n 7, includes an import right for the patent owner; this is discussed below. And the regime for compulsory licensing arising from the WTO Ministerial Conference, Fourth Session, Doha, 9–14 November 2001, *Declaration on the TRIPS Agreement and Public Heath*, WT/MIN(01)/Dec/2, also prevents controls on parallel imports made under compulsory licence. See Chapter 1, footnote 25.

[9] Some would go further and suggest it would require 'great imagination' to do so; see Heath, *Parallel Imports and International Trade*, above n 4.

[10] See also discussion in Chapter 3. [11] See also discussion in Chapter 4.

[12] TRIPS Agreement, above n 7, art 7. See also discussion of the TRIPS Agreement objectives and principles in Chapter 3.

[13] See also Chapter 3 for discussion of interpretation and object and purpose.

[14] See M. Coull, 'New Zealand's Approach to Parallel Imported Goods and the Copyright Amendment Act 1998', *Victoria University of Wellington Law Review*, 29 (1999), 253, at 270–271.

sound recordings and computer programs in particular have made the argument that checking if the goods are genuine is difficult and burdensome, whereas the existence of proof of ownership or a licence can be more readily confirmed.[15] Developments in technology have resulted in imports of copyright works often occurring online, making such arguments close to, if not entirely, redundant.[16] In any event, while it is true that copies of goods have become more sophisticated and in some areas, such as sound recordings, not necessarily of lesser quality, parallel importing whether online or through hard products is not piracy.

Restrictions on parallel importing utilise territoriality principles. The basic territorial principle of copyright is that there is no global copyright and each instance of copyright vests according to the laws of the country in which copyright is sought, subject to the minimum standards of the Berne Convention[17] and the TRIPS Agreement.[18] This territoriality allows owners to decide how to control markets, including having separate rights owners in different jurisdictions. The distribution-related issue is whether in any particular market copyright owners have rights to control first and subsequent distribution of copyright works or only first distribution (first sale).

Rights to control distribution

Under the Berne Convention, there is no general distribution right that members are obligated to enact in their national laws.[19] As Ricketson and Ginsburg note, 'distribution' is an ambiguous word in the English language because it could refer not only to first but also to subsequent distributions. They also note that the French version of the Berne Convention, which is its authoritative version, says, 'la mise en circulation des oeuvres ainsi adaptées ou reproduites', of which an appropriate English translation would be, 'the putting into circulation of the works thus adapted to be reproduced'.[20]

[15] See, for example, 'Price Surveillance Authority Inquiry into the Prices of Sound Recordings – Final Report' (Canberra, Australia, December 1990).

[16] See Frankel et al., *The Challenges of Trans-Tasman Intellectual Property Coordination*, above n 3. This research is also discussed further below.

[17] Berne Convention for the Protection of Literary and Artistic Works (Paris text), 1161 UNTS 3, 24 July 1971 ('Berne Convention').

[18] TRIPS Agreement, above n 7, art 9.

[19] S. Ricketson and J. Ginsburg, *International Copyright and Neighbouring Rights: The Berne Convention and Beyond* (Oxford University Press, 2005) ('*International Copyright*') at 11.42. There is a limited right of distribution for cinematic reprographic adaptations and reproductions in the Berne Convention, above n 17, art 14ter, explained in *International Copyright*, at 11.49–11.52.

[20] Ricketson and Ginsburg, *International Copyright*, above n 19, at para 11.50.

Subsequent to the TRIPS Agreement, members of WIPO entered into another copyright treaty, known as the WIPO Copyright Treaty (WCT).[21] The WCT provides a right of distribution which is independent from the right of reproduction. The distribution right gives the copyright owner the 'exclusive right of authorizing the making available to the public of the original and copies of their works through sale or other transfer of ownership'.[22] It states that parties are free to determine 'the conditions, if any, under which the exhaustion of the right . . . applies after the first sale or other transfer of ownership of the original or a copy of the work with the authorization of the author'.[23]

Prior to the WCT, a committee of Berne Convention experts suggested that the right of distribution is an 'inseparable corollary' to the right of reproduction.[24] Even if a link is required between reproduction and distribution, that does not fully address the parallel importing question. Parallel imports are primarily about further distribution after the first distribution, that is, the first time the work is made available.[25] As noted above, a first distribution right can exist at national law and parallel importing may also be permissible. In New Zealand, for example, the right to issue a work to the public (or right of first distribution) is

[21] WIPO Copyright Treaty (WCT), 36 ILM 65 (1997) (adopted 20 December 1996, entered into force 6 March 2002).

[22] WCT, above n 21, art 6.1.

[23] WCT, above n 21, art 6.2. The agreed statement in relation to this article provides 'As used in these Articles, the expressions "copies" and "original and copies," being subject to the right of distribution and the right of rental under the said Articles, refer exclusively to fixed copies that can be put into circulation as tangible objects.' See Chapter 3 for discussion of the interpretative value of agreed statements.

[24] See Document prepared for the Committee of Experts on a Possible Protocol to the Berne Convention, BCP/CE/III/2-III, 12 March 1993 in *Copyright*, Monthly Review of the World Intellectual Property Organization, 6 (June 1993) at 87 (para 22), at www.wipo.int/edocs/pubdocs/en/copyright/120/wipo_pub_120_1993_06.pdf and cited in Gervais, above n 8, 2.100. It is notable that although this document is prepared by experts, it is in no way determinative of the interpretation under the Vienna Convention on the Law of Treaties, 23 May 1969, 1115 UNTS 331 (entered into force 27 January 1980) ('VCLT') as it does not amount to a subsequent agreement between the parties; see discussion below.

[25] 'While the debate over parallel importation focuses on the perceived practical effects, the importation right sits in the conceptual border between intellectual property and personal property law. The debate over parallel importation reflects wider issues concerning the degree to which the owner of intellectual property should be able to control the fate of physical objects once the owner has consented to their first sale. This clash of fundamental concepts, as well as confusing statutory language, has resulted, especially in trade mark law, in an unsatisfactory mish-mash.' See S. Frankel, *Intellectual Property in New Zealand*, 2nd edn (LexisNexis, Wellington, 2011), at 2.5.1(c).

a right of copyright owners,[26] but copyright works may also be parallel imported. Hence, copyright is territorial, but distribution is both territorial and non-territorial.[27] Put differently, even if the distribution right and reproduction right are 'inseparable', this linkage at most addresses first distribution and not subsequent distribution.

The hooking together of the reproduction and distribution rights is also questionable because it is not explicit in the Berne Convention and the WCT has them as separate rights. At best, state practice reveals disagreement over this, especially as it relates to parallel importing. When interpreting a treaty, state practice is relevant where it reveals agreement between members over the practice subsequent to the treaty.[28] One, two or even a handful more states' practices at the time of entering a treaty, or after the treaty is in force, will not determine the meaning of a treaty or part of a treaty. Furthermore, state practice could illustrate both compliance with and breach of a treaty. It may explain the negotiating positions and even why a party submitted draft wording. However, adoption of that wording as an international agreement does not mean that the state practice determines the internationally agreed meaning. That is not the method of interpretation that is agreed to under the Vienna Convention. In sum, state practice is informative, but not determinative.[29]

The intent of linking the reproduction and first distribution rights seems to be that the owner of copyright can control supply of a product

[26] Copyright Act 1994, s 31 makes it an infringement to issue copies of a work to the public. Section 9 defines 'issue to the public' as:

(1) References in this Act to the issue of copies of a work to the public mean the act of putting into circulation copies not previously put into circulation; and do not include the acts of –
  (a) subsequent distribution or sale of those copies; or
  (b) subject to subsections (2) and (3), subsequent hiring or loan of those copies; or
  (c) subsequent importation of those copies into New Zealand; or
  (d) distribution of imported copies that are not infringing copies within the meaning of section 12 subsequent to their importation into New Zealand.

[27] This territorial and non-territorial combination is also seen in tax law as it applies to intellectual property related income. The intellectual property rights are exploited on a territorial basis and royalties are paid in a territory, but corporates are often structured such that those royalties are not taxed where they are earned, but they flow back to corporate headquarters and are taxed according to the relevant laws there. Some dispute the legitimacy of this. It is arguably a considerable policy contradiction to say that intellectual property rights are needed offshore for creativity and innovation, but the royalties are not invested in those offshore places. See also discussion in Chapters 2 and 4.

[28] VCLT, above n 24, art 31, 3(b) which provides, 'There shall be taken into account, together with the context . . . (b) any subsequent practice in the application of the treaty which establishes the agreement of the parties regarding its interpretation'; see discussion in Chapter 3.

[29] See Chapter 3.

in a market and prevent parallel importing until the owner has supplied the market.[30] This view of the committee of experts was also expressed, somewhat unconvincingly, as 'taking into account the differing economic, social, cultural and legal conditions of the two countries'.[31] It seems, however, to do the exact opposite and suggest a one-size-fits-all rule meaning those factors are not taken into account.

Controlling distribution can also mean denying supply. Also, controlling first distribution raises different normative concerns than control over subsequent supply. In the world of technology and online purchase, attempts to prevent supply of a market for many copyright works are unlikely to be sustainable.[32] If someone in Singapore, for example, can purchase something from the United States online, it hardly makes sense to say the product has not been 'distributed' in Singapore. 'Distributed' in this context is perhaps better expressed as 'made available' in Singapore.

Trade rules and parallel importing

The incorporation of the Berne Convention into the TRIPS Agreement links copyright (and other intellectual property rights) to trade rules. A key principle of trade and another WTO agreement, the GATT,[33] is the free movement of goods.[34] The free movement of goods and the way in which territorial intellectual property rights can legitimately be used to create trade barriers are in conflict.[35] On the one hand, a one-size-fits-all rule of

[30] See Document prepared for the Committee of Experts, above n 24, which states, 'The author or owner of the right of reproduction in a certain country would not be able to exploit this right in a normal way without the possibility to authorize or prohibit the importation of copies (particularly for distribution) into that country, even if the copies have been made with the authorization of the owner of copyright in another country. The situation is not different if the owner of copyright in the same countries concerned because, flowing from the territorial nature of copyright, two separate rights are involved which he should be able to exercise separately.'

[31] Document prepared for the Committee of Experts, above n 24.

[32] However, this does not appear to have curbed attempts to restrict parallel importing through free trade agreements. See also discussion in Frankel et al., *The Challenges of Trans-Tasman Intellectual Property Coordination*, above n 3, at 17–62.

[33] General Agreement on Tariffs and Trade (GATT), 30 October 1947, 55 UNTS, 194.

[34] See discussion in S. Frankel, 'The Applicability of GATT Jurisprudence to the Interpretation of the TRIPS Agreement', in C. M. Correa (ed.), *Research Handbook on Intellectual Property Law and the WTO* (Edward Elgar Publishing, Cheltenham, 2010), pp. 3–23. See also Paul J. Heald, 'Trademarks and Geographical Indications Exploring the Contours of the TRIPS Agreement', *Vanderbilt Journal of Transnational Law*, 29 (1996), 635–660 at 658 where he suggests that 'protecting the profit margin of certain producers by stopping goods at the border is precisely the sort of activity that the GATT was meant to discourage'.

[35] This is why the GATT, above n 33, art XX(d), recognised that intellectual property laws could amount to an exception to GATT principles.

international exhaustion of intellectual property rights and associated free movement of goods may seem undesirable to some countries. Such countries have the autonomy to prevent parallel imports within their own borders. On the other hand, attempting to prevent other countries from utilising international exhaustion and thus creating barriers to trade cannot be fully justified in light of the goals of global trade.[36] Additionally, aspects of the underlying reasons that intellectual property rights are given in some jurisdictions support allowing parallel imports. The intended effect of the grant of intellectual property rights is to incentivise the availability of innovation and creativity. When that domestic law rationale is translated to a global rationale, the intended effect of protecting foreign copyright is to promote the availability of legitimate copies, not the non-availability.

One of the reasons to prevent parallel importing is that to do so may allow copyright owners (and other intellectual property rights owners) to create market differentiation among products and price discrimination between markets.[37] Put differently, cheaper prices for genuine goods can be charged in countries that cannot afford developed country prices and, at the same time, higher prices can be maintained in developed countries. Even if this is theoretically possible, it is not a dominant practice. In fact, intellectual property owners often express reluctance to make cheaper goods available because of the possibility that those cheaper goods will flow over borders and into markets that can afford higher prices.[38] In any event, determinations as to price are not the direct business of copyright law. Setting the price may be something that copyright owners can do, but the law is not premised on the ability to charge a particular price in any one or in multiple markets.

Related to the debate over whether copyright owners should control distribution and thus be able to prevent parallel imports is[39] the preservation

[36] For further discussion of the object and purpose of the TRIPS Agreement and combining intellectual property with trade rules, see Chapters 2 and 3.

[37] For a general summary, see K. E. Maskus, 'Benefiting from Intellectual Property', in B. M. Hoekman, A. Mattoo and P. English, *Development, Trade, and the WTO: A Handbook* (The World Bank, United State, 2002), 369–381 at 376–379. See also I. Calboli, 'Corporate Strategies, First Sale Rules, and Copyright Misuse: Waiting for Answers from Kirtsaeng v. Wiley and Omega v. Costco (II)', *Northwestern Journal of Technology and Intellectual Property,* 11 (2013), 221–238, at 227.

[38] In the copyright context, making affordable (and translated) copies available was the goal of the Berne Appendix for developing countries to have better access to literary works and translations, see Berne Convention, above n 17, Appendix. The complexity of the Appendix is generally agreed to have contributed to its failure. See, for example, D. J. Gervais, 'The Internationalization of Intellectual Property: New Challenges from the Very Old and Very New', *Fordham Intellectual Property Media & Entertainment Law Journal,* 12(4) (2002), 929–990, at 942 n 70.

[39] See, generally, N. T. Gallini and A. Hollis, 'A Contractual Approach to the Grey Market', *International Review Law & Economics,* 19 (1999), 1–21.

of the local over the global. Globalisation affects the preservation of local copyright content whether parallel importing is restricted or not; restricting parallel importing does not prevent the spread of globalisation. Arguably, local businesses that develop local culture are less affected by parallel importing than local exclusive distributors of globalised culture. Protecting the local book business was a position that the Australian government purportedly followed when it did not lift restrictions on parallel imports of books.[40] This contrasts to the approach of New Zealand (and others) as discussed below.

New Zealand, Israel and Singapore

The 'Copyright' chapter of this book, Chapter 6, discusses how industrial design is included in New Zealand copyright law. The protection of industrial design motivated the need for parallel importing. In the 1980s, New Zealand progressively instituted a free market and deregulated economy and stopped manufacturing goods which could be made more cheaply elsewhere. Major car manufacturers, including Ford, Mitsubishi and Toyota, closed their New Zealand assembly operations because there was, and is, no comparative advantage in car assembly in New Zealand. Cars were then only imported and this resulted in cars being expensive. The appointed New Zealand distributors of the car manufacturers used copyright law to make sure that cheaper imports did not enter New Zealand and this provided the political incentive for the law to be changed to allow copyright goods to be parallel imported. The solution to escalating car prices was parallel imports, which would eventually come primarily from Japan and Korea.

The New Zealand reform of copyright law to allow parallel importing involved some legal innovations which are described here. As noted above, parallel importing is about allowing genuine copyright works to be imported. Prohibitions on importation of infringing works do not affect the ability of countries to allow parallel importing.[41] The legislative method used to allow parallel importing was to redefine 'infringing copy'

[40] Australian Productivity Commission *Restrictions on the Parallel Importation of Books* (Research Report, June 2009), at XVIII. The Productivity Commission recommended that all remaining parallel importing restrictions be repealed. As an illustration, the report's findings showed that book prices in Australia were, on average, 35 per cent higher than those in the United Kingdom and the United States.

[41] Copyright Act 1994 (NZ), s 35. An infringing copy is defined by s 12(3) as including an object the making of which 'constituted an infringement of the copyright in the work in question in the country in which the object was made'. Therefore, the focus of s 35 is on whether the goods being imported have been legally produced in their country of origin.

so that parallel imports were not caught.[42] Consequently, 'an object that a person imports or proposes to import into New Zealand is not an infringing copy if it was made by or with the consent of the owner of the copyright, or other equivalent intellectual property right, in the work in question in the country in which the object was made'.[43]

In essence, the requirement for parallel importation is that the product being imported must be a legitimate copy in the place from which it is imported. There may be exceptions such as legitimate copies made under a compulsory licence, a term of which is that the product made is for the domestic market and not for export, or only for export to places named in the compulsory licence.[44] While the legitimate copy requirement makes sense, it necessarily requires evidence of foreign law of copyright infringement, which often is not straightforward to obtain or for a court to interpret.[45] Under New Zealand law the importer will need to show that the imports are legitimate copyright works. This reverses the onus of proof, as normally a plaintiff in an infringement of copyright claim has the onus of proof. Reversing the onus of proof is a legal innovation, which overcomes the hurdle that the copyright owner cannot easily prove infringement. The approach of changing the onus of proof was extended to other aspects of parallel importing laws in 2003.[46] Importers of sound recordings, films and computer programs need to demonstrate, if challenged, that their imports are legitimate and not an infringement.[47]

New Zealand's parallel importing regime also illustrates the relationship between distribution and reproduction. Even though parallel imports are permitted, the TRIPS Agreement also requires that countries give rental rights to copyright owners.[48] Therefore, there are some restrictions on the uses of parallel imported works. A case in point was where the copyright owner, Roadshow Entertainment, brought proceedings against a video and

[42] For a full discussion of the old regimes, see Frankel, *Intellectual Property in New Zealand*, above n 25, at 94–96. Copyright Act, s12(3)(b) now limits 'infringing copying' to situations in which: 'The importer would have infringed the copyright in the work in question in New Zealand had the importer made the object in New Zealand, unless the object is one to which subsection (5A) or subsection (6) applies.'

[43] Copyright Act 1994 (NZ), s 12(5A).

[44] This would be the situation where a patented product is made under the TRIPS Agreement, above n 7, art 31bis system. See also Chapter 1, footnote 25.

[45] *Massive NV* v. *Lighting Plus Ltd* [2003] 1 NZLR 222 (HC) at [47]: '[T]he defence established by the new provision requires proof of foreign law. Its purpose is to enable a party to establish affirmatively that a product in question was lawfully made in an overseas country . . . In these circumstances the importer carries the burden of establishing, first, that no person owned the copyright in the subject country'.

[46] Copyright (Parallel Importation of Films and Onus of Proof) Amendment Act 2003, incorporated into the 1994 Act.

[47] Copyright Act 1994 (NZ), s 35.

[48] TRIPS Agreement, above n 7, art 11.

DVD rental company for renting out parallel imported DVDs.[49] Roadshow successfully claimed that rental subsequent to importation was an infringement of copyright, even though the parallel importation was legitimate. Paterson J. concluded that the rental right was unaffected by the parallel importation reforms. He focused on the statutory construction of the right to issue to the public[50] and New Zealand's obligation to give effect to the rental right under Article 11 of the TRIPS Agreement.[51] His reasoning is questionable. It does not consider Article 6 of TRIPS and that there is no international agreement on rules of exhaustion. The best reason for the result, and not one given in the judgment, is that the copyright owner would have rental rights relating to non-parallel imported copies and, therefore, it would be odd if those rights could be defeated by parallel importation without the legislature having expressly said so. The opposite result was reached in a case in Singapore where the Court found that as long as the copies were genuine, they could be rented.[52]

One description of Singapore's law is that it 'has adopted a mercantile policy of allowing . . . a free market where copyright articles, whether parallel imports or made under licence in Singapore, may be sold or dealt with in competition with one another'.[53] Early case law in Singapore suggested that parallel imports of copyright works were only permitted if the copyright owner in Singapore was the same as the copyright owner in the country of origin. A legislative change was made in 1994 to allow international exhaustion and parallel importation of genuine copyright goods in all circumstances.[54] One study has shown that this reduced the price of CDs.[55]

Perhaps of all three small market economies, Israel has overall the broadest approach to international exhaustion. However, unlike either New Zealand or Singapore, copyright law was the last bastion of national

49 *Video Ezy International Ltd* v. *Roadshow Entertainment (NZ) Ltd* [2002] 1 NZLR 855 (HC).

50 Copyright Act, s 9(1). The judge concluded that the issue of copies of a work to the public, in relation to sound recordings and films, includes the rental of copies of those works to the public. In 2003, the words 'and rental subsequent to those works having been put into circulation' were added to the statute.

51 See discussion in Frankel, *Intellectual Property in New Zealand*, above n 25, at 2.5.3(e) where this is questioned.

52 See *Television Broadcasts Ltd* v. *Golden Line Video & Marketing Pte Ltd* [1988] SLR 930.

53 *Television Broadcasts Ltd* v. *Golden Line Video & Marketing Pte Ltd* [1988] SLR 930, 937.

54 See W. L. Ng-Loy, *Law of Intellectual Property of Singapore*, revised edn (Sweet & Maxwell, 2009) [10.3.15]–[10.3.19] ('*Law of Intellectual Property of Singapore*').

55 Y. Chen and I. Png, 'Parallel Imports and Music CD Prices', available at http://128.118.178.162/eps/it/papers/0401/0401005.pdf; The authors concluded, 'Our empirical results show that legalization of parallel imports reduced the average price of music CDs by 7.2–7.9%.'

exhaustion in Israel. Now, however, as long as the copy imported is made legitimately in the country of origin (i.e. it does not infringe copyright), the copyright work can be parallel imported into Israel.

The issue came to a head in an industrial design case involving both copyright and registered designs, *Dyson Ltd* v. *Y Shalom Ltd.*[56] There the overseas manufacturer and local exclusive distributer of Dyson products complained about imports of Dyson vacuum cleaners and an unauthorised translation of the manufacturer's user manual into Hebrew. The Haifa District Court held that the parallel importing was allowed. Its reasoning was that as parallel imports of trade marked products are allowed,[57] the other intellectual property rights should not be used to prevent the parallel importation of trade marked goods. The court explicitly rejected the claim of copyright infringement because the imported goods were genuine. In addition, it held that the right to parallel import included the right to supply explanatory materials in the local language.

Effects of copyright parallel imports on creative sectors

An argument often made against parallel importing is that local creative industries and distributors will not be able to compete with the imports. The effect on local authorial production and distribution of books, music and film was the subject of extensive reviews of the New Zealand regime.[58] An important background to these reviews is that New Zealand's decision to allow for international exhaustion has been controversial. The United States placed New Zealand on an intellectual property watch-list, under s 103 of the Omnibus Foreign Trade Competitiveness Act 1988, and the reforms still appear to be a source of friction between New Zealand the United States in trade negotiations, although New Zealand is no longer on the watch-list.[59] The music and computer industries both expressed concern that parallel importing would lead to a greater amount of pirated goods entering New Zealand, despite the strengthening of border control measures. But that has not happened. However, as a consequence of those concerns, the government

[56] *Dyson Ltd* v. *Y Shalom Ltd* (Case 1089/05, 14 November 2007).

[57] Citing *Geigy* v. *Pazchim* (Case 471/70) and *Leibovitch* v. *Eliyahu* (Case 371/89).

[58] For a summary of these, see Frankel et al., *The Challenges of Trans-Tasman Intellectual Property Coordination*, above n 3, Appendix, where the authors examine the relevance of parallel importing restrictions on New Zealand through a cost–benefit lens. The same sorts of reviews do not seem to have taken place in either Israel or Singapore.

[59] See above n 2 for summary of different approaches in the Trans-Pacific Partnership negotiations.

that took office in 1999 stated that it was going to reintroduce parallel importation restrictions in the 'cultural', musical, literature and retail software sectors, as a way of promoting local industry. But it did not do so. However, after a review, it decided to prevent the parallel importation of films, videos and DVDs within nine months of international release.[60] Nine months was in 2013 reduced to five months.[61]

In 2007, a further review was undertaken of the parallel importing laws and their effect on the production and distribution of books, sound recordings, films and computer programs.[62] In that review, a recommendation was made to shorten the restriction period from nine to six months. The report also found that the parallel importing law overall had benefited New Zealand and should not change. The findings included the following:

> In general, we have not found any case for concern in relation to the impacts of parallel importing within the book publishing or computer software industries. There is some cause for concern in the music industry.[63]
>
> We recommend that thought be given to government policies for the sound recording industry, and whether [the music industry] warrants protection from the impacts of parallel importing.[64]
>
> Parallel importation adds some uncertainty to long-term investment decisions by authorised distributors, but it is not a high level consideration at present (should the amount of parallel importation increase drastically this may change).
>
> Within various distribution chains there are some industry participants more affected than others. One distribution industry segment brought to our attention was the authorised importers of educational and technical books, where the impact of parallel importing was greater than in other segments of the industry. Also within the book publishing industry, the parallel importation and sale of remaindered books, and remaindered children's illustrated books in particular, has not had the negative impact on domestic industry that some thought it might have.[65]

In addition to the above-quoted study, there have been other studies on the impact that removing parallel importing restrictions has had on the New Zealand economy.[66] All of the reports come to 'remarkably similar

[60] Copyright (Parallel Importation of Films and Onus of Proof) Amendment Act 2003, incorporated into the Copyright Act 1994, s 35(3)(a).

[61] Copyright Act 1994, s 35 (3)(a) was on 31 October 2013 replaced by Copyright (Parallel Importing of Films) Amendment Act 2013, s 4(1).

[62] D. Moore, Dr M. Volkerling and B. van der Scheer, *MED Parallel Importing Review: Impact upon Creative Industries* (LECG, Wellington, 2007).

[63] *Parallel Importing Review: Impact upon Creative Industries*, above n 62 at ii.

[64] *Parallel Importing Review: Impact upon Creative Industries*, above n 62 at i *Parallel Importing Review: Impact upon Creative Industries*, above n 62 at iii.

[65] *Parallel Importing Review: Impact upon Creative Industries*, above n 61, at 38.

[66] Network Economics Consulting Group, *The Impact of Parallel Imports on New Zealand's Creative Industries* (Ministry of Economic Development, Wellington, 2004); NZIER,

conclusions: [that] the net impact of removing parallel import restrictions would likely to be positive'.[67]

New Zealand and Australia have free movement of goods between them and many international companies treat them as one market. Australia has also reviewed whether or not it should allow parallel importing. This resulted in the restrictions on parallel imports of sound recordings as well as computer programs being removed, but print music and books cannot be parallel imported.[68] A 2009 report of the Australian Productivity Commission recommended that parallel importing restrictions on books be lifted.[69] The Australian government did not follow those recommendations. The New Zealand and Australian studies have been analysed together and found to support the following conclusions:[70]

> Removing parallel importing restrictions leads to lower prices and little impact on domestic innovation. The evidence documented in these reports suggests that:
> (1) real CD prices in both Australia and New Zealand had fallen dramatically;
> (2) parallel import restrictions in Australia resulted in book prices that were 10 per cent higher than they otherwise should be;
> (3) parallel importing had little impact on trans-Tasman music industries (sales of singles by New Zealand artists had risen eightfold and employment remained stable in music-related employment categories);
> (4) the number of authors in New Zealand has remained stable after increasing just after the introduction of parallel importing in New Zealand;
> (5) the temporary ban of imports of new motion pictures has not had a positive domestic impact in New Zealand (attendance at cinemas has

'Parallel Importing: A Theoretical and Empirical Investigation', Report to Ministry of Commerce, Working Paper 98/4, February 1998; NZIER, 'Parallel Importing Review: The Economic Effects of Lifting the Ban in NZ', Report to the Australian Federal Government, February 2000; Australian Productivity Commission, 'Restrictions on the Parallel Importation of Books', Research Report, June 2009.

67 Frankel et al., *The Challenges of Trans-Tasman Intellectual Property Coordination*, above n 3, at 134.

68 Books which are privately purchased over the Internet and eBooks can be parallel imported; see Copyright Act 1968 (Cth), ss 37–38 (44A and following) and ss 102–103 (103C and following). Other qualifications include that if a book is not released in Australia within 30 days of its being published elsewhere or there is no capacity to resupply it within 90 days, the parallel import restrictions do not apply.

69 See Australian Productivity Commission, 'Restrictions on the Parallel Importation of Books', Research Report, June 2009, available at www.pc.gov.au/projects/study/books/report.

70 Frankel et al., *The Challenges of Trans-Tasman Intellectual Property Coordination*, above n 3, at A4.4(c).

fallen since 2003 and the length of the format release window has narrowed); and

(6) little impact has been felt by the computer software industry with the introduction of parallel importing.

Patents and parallel imports

Patents in England and in British Commonwealth countries, including New Zealand, were sometimes awarded to the first importer rather than to the first inventor or the first to file a patent for an invention.[71] This was to encourage imports and was also based on a local novelty requirement.[72] As trade grew, having patent rights for importers who were not otherwise connected with the inventing process became defeating of rather than supportive of trade and thus patent owners could no longer just be importers but had to be inventors. Of course, a patent owner may now authorise an entity to import its products, but that does not make the authorised entity a patent owner.[73]

The Paris Convention confirms the territorial nature of patents.[74] For some countries, the independence of patent rights is used as the basis of the rule that prevents the parallel importing of patented products. As discussed above, the territorial nature of intellectual property is relevant to parallel importing. Territoriality can be used to separate markets, but

[71] In *Marsden* v. *The Saville Street Foundry and Engineering Company Ltd* (1878) 3 Ex D 203, 205 (CA) Jessel MR said, 'I have never been able to discover the principle [behind giving a patent based on importation], and although I have often made inquiry of others, and of some who are more familiar with the patent law than even I am, ... I could never get a satisfactory answer. The only answer was, it has been so decided, and you are bound by the decisions. But it is an anomaly as far as I know, not depending on any principle whatever. It has never been declared by any judge or authority that there is such a principle, and, not being able to find one, all I can say is, that I must look upon it as a sort of anomalous decision which has acquired by time and recognition the force of law.' In 2000, achieving novelty by importation was upheld by a first instance judge in New Zealand; see *Sherman* v. *Merck & Co* (11 April 2000) HC WN AP 184/98 McGechan J. As local novelty also included looking at the Internet, novelty by importation has not again been asserted and seems to have faded away as it has become unlikely with the expansion of the Internet. The Patents Act 2013 (NZ), s6 and s8 changed the local novelty to an international standard.

[72] Local novelty means novel in a country rather than novel on a global basis.

[73] A related issue is whether countries can require that patents be locally worked; see discussion R. Dreyfuss and S. Frankel, 'From Incentive to Commodity to Asset: How International Law is Reconceptualizing Intellectual Property', *Michigan Journal of International Law*, 36 (2015) (forthcoming).

[74] Paris Convention for the Protection of Industrial Property ('Paris Convention') (Stockholm text 1967), 828 UNTS, 303, art 4bis states, 'Patents applied for in the various countries of the Union by nationals of countries of the Union shall be independent of patents obtained for the same invention in other countries, whether members of the Union or not.'

territorial law does not necessarily mean that parallel importing is not legitimate.

In addition to the rule that issues about exhaustion cannot be subject to dispute settlement, the TRIPS Agreement provides that patent owners have the exclusive right to prevent others from importing patented products.[75] It does not define 'importing'. There are some limits in national laws to the patent holder's ability to control importation. One such limit is that the denial of supply of a patented product may lead to a compulsory licensing regime.[76]

Exclusive right to import

The TRIPS Agreement states that the patent owner has the importation right, but it does not specify the scope of that right and it is well known that members of the WTO do not agree on the scope of the right.[77] The patent importation right is effectively a right relating only to initial importation. It is not a right against parallel importation. Put differently, the wording of the TRIPS importation right does not prohibit parallel importation. However, the importation right is not empty. Arguably, some sort of importation right makes sense in a situation where a patent owner does not necessarily make goods locally, but imports them. As noted above, the WTO regime encourages countries to only import and not make products locally where they do not have a comparative advantage in local production. Also, countries are not able to subsidise industries in order to adjust their comparative advantage. Such subsidies are usually against trade rules because they distort the market.[78] Consequently, giving rights over importation to patent owners arguably

[75] TRIPS Agreement, above n 7, art 28. The right is footnoted that it is subject to Article 6, which provides that for dispute settlement 'nothing in this Agreement shall be used to address the issue of the exhaustion of intellectual property rights'.

[76] See, for example, Patents Act 2013 (NZ), s 46, Patents Act (221 – revised 1995) (Sing) s 55; Patents Act (5727–1967), s 119 (Israel). See also S. Frankel and J. Lai, 'Recognised and Appropriate Grounds for Compulsory Licences: Reclaiming Patent Law's Social Contract', in R. M. Hilty and K.-C. Liu (eds.) *Compulsory Licensing: Practical Perspectives and Ways Forward* (Springer, 2015) for a discussion of the role of compulsory licences in the patenting social contract pp.149–164.

[77] This is why Article 6 was included in the Agreement. Importing is also subject to border enforcement regimes. With patents, this has given rise to complex questions as to whether a country with national (or regional) exhaustion can stop, in transit, products legitimately made in the originating country from reaching a country with international exhaustion rules. See, generally, F. M. Abbott, 'Seizure of Generic Pharmaceuticals in Transit Based on Allegations of Patent Infringement: A Threat to International Trade, Development and Public Welfare,' *World Intellectual Property Organization Journal*, 1 (2009), at 43.

[78] See discussion in Chapter 4.

makes sense as it fits the trade purpose connected to intellectual property through the TRIPS Agreement.

Other factors are also relevant to the trade-related analysis. If a patent owner makes a product locally, then, after that product is sold, the buyer can resell it.[79] Those in favour of parallel importation would say that the same should apply after the first sale of an imported product on the basis that there is no reason to distinguish between first sales nationally and internationally. Put differently, if exhaustion can occur nationally after first sale, then why should it not occur internationally? Some would suggest that a distinction between national and international exhaustion is justified so that the local patent owner, who may or may not be the patent owner in other territories, is in control of the local market. However, the justifications for this local control ought to be tied to the underlying purpose of the right, which in the content of patents is supporting innovation.[80] Controlling all imports is not necessary to incentivise innovation.[81] The reason for controlling all imports is not to grow local innovation, but rather to gain local royalties and sales. Consequently, with a perspective that takes into account the object and purpose of trade-related intellectual property rules, the patent import right can be interpreted as limited to first sale and that subsequent parallel imports do not infringe that right.

Article 27 (1) of the TRIPS Agreement provides relevant interpretative context for this argument. It provides that 'patents shall be available and patent rights enjoyable without discrimination as to the place of invention, the field of technology and whether products are imported or locally produced'. This Article was discussed in the WTO *Canada Pharmaceuticals*[82] dispute where the panel found that it was relevant to the interpretation of Article 30.[83] It is perhaps more obviously relevant to

[79] This is often called the first sale principle.

[80] It is generally accepted that patents have an innovation-supporting role.

[81] Again, this may also have an impact on the legitimacy of a local working requirement, and on whether such requirements found in the Paris Convention and incorporated into the TRIPS Agreement survive that incorporation or whether TRIPS and its provisions mean that local working no longer means local production but can be satisfied by importation. For discussion of this issue, see Dreyfuss and Frankel, *Reconceptualizing Intellectual Property*, above n 73.

[82] WTO Panel Report, *Canada – Patent Protection of Pharmaceutical Products*, Complaint by the European Communities and Their Member States, WT/DS114/R (17 March 2000).

[83] There are problems with the way Article 27 was applied to Article 30 of the TRIPS Agreement, above n 7. The point of Article 30 is to create exceptions which are limited. This is likely to mean some kind of identifying of a technology or a field where a particular issue needs to be addressed. See discussion in G. B. Dinwoodie and R. C. Dreyfuss, 'Diversifying without Discriminating: Complying with the Mandates of the TRIPS Agreement', *Michigan Telecommunications and Technology*

the interpretation of Article 28 (the exclusive rights). To prevent parallel importing after initial distribution arguably discriminates against imported goods. Singapore's law, which is discussed below, reflects this analysis.

An argument against such an interpretation is that the importation right is not so expressly limited. However, similar conclusions can be drawn about 'import' in the TRIPS Agreement to 'distribution' in copyright, which, as discussed above, is ambiguous in the sense of whether on its face it applies only to initial imports or otherwise.

Overall, I suggest that the arguments weigh in favour of the import right applying to the patent owners' rights of import in a way that recognises the legitimacy of parallel importing. To do so recognises that countries can calibrate their laws to their national needs and can also be compliant with international rules. Patent law should not be used to deny supply to a market or to divide markets in a way that does not support the purposes of a country granting patents in the first place.[84] As noted above, sometimes patent owners may wish to sell their products for a lower price in some countries. If they want to do this, they should do so more often than is currently evident. For those countries (large developed countries), preventing parallel imports at home is an economic choice that they are free to make. That choice does not mean that parallel importing should be prevented elsewhere. Put differently, the ability to price discriminate is not reason enough to prevent parallel imports, particularly not from an intellectual property, competition or liberalised trade perspective. Patents are strong property rights, but like all property rights they are not absolute and the extent of property protection should be consistent with the object and purpose of protecting that property.

Finally, the interpretation that TRIPS gives control to patent owners over all imports seems entirely improbable in view of the many negotiators who support international exhaustion, and the practice of some countries both before and after TRIPS came into being.[85] It seems very unlikely that the TRIPS negotiators agreed only to prevent disputes over exhaustion of rights, as Article 6 provides, but otherwise gave away the option of parallel importing. They obviously did not do so.

Law Review, 13 (2007), 445–456. The situation here is different as art 27 subject matter is a context directly relevant to the exclusive rights given to that subject matter in art 28.

[84] For further discussion, see Chapter 6.

[85] Countries other than small market economies which support the international exhaustion rule include large developing countries such as India and Brazil.

New Zealand, Singapore and Israel

New Zealand allows parallel imports of copyright and trade marked goods but it does not allow parallel imports of patented products.[86] This has not always been the case. Prior to 1992, the New Zealand law permitted compulsory licences under which medicines or food products could be imported into New Zealand. These were subject to conditions including the need to provide reasonable remuneration.[87] This provision was stunningly underused and speedily repealed when an application was pending for the supply of an extremely lucrative ulcer treatment.[88] Both the trade mark and copyright law, however, cannot prevent the importation of drugs when the relevant patents have expired.[89]

The late 1980s and early 1990s saw an escalation of prices for imported drugs. Consequently, the health reforms of the same period included changes designed to enable the Crown to parallel import pharmaceuticals.[90] Estimates suggested that parallel importing might save some NZ$50 million.[91] There were never any significant parallel imports under that law and the legislative changes were reversed within three months. The official position is that it was never intended to parallel import pharmaceuticals.[92]

[86] Patents Act 2013 (NZ), s18(1) gives the import right, which seems to be interpreted as preventing parallel importing, although parallel importing or exhaustion are not specifically referred to.

[87] Section 51 of the Patents Act 1953 was repealed by the Patents Amendment Act 1992, s 8(1).

[88] For litigation associated with that application, see *Glaxo Group* v. *Commissioner of Patents* [1991] 3 NZLR 179 (CA).

[89] Section 76 of the Copyright Act 1994 (NZ) provides:
'The copying or adaptation or publication of a literary work or an artistic work does not infringe copyright in that work if that work –
(a) Relates to a medicine that has been imported by the Crown pursuant to section 32A of the Medicines Act 1981; and
(b) Has been made, copied, published, adapted, or distributed, in an overseas country, by or with the licence of the owner of the copyright in the work in that country.'
Section 98 of the Trade Marks Act 2002 (NZ) expressly provides that 'the trade mark provider is deemed to have consented to the use of a trade mark: ... if a person with whom the owner or licensee has an arrangement that relates to the use of the trade mark by the owner or licensee has consented to its use (whether or not that consent is subject to any conditions)'.
Subsection (2) specifies that subs (1) applies only to the use of a trade mark in relation to a medicine imported by the Crown under s 32A of the Medicines Act 1981.

[90] Section 32A of the Medicines Act 1981, introduced by the Medicines Amendment Act 1989, provided that the Crown could import or sell approved medicines 'notwithstanding anything in this Act or any other Act'.

[91] Referred to by Hon Don McKinnnon MP (24 July 1989) NZPD 3174.

[92] In the select committee report, considering the repeal, Dr Bill Sutton disclaimed that the government had ever intended to parallel import drugs. Bill Sutton MP (23 May 1989) NZPD 1739.

Recognising that small markets need greater competition, Singapore embraced parallel importing of patented, copyright and trade marked goods and then curbed some aspects relating to pharmaceuticals as a result of its free trade agreement with the United States. The issue of parallel imports and pharmaceuticals was described as a sticking point in the negotiations.[93] Singapore allows parallel importation of patented products even when the owner outside of Singapore is different from the owner in Singapore. Also, a label indicating 'not for sale' outside of a particular country will not prevent parallel importation into Singapore.[94] These are general rules, but the rules differ for pharmaceuticals.[95] In particular, importation of a pharmaceutical is not permitted if 'the product has not previously been sold or distributed in Singapore'.[96] But once the drug has been brought into Singapore, parallel imports can occur. Put differently, there is a first sale right for pharmaceuticals in Singapore, but that first sale right does not prevent subsequent parallel importation. But there is a qualification. The patent owner also has a right against a parallel importer who has actual or constructive knowledge that the pharmaceutical product has been distributed in breach of a distribution agreement.[97]

The Supreme Court of Israel found that patented goods and pharmaceuticals in particular could be parallel imported into Israel.[98] Interestingly, prior to this decision, Israel manufactured a significant amount of pharmaceuticals locally, but local manufacture has declined. Perhaps now parallel importing is more advantageous.

Trade marks and parallel importation international rules

Trade marks are often attached to goods and services where there are no other intellectual property rights and some countries allow parallel imports of these goods. Parallel imports of copyright and patent goods often carry trade marks. Many countries allow parallel importation of trade marked goods. This has been the case in the United States where international exhaustion is the rule for imports of trade marked goods.[99] Sometimes trade mark law has been used to both prevent and permit parallel imports in other areas of intellectual property law. If the law

93 Tommy Koh and Chang Li Lin (eds.), *The United States–Singapore Free Trade Agreement: Highlights and Insights* (Research Associate, Institute of Policy Studies, Singapore, 2004).

94 Ng-Loy *Law of Intellectual Property of Singapore*, above n 54, at [34.3.13]–[34.3.23].

95 Singapore US FTA, art 16.7.2. 96 Patents Act (Sing.), s 66(3)(a).

97 Patents Act (Sing.), s 63(3)(b) and (c). See also discussion in Ng-Loy, *Law of Intellectual Property of Singapore*, above n 54, at [34.3.1]–[34.3.6].

98 *Bristol Myers Squib Company* v. *The Minister of Health*, 5379/00.

99 See Caboli, '*Corperate Strategies, First Sale Rules and Copyright Misuse,*' above n 37, at 221–238.

permits parallel imports of copyright works or patented products, then to defeat that goal through the use of trade marks is not desirable. Additionally, if parallel importation of trade marked goods is permitted, but copyright or patent is not, then defeating the import of trade marked goods by use of copyright or patent is also not desirable.

The greatest complexity seems to have arisen where a country allows parallel importation of trade marked goods, but not copyright goods. The distinction between trade mark and copyright is increasingly blurred.[100] As one commentator has pointed out, the trade mark-like features of products may also attract copyright protection and this has resulted in trade mark owners in the United States, who cannot prevent parallel imports under trade mark law, using copyright to do so.[101] The US Supreme Court decision in *Kirstaeng*[102] may have ended this use of copyright law.[103] When this use of copyright to defeat parallel importing occurred in Singapore (prior to Singapore allowing parallel imports of copyright works), it enacted a provision preventing the use of copyright for 'accessories'.[104] The law provides that importing and distributing an accessory to an article is not a copyright infringement.[105] Accessories include what might otherwise fall under trade mark law, such as labels, packaging and containers. It also includes leaflets, instructions, certificates and the like that are 'incidental' to the article being imported.[106]

Trade mark law in some jurisdictions initially led to cases where those seeking to prevent parallel imports have relied on issues about whether

[100] G. M. Prévost, 'Canada: Using Copyright to Prevent Parallel Importation in Canada', *INTA Bulletin*, 62 (2007), available at www.inta.org/INTABulletin/Pages/CANADAUsingCopyrighttoPreventParallelImportationinCanada.aspx.

[101] See I. Calboli, 'The (Avoidable) Effects of Territorially Different Approaches to Trademark and Copyright Exhaustion', in I. Calboli and E. Lee (eds.), *Trademark Protection and Territoriality Challenges in a Global Economy* (Edward Elgar, Cheltenham, 2014) pp. 151–177 at 152, 'Even though these products cannot be copyrighted in their entirety because they are non-copyrightable articles, they frequently carry 'incidental features' such as decorations, product design, product packaging, creative labels, logos, and so forth that can qualify for copyright protection. In recent years, copyright protection for these incidental product features has become increasingly popular in the business world.'

[102] *Kirstaeng* v. *John Wiley & Sons Inc.* 133 S.Ct 1351 (2013).

[103] See I. Calboli and M. LaFrance, 'The Case for a Legislative Amendment Against "Accessory Copyright" for Grey Market Products: What can the U.S. Learn from Singapore and Australia?', *Singapore Journal of Legal Studies* (2013) 253–277, at 255. The authors explain how copyright law has been used in the United States to prevent parallel imports and some of the exceptions to the international exhaustion rule for trade marks under US law.

[104] Copyright Act (Sing.), s 40A. [105] Copyright Act (Sing.), s 40A(1).

[106] Copyright Act (Sing.), s 7(1). See discussion of this in Calboli and LaFrance, *The Case for a Legislative Amendment against Accessory Copyright*, above n 103, at 263–264.

the owner is the local trade mark owner or not.[107] This means court rulings were based on corporate structure rather than intellectual property rationales, or arguments about distinct products in different markets.[108] There is little international coordination on the point and the TRIPS Agreement does not directly address it. Trade marks, like other intellectual property rights, are territorial, but the exclusive rights of the trade mark owner in the TRIPS Agreement do not extend to preventing imports of trade marked goods.[109]

The Singaporean rule for imports of trade marked goods is international exhaustion, but there are some limitations. In particular, goods must have been put on the market in Singapore under the trade mark registered in Singapore.[110] However, if the owner is a parent or subsidiary company, then international exhaustion can apply. In other words, if there is a different registered proprietor in Singapore than in the place of the origin of the goods, the trade marked goods cannot be parallel imported.[111] This may very well reflect the value of trade marks in small market economies, which was discussed in Chapter 7.

International exhaustion will not apply, in Singapore, if the physical condition of goods has been altered in such a way that they are changed or impaired.[112] In one case, because there was no relationship between the Singapore trade mark owner and the overseas trade mark owner, parallel imports were not permitted.[113] However, if there is a relationship then consent to the importation may be established.[114]

107 See, for example, INTA, 'Trademark Owner's Guide to Parallel Imports in the United States' (February 2012), available at www.inta.org.

108 See, for example, *Revlon Inc* v. *Cripps & Lee Ltd* [1980] FSR 85 (EWCA); *South Pacific Tyres NZ Ltd* v. *David Craw Cars Ltd* (1989) 24 IPR 99 (NZHC); *Colgate Palmolive Ltd* v. *Markwell Finance Ltd* [1989] RPC 497 (EWCA); *Zino Davidoff SA* v. *A & G Imports Ltd* [2000] Ch 127 (Ch D) at 136–137; *Transport Tyre Sales Pty Ltd* v. *Montana Tyre Rims & Tubes Pty Ltd* (1999) 43 IPR 481 (FCA).

109 There may be rules at domestic law which prevent someone obtaining a trade mark unless it is used in a jurisdiction. Also, well-known marks may obtain protection even when they are not used (although this should not prevent parallel imports but such a case is likely to depend on facts); see the chapter 7 in this volume.

110 Trade Marks Act (Sing.) s 29(1).

111 See W. L. Ng-Loy, 'Exhaustion of Rights in Trade Mark Law: The English and Singapore Models Compared', *European Intellectual Property Review*, 22(7) (2000), 320.

112 Trade Marks Act, s 29(2). A leading commentator suggests this alteration must be to the goods, not the packaging; see Ng-Loy, *Law of Intellectual Property of Singapore*, above n 54, at [24.8.10].

113 *Pan–West (Pte) Ltd* v. *Grand Bigwin Pte Ltd* [2003] 4 SLR 755. See also B. Ong, 'The Interface between Intellectual Property Law and Competitor Law in Singapore', in S. D. Anderman (ed.), *The Interface between Intellectual Property Rights and Competition Policy* (Cambridge University Press, 2007), p. 375, explaining that consent includes express and implied consent under Singapore law.

114 See Ng-Loy, *Law of Intellectual Property of Singapore*, above n 54, at 24.8.8.

The issue of preventing parallel imports of goods of a different quality than those the trade mark owner supplies to the local market has not been before the courts in Israel. In fact, international exhaustion of trade marked goods is well established in Israel. '[I]t was held that such activity fosters competition, lowers prices and should be encouraged'.[115]

In New Zealand, the local owner of the relevant trade mark successfully prevented the importation of used Japanese tyres bearing Dunlop's registered trade mark 'flying D'. A statement on the tyres that they were made in Japan to differentiate them from the New Zealand proprietor's tyres was not enough and according to the Court did not change the fact that the plaintiff's trade mark had been embossed on the tyres. There was no relationship between the Japanese manufacturer and the New Zealand registered proprietor.[116] The decision is questionable because the tyres were second-hand and there was insufficient discussion of exhaustion of rights.[117]

After the initial reforms of copyright law in New Zealand, it soon became apparent that allowing parallel imports for copyright goods would not work unless trade marked goods could also be parallel imported. Trade mark law had allowed some parallel importing based on consent rules, but these could sometimes be used in a way that defeated the copyright rules.[118] Consequently, there was amendment to trade mark law in 2003, which provides that 'a registered trade mark is not infringed by the use of the trade mark in relation to goods that have been put on the market anywhere in the world under that trade mark by the owner or with his or her express or implied consent'.[119] This provision was enacted in addition to an existing section (the subject of the Dunlop trade mark dispute discussed above) which allowed parallel imports only if the New Zealand-based trade mark owner had consented to the trade mark being applied to the imported goods. The intention of the above-quoted amendment was to ensure that parallel imports could not be defeated by requiring consent of the New Zealand trade mark owner to the import, when the trade mark had been applied with consent

[115] E. Liss and D. Adin, *Intellectual Property Law and Practice in Israel* (Oxford University Press, 2012), at 314.

[116] *South Pacific Tyres NZ Ltd* v. *David Craw Cars Ltd* (1989) 24 IPR 99 (HC), at 104.

[117] A full discussion of this and related cases can be found in Frankel, *Intellectual Property in New Zealand*, above n 25, at 100–109.

[118] Copyright (Parallel Importation of Films and Onus of Proof) Amendment Act 2003, incorporated into the 1994 Act. See copyright discussion above.

[119] Trade Marks Act 2002 (NZ), s 97A.

of the relevant trade mark owner anywhere in the world. As the legislative history explained,[120]

Consequential amendments are made to the Trade Marks Act 2002 to ensure that registered trade marks cannot be used to frustrate legitimate parallel importing, in line with the Government's parallel importing policy. For the avoidance of doubt, these amendments provide that a registered trade mark is not infringed by the use of the trade mark on parallel imported goods (including for the purpose of advertising) when a trade mark has been legitimately applied, whether that was in New Zealand or anywhere else in the world. The amendment to the Trade Marks Act 2002 (a Bill currently before Parliament) is appropriate in the context of this amendment to copyright legislation. While parallel importation is more generally perceived as a copyright issue in New Zealand, copyright goods may also be trade marked. It is therefore appropriate that a consistent approach towards parallel importation is taken in both copyright and trade mark legislation.

Conclusion: analogous concerns resulting in three different approaches

The evolution of parallel importing law perhaps sharply illustrates the difficulty of making international exhaustion of rights work when intellectual property law is territorial and there is no international agreement over when intellectual property rights are exhausted.

Parallel importing is simple to the consumer (why should they not have access to cheaper goods?), but the law of intellectual property has made it complex. The small market economies illustrate some ingenuity in ironing out some of the complexities, such as reversing the burden of proof and creating windows of opportunity for rights holders to supply markets before competition from parallel imports is permitted.

The different approaches found in the small market economies may also reflect the different needs of local industry and consumer demand. New Zealand's ban on parallel imports for patented products and Singapore's adjustments to pharmaceutical parallel imports are trade-related concessions. Because of these trade-related exceptions, the overall small market economy approach to parallel imports does not illustrate an entirely consistent distinct normative underpinning from a legal perspective, except that small markets often need to rely on parallel imports for effective

[120] See Trade Marks Bill (leading to Trade Marks Act 2002) Explanatory Notes. See also this passage quoted in *Leisureworld Ltd* v. *Elite Fitness Equipment Ltd*, HC Auckland CIV-2006-404-003499, 21 July 2006, para [67]. There the judge failed to give proper effect to this provision and, as I have said elsewhere, this case must have been incorrectly decided; see Frankel, *Intellectual Property in New Zealand*, this case above n 25, at 108–09.

competition. Overall, therefore, the small market economies prefer international exhaustion, but compromises are made.

Globally the position of parallel importing is complex and different rules proliferate. There are two forces that will continue to push, even if haphazardly, towards international exhaustion. Those are global trade and the Internet.

9 An insight into protecting traditional knowledge and innovation

Consider the following:

New Zealand has led the world in recognising the indigenous place in its constitutional, political, and cultural institutions in the past. Finding ways to protect the Māori interest in taonga works and mātauranga Māori while also acknowledging the interests of others in free access to knowledge and ideas is potentially another milestone in that history.[1]

There are anecdotal reports that overseas entrepreneurs have been searching New Zealand for IP that has value and has not been commercialised. Apparently, New Zealand organisations, including government agencies, that are ignorant of the value of some of the IP that they own, or lack the capital to invest in commercialisation, have sold off IP.[2]

With this greater respect and acknowledgement comes a clearer, wider recognition that traditional knowledge systems are indeed innovative, dynamic and directly relevant to practical needs; that collective and cumulative forms of innovation and creativity have value and worth in themselves; that Indigenous Peoples do trade and do engage with the wider community, have done so for millennia, and today simply seek to do so on terms that are more equitable and culturally attuned.[3]

We recognize that WTO Members are, subject to existing rights and obligations, free to protect traditional knowledge above and beyond the protection for objects of intellectual property rights contained in the Agreement on Trade-Related Aspects of Intellectual Property Rights (TRIPS), subject to rights and obligations contained in that Agreement.

[1] Waitangi Tribunal, Ko Aotearoa Tēnei: A Report into Claims Concerning New Zealand Law and Policy Affecting Māori Culture and Identity (2011) Wai 262 ('*Ko Aotearoa Tēnei*'), at 32. Translated, Ko Aotearoa Tēnei means 'This Is Aotearoa/New Zealand'. Aotearoa is the Māori name for New Zealand. For a discussion of this report, see J. C. Lai, *Indigenous Cultural Heritage and Intellectual Property Rights: Learning from the New Zealand Experience?* (Heidelberg: Springer, 2014), at 223–310.

[2] Auckland Uniservices Ltd, 'Review of the New Zealand Intellectual Property System', Report for the Ministry of Economic Development, April 2010, at 7.

[3] A. Taubman, Preface 'Indigenous Innovation: New Dialogues, New Pathways', in P. Drahos and S. Frankel (eds.), *Indigenous Peoples' Innovation: Intellectual Property Pathways to Development* (ANU E-press, Canberra, Australia, 2012) ('*Indigenous Peoples' Innovation*'), pp. xv–xxiv, at xv–xvi.

We encourage the adoption of private and public measures destined to take account of the needs of traditional knowledge holders in the exploitation of indigenous and genetic resources and to foster the adequate transfer of technologies developed on the basis of such resources.[4]

New Zealand is a country where there is an advanced discussion about and analysis of the protection of mātauranga Māori (traditional knowledge of Māori, the indigenous people of New Zealand). This activity has not yet resulted in a great legislative change, although the recognition of Māori concerns in intellectual property statutes is arguably the strongest recognition in any jurisdiction in the developed world.[5] The protection of traditional knowledge has apparently not been a major concern in other small market economies. Arguably, however, it is precisely because New Zealand is a small market economy that it has been possible, perhaps even made expedient, for it to advance the debate on the protection of traditional knowledge. It is important for its economic growth (and for its political and cultural life) to do so.

The developed world countries with indigenous populations (New Zealand, Australia, Canada and the United States) have been a focus of the protection of traditional knowledge discussion,[6] even though those countries have had markedly different approaches to the issues both in international negotiations and nationally. There is also much interest in traditional knowledge protection in developing countries, which have been at the forefront of discussions at the World Intellectual Property Organization (WIPO) and the World Trade Organization (WTO).

If there ever was a test tube for the global issue of protecting traditional knowledge, it is New Zealand. Of course, there are things about New Zealand and the political situation of the Māori people that, some may say, make New Zealand different. That is undoubtedly so, but it is not a dispositive reason to dismiss the New Zealand example and it is possible to overstate the difference. To the extent that all protection of traditional knowledge is premised on protecting the customs and unique heritage of the people from whom the knowledge comes, there will be differences in that protection at a practical level. These differences may, as discussed below, point to the necessity of pluralistic approaches to domestic law. Those differences create certain difficulties in finding

[4] An extract of a proposed declaration on the protection of traditional knowledge from D. Gervais, 'Traditional Knowledge & Intellectual Property: A TRIPS-Compatible Approach', *Michigan State Law Review* (2005), 137–166, at 162.

[5] As discussed below, there is a Trade Marks Advisory Committee and a Patents Advisory Committee.

[6] See, for example, C. B. Graber, K. Kuprecht and J. C. Lai, *International Trade in Indigenous Cultural Heritage: Legal and Policy Issues* (Edward Elgar, Cheltenham, 2012).

common ground at an international level. That does not mean there are no commonalities or indeed international frameworks which are developing to accommodate both minimum standards of agreement and differences. That is also the structure of the Agreement on Trade-Related Aspects of Intellectual Property Rights (TRIPS);[7] some commonalties are expressed as minimum standards, but they include the possibility for differences at national level.[8]

The international issue

So why has the protection of traditional knowledge become an international issue? The increase in global trade and the consequent cross-border flows of cultural and intellectual property related goods and services have led to an increase in the desire for the protection of local culture. They have also led to an increased market in the developed world for the 'exotic', the 'traditional' and the 'natural'. The availability of products of culture (protected by intellectual property rights) worldwide has shined a spotlight on the role of international legal norms. Questions have arisen, such as why those norms which are found in the TRIPS Agreement give legal force to the protection of some cultural products but not to others. Countries that are not significant exporters of intellectual property may also be net importers of intellectual property and would often find themselves paying a considerable price for it. Yet, residents of those exporting countries often pay no price at all for using the traditional knowledge assets of many intellectual property-importing countries or their indigenous populations. Such an imbalance has substantially contributed to the call for the protection of traditional knowledge at the international level. The debate over the protection of traditional knowledge has occurred at a time when the role of intellectual property more broadly is being questioned and challenged in a variety of ways. The traditional knowledge debate has contributed to that wider discussion. In addition, the discussion over the protection of traditional knowledge has provoked a broader discussion over why we have intellectual property rights at all.[9]

What is traditional knowledge?

But what is meant by the phrase 'traditional knowledge'? Defining traditional knowledge is fraught with difficulty. The reason is at once obvious

[7] WTO, Agreement on Trade-Related Aspects of Intellectual Property Rights, Marrakesh Agreement Establishing the World Trade Organization, Annex 1C, 1869 UNTS 299; 33 ILM 1197 (adopted on 15 April 1994, entered into force 1 January 1995) ('TRIPS Agreement').

[8] See discussion in Chapter 4 of this volume. [9] See Taubman, *Preface*, above n 3.

if the scope of the notion of the knowledge of a culture is considered. Definition is a mechanism of legal rules to give supposed certainty, particularly to concepts of ownership. Where traditional knowledge is concerned, there are many reasons not to struggle with precise definition, including that the term 'traditional knowledge', while widely used, is at face value misleading. It suggests that the knowledge is wholly traditional, that it is a relic of the past. The phrase does not capture the full scope of cultural heritage or indeed of the innovation systems for which indigenous peoples use traditional knowledge. The nature of such knowledge is not that it remains in the past, but rather that its long-standing basis and mode of transmission from generation to generation (often involving complex detail) are crucial to future developmental and innovative uses of the knowledge.

Attempts at definition can run into varying problems and may look different depending on the discipline or perspective creating the definition. Anthropological definitions, for example, look different from international law definitions, which are by comparison open-ended.[10] A co-author and I have suggested the following:[11]

> Without definitions, the discipline of law treats itself as undefined and uncertain. This has contributed to a plethora of definitions relating to traditional knowledge. Indigenous peoples do not usually attach the same value to abstract definition. If called upon to define their traditional knowledge, they will emphasise not the analytical facets of knowledge, but rather the relational boundaries and dynamics created by the possession of knowledge. This includes indigenous peoples' relationship with their knowledge, and their responsibility to maintain and develop the knowledge for the good of society and future generations. Māori, for example, are kaitiaki (guardians) of their knowledge. Additionally, being kaitiaki in part defines Māori culture and identity.

The openness of the approach which describes relationship boundaries is a different kind of openness from the international law approach. The relationship boundaries approach draws on the customary law of the relevant community for its definition. It is therefore in some aspects pluralistic. The extent of that pluralism may vary depending on the particular jurisdiction and how it recognises minority rights, which may or may not be recognised by the dominant legal system. The international law approach could be seen as being sufficiently broad so

[10] The UNDRIP definition, for example, gives the opportunity for anyone to be indigenous; see below n 40 and the related text.

[11] P. Drahos and S. Frankel, 'Indigenous Peoples' Innovation and Intellectual Property: The Issues', in Drahos and Frankel, *Indigenous Peoples' Innovation*, above n 3, pp. 1–28, at 9.

as not to exclude minority rights, but its broadness is also a problem. The broadness can lead to endless ways in which opponents of protecting traditional knowledge can eternally question the necessity for protection and the appropriate mechanisms for that protection.[12]

Because the phrase 'traditional knowledge' carries with it implications that seem to 'contradict' conventional understandings of intellectual property (for example, that copyright protects expression, not knowledge or ideas) and because the phrase does not convey the concerns that indigenous peoples have over the uses of their knowledge, a co-author and I have suggested that the focus should not be on that knowledge. 'Perhaps the most important thing for indigenous innovation is to make "indigenous innovation" rather than traditional knowledge the primary term of art in this field. Then policy-makers would have to start asking how they might support indigenous innovation, as opposed to dividing the spoils from traditional knowledge.'[13]

Definition at a domestic level may be a little more straightforward than definitions which, because they are designed at international level, attempt to accommodate all. In domestic law, the number of cultures relevant to the definition will not necessitate including the entire world. That said, making a national definition is by no means easy. The New Zealand discussion explains traditional knowledge and Māori peoples' relationship with it in some depth. An introductory explanation is as follows:

> In the 1,000 years or so in which Māori have lived on the island of Aotearoa, they have developed – among other things – artistic and cultural traditions that are uniquely of this place. The underpinnings of these traditions are found in the environment itself – mountains, rivers, sea and sky, plants and animals – and their expression takes many forms, ranging from the architectural achievements of the great meeting-house and canoe builders, to the work of weavers, carvers, tohunga tā moko, musicians and the like, as well as in te reo Māori, the language itself. These works are founded in and reflect the body of knowledge and understanding known as mātauranga Māori. Some of them are ancient, others not, but those who are responsible for safeguarding them, whether or not they are original creators of the works, have a very particular relationship with them. We call this the kaitiaki relationship.[14]

[12] For a discussion of why the United States' broad objections to the protection of traditional knowledge are unfounded when considered through examples, see S. Frankel, '"Ka Mate Ka Mate" and the Protection of Traditional Knowledge', in R. Dreyfuss and J. Ginsburg (eds.), *Intellectual Property at the Edge* (Cambridge University Press, 2014), pp. 193–214.

[13] Drahos and Frankel, *Indigenous Peoples' Innovation*, above n 11, at 28.

[14] *Ko Aotearoa Tēnei*, above n 1, at 31.

This chapter will further explain the New Zealand approach to traditional knowledge protection, a global balancing act in a national setting. It will also look at the voluntary protection mechanisms and how other countries, for example Norway, have implemented them.

Recognition of Māori interests in intellectual property statutes

There are instances in New Zealand law where there is a kind of legal interface between the protection of Māori interests and the intellectual property system.[15] The mechanisms do not form the basis of protection of the wider Māori interest in Māori knowledge, and uses thereof. They provide a way to deal with potential conflicts as they may arise in certain circumstances. These interfaces are found in trade mark and patent law in particular.

New Zealand trade mark law includes a ground that a trade mark should not be registered if it is offensive to Māori.[16] The provision does not only apply to Māori, but also applies to a significant section of the community, although Māori are the only section of the community named in the statute. The Commissioner's role in not allowing such registrations is supported by the advice of the Māori Advisory Committee.[17]

That Committee also provides guidelines of general application about what may or may not be offensive. The Committee has issued guidance which concludes that the word 'kiwi' is not offensive to Māori when used as a trade mark.[18] It has also found that the koru symbol (also

[15] For a full discussion of the role of the interface between intellectual property law and sui generis traditional knowledge protection, see S. Frankel, 'A New Zealand Perspective on the Protection of Matauranga Maori (Traditional Knowledge)', in Graber, Kuprecht and Lai, above n 6, pp. 439–459.

[16] Trade Marks Act 2002, s. 17(1)(c).

[17] Trade Marks Act 2002, s. 178. Elsewhere, I have contrasted this system with the now repealed provision that allowed the Commissioner of Trade Marks to refuse registration of trade marks on the basis of morality. S. Frankel, 'Third-Party Trade Marks as a Violation of Indigenous Cultural Property – A New Statutory Safeguard', *Journal of World Intellectual Property Law*, 8 (2005), 83–98. Similar morality provisions are also found in other countries. I have also contrasted New Zealand's culturally offensive ground for objection to trade mark registration to the US objection system and concluded that New Zealand's law is stronger and gives greater weight to indigenous peoples' interests. S. Frankel, 'Trade Marks, Traditional Knowledge and Cultural Intellectual Property', in G. B. Dinwoodie and M. D. Janis (eds.), *Trade Mark Law and Theory: A Handbook of Contemporary Research* (Edward Elgar Press, Cheltenham, 2007), pp. 433–463.

[18] See IPONZ, Guidelines of the Maori Advisory Committee, 'Kiwi', available at www.iponz.govt.nz/cms/trade-marks/practice-guidelines-index/practice-guidelines/16-maori-advisory-committee-maori-trade-marks/6-annexure/6-1-kiwi.

known as pitau – a spiral shape) is not offensive.[19] This function of the Committee is extremely important as it provides a way to overcome the hurdle (real or perceived) of businesspeople not knowing what aspects of Māori culture can be legitimately used and how.[20]

As a legal matter, the Committee is advisory. The final decision is made in the name of the Commissioner.[21] The Commissioner has to date followed the Committee's advice. Māori who brought a claim against government intellectual property policy (the claim is known as WAI 262 and is discussed further below) claimed that Māori should have more than an advisory committee role. The Tribunal Report on the claim agreed and recommended that Māori have a decision-making role.

The ground of offensiveness as a reason against registration may also be the basis of a pre-grant opposition and a post-grant revocation action. Interestingly, the post-grant process uses the phrase 'culturally aggrieved' rather than 'offensive'.[22] The Māori Advisory Committee will be relevant to these actions also.

The Committee has, within the confines of registered trade marks, worked effectively and its broad model has now been included in patent law.[23] The Patents Act 2013 includes a statement that one of the Act's purposes is to

> address Māori concerns relating to the granting of patents for inventions derived from indigenous plants and animals or from Māori traditional knowledge[24]

The Act requires that the Intellectual Property Office of New Zealand (IPONZ) establish a Patent Advisory Committee.[25] The role of the Committee is to advise the Commissioner of Patents on whether a patent application conflicts with Māori values.[26] More specifically, the advice is to be directed to whether a claimed invention is derived from Māori traditional knowledge or indigenous plants or animals, and if so whether the commercial exploitation thereof is likely to be contrary to Māori values.[27] In terms of the patent registration system, this advice would be

[19] See IPONZ, Guidelines of the Maori Advisory Committee, 'Pitau (koru)', available at www.iponz.govt.nz/cms/trade-marks/practice-guidelines-index/practice-guidelines/16-maori-advisory-committee-maori-trade-marks/6-annexure/6-3-pitau-koru.

[20] An oft-stated claim against the protection of traditional knowledge is that people do not know from whom to seek permission.

[21] Trade Marks Act 2002, s. 178. [22] Trade Marks Act 2002, s. 178.

[23] Lai, above n 1, at 135–142. [24] Patents Act 2013, s 3(d). [25] Patents Act 2013, s 225.

[26] Patents Act 2013, s 226. The committee can make its own procedure, s 228(4).

[27] Patents Act 2013, s 226(a).

relevant to any assessment of the prior art[28] as it relates to novelty and inventive step[29] and any objection made on the grounds of *ordre public* or morality.[30]

The Waitangi Tribunal, in an inquiry about intellectual property, which is discussed in the next section, recommended that patent reform should go further than the 2013 Act has. The Tribunal recommended that the Committee should have a joint decision-making role, with the Commissioner of Patents not merely playing an advisory role,[31] and that there should be a requirement in the patent law to disclose the origin of genetic or biological resources used in patents.[32]

The New Zealand position beyond the legal framework

The WAI 262 claim

In 1991 several iwi (tribes) lodged a claim before the Waitangi Tribunal[33] about the protection of Māori culture.[34] The claim included many details about several areas of New Zealand law, including intellectual property statutes and the international treaties (that New Zealand is a member of) which are relevant to intellectual property. The overarching issue in the claim was that successive New Zealand governments had failed to allow Māori to exercise te tino rangitiratanga[35] (self-determination and control) over things which are taonga (sacred or treasured) to Māori. This included a claim that governments of New Zealand should not have unduly interfered with the body of Māori knowledge and understanding

[28] Patents Act 2013, s 8. 'For the purpose of deciding whether or not an invention is novel and for the purpose of deciding whether or not an invention involves an inventive step, the prior art base, in relation to an invention so far as claimed in a claim, means all matter (whether a product, a process, information about a product or process, or anything else) that has at any time before the priority date of that claim been made available to the public (whether in New Zealand or elsewhere) by written or oral description, by use, or in any other way.'

[29] Patents Act 2013, ss 6–7. [30] Patents Act 2013, s 15(1).

[31] Patents Act 2013, s 227 provides that the Commissioner must consider, but is not bound by, the advice given by the Māori Advisory Committee.

[32] This is discussed below. For a discussion on the recommendations pertaining to patent law, see Lai, above n 1, at 264–271.

[33] I was the Waitangi Tribunal's expert intellectual property law adviser for this claim.

[34] Six claimants brought the proceedings on behalf of their iwi (tribe) and as individual claimants. The claimants were Haana Murray of Ngāti Kurī, Hema Nui a Tawhaki Witana of Te Rarawa, Te Witi McMath of Ngāti Wai, Tama Poata of Ngāti Porou, Kataraina Rimene of Ngāti Kahungunu and John Hippolite of Ngāti Koata. It is important to record the people who brought that claim. At the core of Māori culture lies that belief that who a person is and what they do is interconnected with their ancestors and their whakapapa (genealogy and connection between all people and the environment).

[35] Te tino rangitiratanga is guaranteed to Māori under Article 2 of the Treaty of Waitangi.

(mātauranga Māori) and should have supported Māori control over it. As successive governments had not allowed that control, the claim was that there had been a major loss of Māori culture and a constraint on Māori development of their culture. The claim also alleged that others could comparatively easily develop Māori culture because intellectual property rights encouraged those others to do so.

The final report of the claim discussed issues of direct relevance to intellectual property law and policy in two chapters. The first chapter is about taonga works (works of culture) and the effect of copyright and trade mark law on taonga works and related mātuaranga Māori. The second chapter is about biological and genetic resources and patent law's effects on those resources and related mātauranga Māori. Both chapters discuss the kaitiaki (guardianship) role of Māori.

The claim was a national example of the global issues around the protection of traditional knowledge and cultural heritage. The report of the claim is conscious of these global issues and discusses them and also New Zealand's potential global role.[36]

What perhaps makes the New Zealand situation different from other parts of the world is the existence of the Waitangi Tribunal that heard the claim and the Treaty of Waitangi,[37] the basis on which the Māori claim against the government was made.[38] These are indeed important differences which give the Māori people an avenue for redress that is not available to all indigenous peoples.[39] The issues before the Tribunal,

[36] *Ko Aotearoa Tēnei*, above n 1.

[37] The key provision provides:

'Her Majesty the Queen of England confirms and guarantees to the Chiefs and Tribes of New Zealand and to the respective families and individuals thereof the full exclusive and undisturbed possession of their Lands and Estates Forests Fisheries and other Preemption over such lands.'

'Ko te Kuini o Ingarani ka wakarite ka wakaae ki nga RaNgātira ki nga hapu – ki nga tangata katoa o Nu Tirani te tino raNgātiratanga o ratou wenua o ratou kainga me o ratou taonga katoa.' Both the Māori and English texts are authoritative. Treaty of Waitangi Act 1975, s 2, which defines 'the Treaty' as including both the English and Māori version set out in schedule 1 of the Act. For further discussion in the intellectual property context, see S. Frankel, *Intellectual Property in New Zealand,* 2nd edn (LexisNexis, Wellington, 2013) at 120–125.

[38] The Tribunal investigates claims made under the Treaty of Waitangi (Te Tiriti O Waitangi). The Treaty is a founding document of New Zealand. For the Treaty's history, see C. Orange, *The Treaty of Waitangi* (Bridget Williams Books, Wellington, 1992). For a discussion of its legal status, see M. S. R. Palmer, *The Treaty of Waitangi in New Zealand's Law and Constitution* (Victoria University Press, Wellington, 2008). For many years, New Zealand courts doubted the legal importance of the Treaty of Waitangi; see Prendergast CJ in *Wi Parata* v. *Bishop of Wellington* (1877) 3 NZ Jur (NS) SC 72.

[39] In P. Drahos and S. Frankel, *Indigenous Peoples' Innovation*, above n 11, at 28 we state: 'In the case of Aboriginal people in Australia the place–time nature of their system means that land rights justice is the primary necessary first step. Land rights justice, although not

however, reflect the global issues and are discussed here in that light. Those global concerns are usefully reflected in the UN Declaration on the Rights of Indigenous Peoples (UNDRIP).[40] Article 31 of UNDRIP provides the following:

> Indigenous peoples have the right to maintain, control, protect and develop their cultural heritage, traditional knowledge and traditional cultural expressions, as well as the manifestations of their sciences, technologies and cultures, including human and genetic resources, seeds, medicines, knowledge of the properties of fauna and flora, oral traditions, literatures, designs, sports and traditional games and visual and performing arts. They also have the right to maintain, control, protect and develop their intellectual property over such cultural heritage, traditional knowledge, and traditional cultural expressions.[41]

As Article 31 of UNDRIP above suggests, the relationship of indigenous peoples with their knowledge (for Māori the kaitiaki relationship) is not static, but rather relates to the past, present and future.[42] According to the Tribunal, this relationship is central to determining whether something is a taonga work or mātauranga Māori.

Taonga works

If the kaitiaki relationship is missing, a work will not be considered a taonga work or mātauranga Māori, even if the work appears to have Māori elements to it. In other words, the Waitangi Tribunal drew a line between taonga works and underlying mātauranga Māori, on the one hand, and works which draw on Māori culture and may obviously have Māori elements but do not have a kaitiaki, on the other. It found that the first category deserved protection and control over commercial uses, but that protecting the second category in that way would go too far. However, the Tribunal recommended the enactment of a law preventing all from using taonga works and the underlying mātauranga Māori in a derogatory or offensive manner, whether there is an identified kaitiaki or not.[43]

completely resolved, is considerably closer to having been achieved in New Zealand through the Waitangi Tribunal and Treaty Settlement Process. That is perhaps why Maori were able to bring the WAI 262 claim about the protection of their knowledge, culture and identity to the Waitangi Tribunal. This claim shows how progress on land rights justice opens the way to progress on the protection of indigenous knowledge and culture more broadly.'

[40] United Nations, Declaration on the Rights of Indigenous Peoples, GA Res. 61/295 (UN Doc. A/61/L.67 and Add.1) (adopted on 13 September 2007) ('UNDRIP').

[41] For discussion of this article, see J. C. Lai, 'The Protection of Māori Cultural Heritage: Post-Endorsement of the UN Declaration on the Rights of Indigenous Peoples', *University of Lucerne, Switzerland*, i-call Working Paper No. 2 (2011), at 33–34.

[42] *Ko Aotearoa Tēnei*, above n 1, at 38–43. [43] *Ko Aotearoa Tēnei*, above n 1, at 84–85.

This distinction between taonga works and what the Tribunal termed taonga-derived works arose from the Tribunal's balancing process where, in analysing the level of protection that ought to be given in recognition of the Treaty of Waitangi obligations, the Tribunal concluded that other interests needed to be taken into account. The other interests at play included that Māori have encouraged and continue to encourage non-Māori to use Māori culture. That is a benefit for both Māori and non-Māori.[44] The Tribunal through this approach recognised that too many legal rules around Māori culture would likely not help its development – too many rules might even have the opposite effect. Some rules are needed because the absence of rules has not achieved the appropriate balance of interests.

When balancing the interests of Māori against other interests, the Tribunal heard evidence from third parties, such as artists, designers, scientists and businesspeople.[45] In addition, the Tribunal talked more broadly of the New Zealand interest and the public interest, including the rights of existing intellectual property owners.

The report of the claim is lengthy and explains its reasoning in full. In summary, the broad recommendations[46] that the Tribunal made in order to achieve the protection of taonga works and mātauranga Māori and to strike an appropriate balance with other interests are as follows:

1. New standards of legal protection governing the use of taonga works, taonga-derived works and mātauranga Māori:
   (a) A general objection mechanism to prohibit the derogatory or offensive public use of taonga works, taonga-derived works or mātauranga Māori;[47]
   (b) A mechanism by which kaitiaki can prevent any commercial exploitation of taonga works or mātauranga Māori (but not taonga-derived works) unless and until there has been consultation and, where found appropriate, kaitiaki consent;[48]
2. An expert commission to have wider functions in relation to taonga works, taonga-derived works and mātauranga Māori.[49]

[44] *Ko Aotearoa Tēnei*, above n 1, at 92. [45] *Ko Aotearoa Tēnei*, above n 1, at 74–77.

[46] The Tribunal's power is one of recommendation to the government.

[47] This recommendation included that anybody should be entitled to object to the derogatory or offensive public use of taonga works, taonga-derived works, or mātauranga Māori.

[48] This recommendation included that only kaitiaki should be entitled to object to any non-derogatory or non-offensive commercial use of taonga works or mātauranga Māori.

[49] The Tribunal recommended that the government establish a commission. The commission should have multi-disciplinary expertise (encompassing mātauranga Māori, IP law, commerce, science and stewardship of taonga works and documents at both commissioner and secretariat levels).

In essence, these aspects of the Tribunal Report engaged with the intellectual property issues, including trade mark, copyright and design law.

The recommended 'general objection mechanism', although about more than intellectual property rights, is a kind of interface mechanism to deal with conflicts between Māori interests and intellectual property rights. The ability for kaitiaki to prevent commercial exploitation goes further than creating the interface with intellectual property and in substance recommends a sui generis law to protect Māori traditional knowledge (mātauranga Māori) and associated taonga works. The Tribunal said,

> This approach is not intended to create a new category of proprietary right, but is rather a way of recognising the relationship of kaitiaki with taonga works and some aspects of mātauranga Māori where it is proposed to exploit those things commercially. It is important to understand that our recommendations do not represent a wholesale change to the current system of IP protection, particularly copyright and trade mark protection.[50]

To date these recommendations have not been adopted. As discussed above, the interface mechanism is already found partially in the Trade Mark's Act 2002 (which pre-dates the report)[51] and the Patents Act 2013 (which post-dates the report).

Biological and genetic resources

The report's chapter about biological and genetic resources discusses various aspects of the research process in addition to patent law.[52] It contextualised patent law and plant variety rights as significant aspects of the laws relating to research. The chapter includes a description of how Māori have made very little use of the patent system and plant variety rights and why those intellectual property systems are not designed for and cannot protect the relationship between Māori and biological and genetic resources.[53] This is also the international situation. That said, Māori and other indigenous peoples have used the patent system both successfully and otherwise.[54]

[50] *Ko Aotearoa Tēnei*, above n 1, at 92.

[51] In *Ko Aotearoa Tēnei*, above n 1, the Tribunal recommended that the proposed Commission take over the role of the existing Trade Marks Advisory Committee. It also concluded, as discussed below, that the current role of the committee as advisory should be changed to joint decision-maker.

[52] Discussed by Lai, *Indigenous Cultural Heritage* above n 1, at 260–264 and 271–276.

[53] *Ko Aotearoa Tēnei*, above n 1, at 115.

[54] See for e.g. D. J. Claudie, S. J. Semple, N. M. Smith and B. S. Simpson, 'Ancient but New: Developing Locally Driven Enterprises Based on Traditional Medicines in Kuuku

The Tribunal concluded that Māori have rights in relation to biological and genetic resources that are dependent on the kaitiaki relationship.[55] The existence of the relationship, the Tribunal said, gives rise to an entitlement of a correlated degree of protection;[56] that is, the degree of protection will depend on the kaitiaki relationship.

One of the other recommendations of the Tribunal was a disclosure requirement in patent and plant variety rights applications. The Tribunal recommended that disclosure of the use of genetic and biological resources (and mātauranga Māori) should be made in the patent system if they were used as part of the research process, even if those resources or mātauranga Māori were not strictly part of the resulting invention.[57]

Disclosure of the origins of genetic resources in patent applications is an international issue.[58] The New Zealand government, at least prior to the WAI 262 report, has been part of the international grouping against disclosure requirements.[59]

Disclosure requirements can take many forms and can have varying consequences if not complied with. These might range from no consequence to either re-examination or revocation of the patent. The Waitangi Tribunal recommended that the consequence of failing to make the disclosure should vary depending on the circumstances, but if the effect on the kaitiaki relationship with the biological or genetic resource was great, then revocation of the patent should not be ruled out.

The global position

Disclosure requirements in TRIPS, the CBD and the Nagoya Protocol

At the international level, the debate over the relationship between the use of biological and genetic resources and the use of traditional

I'yu Northern Kaanju Homelands, Cape York, Queensland, Australia' in Drahos and Frankel, *Indigenous Peoples' Innovation*, above n 3, pp. 29–55.

55 *Ko Aotearoa Tēnei*, above n 1, at 114–115. 56 *Ko Aotearoa Tēnei*, above n 1, at 210.

57 *Ko Aotearoa Tēnei*, above n 1, at 205.

58 For a discussion of many issues relating to disclosure requirements, see WIPO, Intergovernmental Committee on Intellectual Property and Genetic Resources, Traditional Knowledge and Folklore, *WIPO Technical Study on Disclosure Requirements Concerning Genetic Resources and Traditional Knowledge*, Third Intersessional Working Group, WIPO Publication No. 786, WIPO/GRTKF/IWG/3/14, 2011.

59 This group includes Australia and the United States. Supporters of disclosure include eight developing countries that submitted a proposal to the WTO for a disclosure requirement to be inserted into Article 29 of the TRIPS Agreement above n 7. See Proposal IP/C/W/474 – 2006, India, Brazil, China, Cuba, Pakistan, Peru, Thailand and Tanzania. Other countries that have co-signed the proposal include The African Group (represented by Uganda), Colombia, South Africa, Ecuador, Venezuela and Paraguay.

knowledge about those biological and genetic resources is well documented. The focus of the TRIPS Council discussion, which has not progressed, became the possible addition of a disclosure requirement of the origin of genetic resources in the patenting system.[60] This sort of disclosure requirement is an example of a possible interface between the protection of traditional knowledge as a sui generis regime and the existing intellectual property regime of patents. The interface is important, even if not a whole solution for traditional knowledge protection, because without the interface there is no effective way for any sui generis protection to succeed. In other words, sui generis protection may fail if there is no way for it to engage third-party patent interests and the disclosure requirement may provide that link. The degrees of engagement will of course vary depending on the nature of the disclosure requirement in any patent law, which may extend from disclosure as a form of notice to an effect (such as re-examination) on the patent if there has not been adequate disclosure.

Article 8 (j) of the Convention on Biological Diversity (CBD)[61] is about the protection of traditional knowledge in conjunction with the protection of biological and genetic resources. There was an ongoing conference of the parties about how to operationalise that provision, which culminated in the Nagoya Protocol[62] of the CBD, which provides for more than disclosure. It also sets out a regime for prior informed consent and access and benefit-sharing for traditional knowledge relating to biological and genetic resources.[63]

In the TRIPS Council, the EU has supported the call for a mandatory disclosure requirement, in patent applications, of the source and country of origin (or legal source) of the resource and any traditional knowledge used in the invention, evidence of prior informed consent from relevant authorities and evidence of fair and equitable benefit-sharing as under the national regime.[64]

[60] For a summary of the proposals before the TRIPS Council, see D. Gervais, *The TRIPS Agreement: Drafting History and Analysis*, 4th edn (Sweet & Maxwell, London, 2012), at 1.79–1.88.

[61] Rio Convention on Biological Diversity, 1760 UNTS 79; 31 ILM 818 (opened for signature 5 June 1992, entered into force 29 December 1993) ('CBD').

[62] Nagoya Protocol on Access to Genetic Resources and the Fair and Equitable Sharing of Benefits Arising from their Utilization to the Convention on Biological Diversity (UN Doc. UNEP/CBD/COP/DEC/X/1) (adopted on 29 October 2010).

[63] Nagoya Protocol, above n 62, arts 4.1bis, 5.1bis and 5bis.

[64] The EU and Switzerland have suggested that failure to disclose cannot affect a granted patent because the WIPO Patent Law Treaty, adopted at Geneva on 1 June 2000, 39 ILM 1047, art 10(1), states that non-compliance with formal requirements does affect a granted patent, except in cases of fraud. This is in part why the EU and Switzerland recommend sanctions outside of patent law,

Outside of some developing countries, which have quite broad traditional knowledge protections of one kind or another,[65] disclosure requirements relating to biological and genetic resources are found in European laws.[66] The relevant European Union (EU) Directive created an optional system.[67] The Netherlands brought a case to the European Court of Justice[68] arguing that the Directive runs counter to the objectives of the Convention on Biological Diversity (CBD).[69] More recently, the EU has taken steps to implement the Nagoya Protocol.[70]

Norway, although not part of the EU, provides an interesting example of compulsory disclosure requirements enacted to comply with the CBD.[71] The law requires that where an invention uses biological material or traditional knowledge, the patent application shall include information about where the inventor collected the material or the knowledge. If the national law of that country requires that access to biological material or use of traditional knowledge is subject to prior consent, the patent application must state whether such consent has

such as through criminal law and fines; see IGC-WIPO, Disclosure of Origin or Source of Genetic Resources and Associated Traditional Knowledge in Patent Applications, 17 May 2005, WIPO/GRTKF/IC/8/11; declaration of the source of genetic resources and traditional knowledge in patent applications: proposals by Switzerland, 6 June 2007, WIPO/GRTKF/IC/11/10. New Zealand is not a party to the WIPO Patent Law Treaty.

65 Examples include China, South Africa, Peru and India.

66 The relevant EU Directive is the *Directive on the legal protection of biotechnological inventions* 98/44/EC, of the European Parliament and of the Council of 6 July 1998. The disclosure requirement is found in Recital 27 of the preamble: 'Whereas if an invention is based on biological material of plant or animal origin or if it uses such material, the patent application should, where appropriate, include information on the geographical origin of such material, if known; whereas this is without prejudice to the processing of patent applications or the validity of rights arising from granted patents.'

67 The recital is in the preamble and is not one of the articles in the Directive. Recital 28 says that the disclosure requirement *does not* affect the patent application examination and the validity of the rights conferred by a granted patent. Thus the directive does not provide for any repercussions such as patent or criminal sanctions in a case of either non-compliance with the disclosure requirement or deliberate misrepresentation.

68 For example, by not providing for equitable sharing of benefits. *Kingdom of the Netherlands* v. *European Parliament and Council of the European Union*, C-377/98, at [67] onwards. All six pleas were rejected by the Court.

69 CBD, above n 61.

70 Proposal for a Regulation of the European Parliament and of the Council on Access to Genetic Resources and the Fair and Equitable Sharing of Benefits Arising from Their Utilization in the Union, 2012/0278 (COD).

71 Patents Act 1967 (Norway), s 8(b). Norway has similar patent filing statistics to New Zealand. In 2008, 5724 patent applications were filed in New Zealand, while 5430 applications were filed in Norway. See IP Statistics Data Centre, WIPO, available at www.wipo.org.

been obtained.[72] Non-disclosure could result in a penalty outside of patent law.[73]

At the WTO, the United States has denied any substantive connection between the CBD and the TRIPS Agreement and has recommended that the relationship be dealt with as a matter of contract law.[74] The problem with reliance on contract law, or any other mechanism outside of the patent system, is that it removes the direct interface that disclosure offers and thus, arguably, reduces the likelihood of competing interests being effectively resolved.

World Intellectual Property Organization

WIPO has an ongoing process of negotiating treaties to address the protection of traditional knowledge. WIPO divides its process into the protection of traditional knowledge as it applies to the technical, genetic resources and the protection of traditional cultural expressions (TCEs).[75] The WIPO process began with a fact-finding mission and then a series of negotiations which ultimately led to a mandate to draft a treaty. No treaty has yet been agreed upon. Drafts consist of broad and detailed objectives and principles and many details in the text are far from agreed and are under ongoing negotiation.[76] There are three separate drafts for the different areas: traditional knowledge, genetic resources and TCEs. However, between the three areas, there are some broad overlaps of principles and objectives.

The proposed treaty for the protection of TCEs, as an example of the three, might prevent the grant of improper intellectual property rights over TCEs and protect and reward creativity based on TCEs.[77] The draft articles under negotiation include protection of the economic and moral

[72] In addition, if the providing country is not the same as the country of origin of the biological material or the traditional knowledge, the application shall also state the country of origin. If the national law in the country of origin requires that access to biological material or the use of traditional knowledge requires prior consent, the patent application shall state whether such consent has been obtained; see General Civil Penal Code (Norway), s 166.

[73] General Civil Penal Code (Norway), s 166.

[74] A summary of the different proposals from members of the WTO, 'Intellectual Property: Geographical Indications and Biodiversity', July 2008 Package: Briefing Notes, is available at www.wto.org/english/tratop_e/dda_e/meet08_brief05_e.htm.

[75] WIPO, *Traditional Knowledge*, available at www.wipo.int/tk/en/.

[76] This is illustrated by the extensive use of bracketed text which represents different negotiating positions. See latest draft provisions, available at http://www.wipo.int/tk/en/igc/.

[77] WIPO, 'The Protections of Cultural Expressions: Draft Articles', WIPO/GRTKF/IC/27/5, 22 January 2014 ('*The Protections of Cultural Expressions: Draft Articles*'), available at http://www.wipo.int/meetings/en/doc_details.jsp?doc_id=261979. For the purposes of

interests in TCEs, including against misappropriation.[78] There are some limitations proposed, such as that the protections must not restrict development or use of TCEs by beneficiaries.[79] Also use of TCEs in museums, archives, libraries or cultural institutions would be prohibited except with the consent of the beneficiaries.[80] The draft also suggests that protections are required to be consistent with other international instruments.[81] The issue of compatibility with other international agreements most clearly arises in the areas which are an interface between the protection of traditional knowledge and the existing intellectual property system. The compatibility of the proposed New Zealand approach is fully discussed in the Waitangi Tribunal Report.[82]

There remains considerable opposition to the WIPO process, including from the United States in particular.[83]

Solutions such as declarations and rules are not always helpful

The WIPO multilateral negotiations have taken a different path from the more common course of international intellectual property agreements. That is, some of the details proposed in the negotiation process exceed the protections found in most national laws. Certainly, in other treaties the multilateral standards may exceed the level of protection found in some national laws, but not to the same degree as appears to be the case in the traditional knowledge context. At least, this was initially the case with the WIPO process, but the longer the international process goes on, there are more domestic laws enacted in national jurisdictions. That perhaps gives the international negotiation momentum, although key economies such as the United States are not likely to enact their own traditional knowledge protecting national laws. The advance of the international process ahead of some national processes may very well be a reflection of the fact, discussed earlier, that the need for protection of traditional knowledge has arisen from recognition of the global effects of the TRIPS Agreement.

the draft treaty, TCEs are defined as tangible or intangible artistic and literary expressions that embody traditional culture or knowledge, art 1.

78 WIPO, *The Protections of Cultural Expressions: Draft Articles*, above n 77, objective 1(a).

79 WIPO, *The Protections of Cultural Expressions: Draft Articles*, above n 77, art 5(1).

80 WIPO, *The Protections of Cultural Expressions: Draft Articles*, above n 77, art 5(4).

81 WIPO, *The Protections of Cultural Expressions: Draft Articles*, above n 77, art 10.

82 *Ko Aotearoa Tēnei*, above n 1.

83 See Frankel, *Ka Mate Ka Mate and the Protection of Traditional Knowledge*, above n 12. See also WIPO, 'The Protection of Traditional Knowledge: Revised Objectives and Principles', WIPO/GRTKF/IC/18/5, 10 January 2011.

The effects of treaties and rules processes can be beneficial, most obviously because they provide a global framework to give protection to those who seek it. The downside might be described as handing over control to those in charge of the regulation. The more those activities are regulated, the more control comes into the hands of those in charge of the regulations and the rules.[84] In the intellectual property field, one can see this, for example, in the degree of control of the shape of the law that resides with patent offices. To be sure, there is always the possibility of appeal of the decisions of such offices, but that does not negate the scope of patent offices' influence over patent law.[85] The WIPO process (or any other international agreement) should not regulate and define traditional knowledge and related protection by norms that are not the norms of those who are seeking protection. To do so would likely result in prescriptive and ill-fitting protection, which would be unlikely to achieve effective protection.

The approach that the Waitangi Tribunal recommended recognises Māori custom and culture as a key factor in the definition of what needs protecting (the relationship of kaitiaki) and the degree of protection (what is the nature of the relationship and to what extent should kaitiaki have input or control over the granting of third-party intellectual property rights in order to protect it).[86] The role of the kaitiaki relationship in the Tribunal's recommendations is a kind of legal pluralism. The WIPO system should support such pluralism through requiring minimum standards of protection in international law, but it should not defeat the functionality and empowerment of pluralism by defining the details of what and who deserves protection in a way that functions as rules that have little to do with the culture involved. Because of this need for recognition of the cultural norms of the culture the rules purport to protect, the splitting of traditional knowledge and TCEs needs to be carefully considered. Such a split is arguably an intellectual property-influenced norm. It is understandable from a functionality viewpoint for an intellectual property institution to make this split, as it in some way accords with how an intellectual property lens sees traditional knowledge issues. But the split is not always apparent from the perspective of those seeking the protection and, as discussed above, the knowledge may have an ongoing developmental role. WIPO acknowledges that traditional knowledge is relevant both in the protection of genetic resource and also as an ingredient of TCEs.

[84] See P. Drahos, *Intellectual Property; Indigenous People and their Knowledge* (Cambridge University Press, 2015).

[85] See, generally, P. Drahos, *The Global Governance of Knowledge: Patent Offices and Their Clients* (Cambridge University Press, 2010).

[86] See *Ko Aotearoa Tēnei*, above n 1.

TCEs are themselves a form of TK: for example, as some of the examples below illustrate, TK related to the production of a traditional creative artifact is embodied and manifested in the design, appearance and artistic form of the artifact. This points to the close relationship between TK and TCEs. TCEs are, therefore, a 'form' in which some TK is embodied.[87]

One commentator, in his discussion of intellectual property's 'sumptuary code',[88] suggests that the protection of TCEs is the most 'ambitious – and reactionary – form of sumptuary intellectual property law that we have'.[89] He highlights that TCEs are distinctive of the communities from which they arise by definition. This is a first sign of TCEs' sumptuary nature.[90] The second sign is that they have attracted 'a lot of dilutive copying' and the third that they are instruments of social ordering.[91] These features are more apparent when the focus is on the TCEs rather than the whole of traditional knowledge and its innovative uses because TCEs are about one embodiment of a knowledge process. Where those TCEs are sacred or are governed by a community's own norms (or social ordering), there Beebe's analysis is correct. However, the knowledge component of TCEs is not necessarily sumptuary. The same knowledge may be applied in ways that are innovative. Some knowledge may be secret, but much traditional knowledge is used for development and innovation. Techniques for growing plants in certain areas, for example, are the result of long-time observation and experimentation about what techniques work best, where and why.

One of the disjunctions between this kind of innovation and that protected by intellectual property rights like patents is that this knowledge is a kind of know-how or systems innovation rather than applied product innovation. In sum, while protecting some traditional knowledge is sumptuary, claims to protect TCEs have developed from normatively defensive grounds as a way of protecting a culture where others use that culture and

87 WIPO-IGC, Traditional Knowledge and Folklore, Seventeenth Session, Geneva, 6–10 December 2010, 'List and Brief Technical Explanation of Various Forms in Which Traditional Knowledge May Be Found', WIPO/GRTKF/IC/17/INF/9, Annex, page 2, [4].

88 B. Beebe, 'Intellectual Property and the Sumptuary Code', *Harvard Law Review*, 123 (2010), 809–889.

89 Beebe, 'Intellectual Property and the Sumptuary Code', above n 88, at 875. One could add that the protection of Flags and Emblems as required under the Paris Convention is even stronger. See Paris Convention for the Protection of Industrial Property, 21 UST 1583, 828 UNTS 305, 1883, art 6ter.

90 Black's Law Dictionary defines sumptuary laws as 'Laws made for the purpose of restraining luxury or extravagance, particularly against inordinate expenditures in the matter of apparel, food, furniture.' Such laws are used to support social hierarchies and morals.

91 Beebe, 'Intellectual Property and the Sumptuary Code', above n 88, at 875–876.

gain intellectual property rights for their uses. TCEs are important, but in fact are a very narrow aspect of the greater claim for traditional knowledge protection. The broader claim to protection for innovative uses as a tool for economic and social development is one that is normatively analogous to – even if functionally distinct from – the claimed rationales relating to innovation and intellectual property.[92] This is precisely what the New Zealand discussion illustrates and why it might be described as a test tube for the global issues of protecting the innovation of indigenous peoples.

Putting the public domain argument in perspective

The notion of what is in the public domain, who defines it and who disagrees with its existence are widely discussed. The boundaries of the so-called public domain are contested. As far as intellectual property law is concerned, there is some general acceptance that what is not protected by intellectual property law may be in the public domain. Thus, if copyright or a patent has expired, what was protected by them will after expiration be in the public domain. Before expiration such things may have been in the public domain, in the sense of being publicly available, but use of them was restricted in various ways because of intellectual property law. This conception of the public domain is one that is constructed around intellectual property law. Those who seek protection of their traditional knowledge may not necessarily agree with a conception of the public domain which is defined by intellectual property law and is time-dependent. The boundaries of intellectual property law do not match the expectations and role that, as discussed above, is a guardianship role.[93] That said, traditional knowledge is not all secret and can be shared and developed, although from the perspective of the traditional knowledge guardian the people who may develop the knowledge may be restricted according to customary law. In public domain terminology the knowledge is public but not in the public domain in the sense of free for all to use.

The public domain can be characterised as a reflection of various strands of domestic public policy and regulation including intellectual property. In some countries, copyright ownership may be so important to some industries that the public domain will be lessened by the copyright term being extended. In other countries, the extension of copyright will

[92] See generally Drahos and Frankel, *Indigenous Peoples' Innovation: Intellectual Property Pathways to Development*, above n 3.

[93] S. Frankel and M. Richardson, 'Cultural Property and "the Public Domain": Case Studies from New Zealand and Australia', in C. Antons (ed.), *Traditional Knowledge, Traditional Cultural Expressions and Intellectual Property Law in the Asia-Pacific Region* (Wolters Kluwer, 2009), pp. 275–292.

not be an important factor (leaving aside for the time being pressure in trade agreements to extend).[94] New Zealand may be such a place. In New Zealand the public domain may on the one hand be greater than elsewhere because the copyright term is shorter. On the other hand, some aspects of traditional knowledge should arguably fall out of the public domain, such as where there is a kaitiaki relationship with a taonga work or a biological or genetic resource. This theme is also found in the Waitangi Tribunal Report:

> there is by no means any agreement . . . about the parameters of the public domain. In short, it is a hotly debated topic. The fact that IP law gives private rights over things in the public domain means that setting its boundaries is an ongoing balancing act between public and private interests. There are no principles that render the line immutable or unmovable, or that dictate that it must be drawn here or there. For example, in 1981 the Flags, Emblems and Names Protection Act . . . ring-fenced from the public domain various cultural symbols perceived to be of national and international importance. Thus, balancing what is in the public domain with what is not – or, put another way, determining what should and should not be protected in law (including IP law) – is a policy choice. And it is a balance that must constantly be recalibrated as circumstances change.[95]

Decisions about what the law regulates and what it does not regulate are a reflection of what a particular jurisdiction considers ought to be protected. What a jurisdiction chooses to protect is consequently out of the public domain. These decisions are a matter of national autonomy but are not entirely free from constraints; after all, international agreements must be complied with. The protection of traditional knowledge, however, is widely recognised as being a measure that does not fall directly within the parameters of the TRIPS Agreement, unless TRIPS measures are used for the protection.[96]

Conclusion

Whether a country chooses to protect traditional knowledge and indigenous innovation or not is almost entirely a matter of national autonomy. If an international agreement is reached, this may change. Even where international law supports protection, such as in the Nagoya Protocol, that treaty defaults to the domestic position.[97] Where a country advocates that all of its population is indigenous or the traditional knowledge

[94] See Chapter 2 in this volume. [95] *Ko Aotearoa Tēnei*, above n 1, at 63.

[96] The TRIPS Agreement requires protection of intellectual property that falls within its definition; see TRIPS Agreement, above n 7, art 1. Things outside this are not governed by TRIPS; see discussion in Chapter 3 of this volume.

[97] Nagoya Protocol, above n 62, art 7.

belongs to all of its peoples, it is more likely to have a general traditional knowledge protection, such as that found in India or China. Where only some people in a country claim traditional knowledge protection, the public domain issue is often raised. Indeed, as the Waitangi Tribunal noted, a concern of third parties was the availability of Māori culture for all New Zealanders to use.

The New Zealand Waitangi Tribunal's recommendations are not a one-size-fits-all model, but they demonstrate an advanced discussion of the balancing that may need to occur to protect traditional knowledge. That balance is evolving in New Zealand, which as a small market economy has both the ability and arguably the need to calibrate intellectual property law to address the protection of mātauranga Māori and its relationship with intellectual property law.

10 Overview

What the international community can learn from the small market economy experience

> Although the institutions of the WTO are not a strong central government in the federal sense, they provide a standing venue for continual discussion of ongoing intellectual property challenges and as a mechanism that allows successful experiments to be elevated from the national to the international level.[1]

This book has analysed complex issues relating to how national lawmakers can strike the right balance among competing interests in intellectual property, while honouring international commitments. Those interests include incentivising local innovation and creativity, addressing other public interests such as ensuring access to innovation and intellectual property products originating from other countries, and being cognisant of the needs of other members of the global community, particularly trading partners. The global issues analysed in this book are infused with the perspective of and examples drawn from three small market economies (Israel, New Zealand and Singapore). These countries have a duality of developed country and developing country interests. They are developed countries, but their national market size results in much intellectual property being imported. These characteristics make small market economies natural global test tubes for experimenting with differences and creating legal innovations to implement intellectual property law and policy.

As noted, small market economies are unique because they share interests with the developing world (which is not homogeneous and is changing). Like many developing countries, small market economies rely considerably on imports of intellectual property and transfer of technology. At the same time, small market economies are developed countries with their own innovation and creative sectors, world-class higher

[1] G. B. Dinwoodie and R. Dreyfuss, *A Neofederalist Vision of TRIPS: The Resilience of the International Intellectual Property Regime* (Oxford University Press, 2012), at Preface ix.

education and consumer demand for quality goods at developed world prices. These small market economies, in their different ways, have each found unique niches in the global intellectual property consortiums and value chains. These niche roles may be more likely to occur in small market economies out of necessity. Nevertheless they illustrate that if intellectual property rules are to enhance the truly global then differing roles in global innovation need to be reflected in intellectual property rules. There are broadly developed and developing country interests, but they are not necessarily polar opposites; there are many nuances to different country interests. International intellectual property rules cannot be a 'one-size-fits-all' because there is no one size.

As set out in this book's Introduction, small market economies do not always get it right and they do not always provide a model that would suit everyone. They do, however, operate at the intersection of global intellectual property issues, and their approaches to balancing interests and calibrating laws to meet local needs are very globally focused, and that is what makes them fertile testing grounds from which the global community can draw information and lessons. In some instances, small market economies also overtly make compromises and enact laws which are not in their best intellectual property related interests, but may be more for the interests of others. There is a growing awareness that to compromise intellectual property in this way, as a trade-off for some other benefit, has long-term consequences which may not be worth it. This is one of the ways in which this book demonstrates that a one-size-fits-all intellectual property model is unsound.

Global Intellectual Property and the Centrality of TRIPS

The global intellectual property regime is made up of international agreements (multilateral, plurilateral and bilateral), international institutions and domestic laws. The many parts of the international regime and its many players have created complex relationships and array of norms which are ever evolving. At the heart of this system are two key institutions: the World Trade Organization (WTO) and the World Intellectual Property Organization (WIPO). Intellectual property is discussed in other multilateral international fora, which have different objects and purposes as their focus, such as biodiversity in the Convention on Biological Diversity.[2] As discussed in this book, there

[2] Rio Convention on Biological Diversity, 1760 UNTS 79; 31 ILM 818 (opened for signature 5 June 1992, entered into force 29 December 1993).

are also FTAs. Some suggest that these multiple regimes mean that the TRIPS Agreement[3] is not as significant as it once was. For several reasons, that is not really so.

The WTO as an administrator of the TRIPS Agreement and institutional home of the only intellectual property dispute settlement process at the multilateral level is a key force in the international intellectual property regime. Disputes over the meaning of and any member's compliance with the TRIPS Agreement include analysis and conclusions not only about TRIPS, but also about other international agreements and particularly the norms from WIPO agreements. This is because the key WIPO agreements (the Berne and Paris Conventions) have been incorporated into TRIPS[4] and because, as norms evolve, TRIPS is structured to absorb some of those norms.[5] The cooperation between WIPO and WTO creates formal conduits for WIPO norms.[6] Other institutions' norms may be taken into account, albeit less directly, in the interpretation of TRIPS. Also, trade agreements build new norms, which, as they multiply in bilateral and emerging plurilateral environments, increasingly flow back into the multilateral.[7] So while much of the norm-making action is presently outside of the WTO, the TRIPS Agreement has provided a platform for those developments to continue. So far the structure of TRIPS has mostly embraced norms which provide more extensive protection than its minimum standards. At the international level, interpretation of the Agreement has yet to be balanced by its own objectives and principles.[8]

3 WTO, Agreement on Trade-Related Aspects of Intellectual Property Rights, Marrakesh Agreement Establishing the World Trade Organization, Annex 1C, 1869 UNTS 299; 33 ILM 1197 (adopted on 15 April 1994, entered into force 1 January 1995) ('TRIPS Agreement').

4 TRIPS Agreement, above n 3, arts 1.3, 9.1, 68.

5 See R. Dreyfuss and S. Frankel, 'How Regime Shifting Reconceptualizes Intellectual Property', forthcoming.

6 Agreement between the World Intellectual Property Organization and the World Trade Organization, 22 December 1995, 35 I.L.M. 754 (1996) and WTO Panel Report, *United States – Section 110(5) of the US Copyright Act*, WT/DS160/R, 27 July 2000.

7 The method by which this happens is largely through interpretation of terms which have a meaning beyond intellectual property. See Chapter 3 of this volume and S. Frankel, 'WTO Application of "the Customary Rules of Interpretation of Public International Law" to Intellectual Property', *Virginia Journal of International Law*, 46 (2006), 365, at 410–415. See also Dreyfuss and Frankel, *How Regime Shifting Reconceptualizes Intellectual Property*, above n 3.

8 These include the multifaceted and thus complex TRIPS Agreement, above n 3, art 7, which provides: 'The protection and enforcement of intellectual property rights should contribute to the promotion of technological innovation and to the transfer and dissemination of technology, to the mutual advantage of producers and users of technological knowledge and in a manner conducive to social and economic welfare, and to a balance of rights and obligations.'

The structure of the TRIPS Agreement can also embrace norms other than those which provide more extensive protection such as the WIPO Marrakech Treaty.[9] Consequently, the TRIPS Agreement remains powerful and also provides a home for integrating new norms, whether they are developed on behalf of rights holders or other interests. The centrality of the TRIPS Agreement should not be underestimated, particularly because the relationship between international and national norms is continuous. They feed and develop each other. National regimes of intellectual property protection only work to support innovation and creativity if they are appropriately framed and calibrated to correlate with development levels and innovation opportunities.

The international regime and relationship between multilateral international agreements and free trade agreements (FTAs) is discussed in Chapter 2. An analysis of the agreements of Singapore and New Zealand (Israel has far fewer FTAs) showed how those countries make adjustments according to the stage of development of the other trading partners. In comparison, large economies tend to have more regularised or template FTAs, which predominantly provide for more extensive intellectual property protections. The technique of using FTAs with extensive protections to develop new norms is now widely known.[10] Despite the well-recognised problems these FTAs cause, they continue to proliferate and are the key technique in driving the increasing intellectual property rights agenda.[11] There is, however, starting to be a greater and more substantial opposition to FTAs and more awareness among some negotiators of the difficulties such agreements can cause.

In addition, such FTAs come with dispute settlement provisions that enable them to be enforced. As more and more countries have FTA-developed norms in their domestic law, the norms make their way in the multilateral system. This book has used examples from small market economies to illustrate the difficulty with FTAs that change and tighten global norms to incorporate heightened intellectual property standards, rather than leaving appropriate space for countries to calibrate their laws to meet their national needs. The intellectual property obligations in the FTAs of New Zealand and Singapore are variable and tend to reflect the

[9] Marrakesh Treaty to Facilitate Access to Published Works for Persons Who Are Blind, Visually Impaired, or Otherwise Print Disabled, 28 June 2013, available at http://www.wipo.int/treaties/en/ip/marrakesh.

[10] These agreements are negotiated in secret and, aside from leaks and expert analysis based on the known terms of other similar agreements, the details are usually not publicly known until they are finalised.

[11] These FTAs include intellectual property chapters and other chapters that affect intellectual property, including pharmaceutical chapters and investment chapters.

level of development of the trading partner in the FTA. This kind of adjustment to the appropriate level of development ideally ought to be achievable through multilateral instruments, so as to avoid the problems of FTAs.

Intellectual property agreements are, however, not yet all one-sided. The key to using TRIPS flexibilities is to interpret the Agreement fully and in ways that recognise the broad suite of objectives and principles of intellectual property, which include that the protection of intellectual property is for the benefit of both producers and users in a way that is conducive to socio-economic welfare.[12] The interpretation chapter of this book (Chapter 3) addresses these issues and how international intellectual property can and should be interpreted in accordance with agreed principles of the customary rules of the interpretation of treaties. The chapter discusses the importance of interpretation to enable the implementation of laws which are suitable for local interests and how local initiatives and needs can be addressed in ways that are compatible with international agreements.

In any economy, how to incentivise innovation and creativity is complex and involves multiple variables of which intellectual property law is one. Chapter 4 focuses on the relationship between intellectual property and innovation policies. It analyses how these linkages are evolving and the choice of intellectual property rules rather than subsidy support for research and development. The chapter includes discussion about when support, such as subsidies and grants, is legitimate under WTO rules and when it may not be so.

The chapters entitled 'Flexing patent law' and 'Approaches to copyright' (Chapters 5 and 6) analyse some legal innovations that small market economies have used in copyright and patent law. The patent chapter shows the disconnect between international patent law and the role of small market economies in global value chains and suggests ways in which the law could be developed to better reflect that role. It is evident that small market economies have been innovative in creating copyright law that both draws on the best models around the world and is framed to meet local needs. The 'Trade mark' chapter (Chapter 7) complements these chapters with a discussion of the centrality of trade marks to small and medium businesses, which are the sizes of the majority of business units of small market economies.

Calibration techniques require both knowledge and skill. Everywhere the ability to make the law 'fit' is a necessity and the fit should take

[12] TRIPS Agreement, above n 3, art 7.

account of, if not be driven by, local circumstances in a global setting. Small market economies' law-making processes often include not only an assessment of local economic needs and cultural imperatives, but also a conscious and sometimes detailed analysis of the compatibility of new laws' international obligations. This approach is illustrated in Chapters 8 and 9, which address areas where the TRIPS Agreement does not predominantly govern, but has a significant impact. These are parallel importing and the protection of traditional knowledge.

In order to introduce competition within their borders, small market economies allow parallel imports. As Chapter 8 shows, Israel, New Zealand and Singapore each have a different approach to the rules and do not parallel import to the same extent as each other. There are also variations in each country's approach across the three main areas of intellectual property. The global debate over parallel imports is not likely to result in a one-size-fits-all rule because such a rule is unlikely to be universally suitable given the varying stages of development and size of countries. The small market economies demonstrate flexibility to trade pressure in their parallel importing regimes, but they also show some unique legal techniques to reconcile competing interests in the parallel importing debate. These include reversing burdens of proof and giving rights holders windows of opportunity to supply the market before parallel imports are permitted.

Developing norms that meet national needs is the subject of Chapter 9, which addresses the way in which indigenous peoples' interests in intellectual property are being developed in New Zealand. This is a global issue and New Zealand's approach provides a detailed insight into the global issue of the protection of traditional knowledge.

Where to from here?

It is well known that as countries become more innovative, they tend to strengthen their intellectual property laws. Equally well known is the observation that strong intellectual property laws alone do not promote innovation. We now see that as large developing countries become key innovators, their interests shift towards the position that large developed countries took when they advocated for the TRIPS Agreement and perhaps when they began the post-TRIPS FTA frenzy. The changing role of the large developing countries also suggests that the developed country incumbent beneficiaries of increased protection of intellectual property may not be the beneficiaries of the future. They too need to calibrate their laws. They should be careful before they make intellectual property law so tight that it boomerangs adversely on them.

Global issues in intellectual property will continue to proliferate because intellectual property is dynamic. Assumptions that the TRIPS Agreement harmonised laws have largely been debunked and a more robust understanding that standards remain minimum and can be complied with in various ways has emerged. This recognition of regulatory autonomy has incentivised national legal innovations to make intellectual property law fit local needs. Distinct national approaches and experiments will continue to develop both through necessity and in response to international development and pressures.

National intellectual property laws do not arise solely because of legal decisions, but they have considerable political dimensions as well. The political dimensions have created a situation where the exceptions model has become the paramount method for calibrating laws to local needs, but that need not necessarily be so. Interpretation of the rights and the extent of their protection are also part of the domestic calibration model.[13] However, this does not mean that international agreements should be flouted but rather that effective interpretation should support multilateral norms. This includes that multilateral norms should not be adjusted and gaps in them filled by interpretative methods that do not give full effect to competing objectives and purposes, in order to prescribe one-size-fits-all rules. Some of the laws and law-making processes of small market economies provide examples of how to balance and reconcile varying and competing interests, how to calibrate to meet local needs and even how to do so innovatively. As the quote at the being of this chapter suggests, ideally these national calibration experiments should filter back to the multilateral.

[13] As discussed in the Chapter 5 of this volume, different approaches to inventive step are illustrative.

Index

Cambridge Intellectual Property and Information Law

Titles in the series (formerly known as *Cambridge Studies in Intellectual Property Rights*)

Brad Sherman and Lionel Bently
The Making of Modern Intellectual Property Law

Irini A. Stamatoudi
Copyright and Multimedia Products: A Comparative Analysis

Pascal Kamina
Film Copyright in the European Union

Huw Beverly-Smith
The Commercial Appropriation of Personality

Mark J. Davison
The Legal Protection of Databases

Robert Burrell and Allison Coleman
Copyright Exceptions: The Digital Impact

Huw Beverly-Smith, Ansgar Ohly and Agnès Lucas-Schloetter
Privacy, Property and Personality: Civil Law Perspectives on Commercial Appropriation

Catherine Seville
The Internationalisation of Copyright Law: Books, Buccaneers and the Black Flag in the Nineteenth Century

Philip Leith
Software and Patents in Europe

Geertrui Van Overwalle
Gene Patents and Clearing Models

Lionel Bently, Jennifer Davis and Jane C. Ginsburg
Trade Marks and Brands: An Interdisciplinary Critique

Jonathan Curci
The Protection of Biodiversity and Traditional Knowledge in International Law of Intellectual Property

Lionel Bently, Jennifer Davis and Jane C. Ginsburg
Copyright and Piracy: An Interdisciplinary Critique

Megan Richardson and Julian Thomas
Framing Intellectual Property: Legal Constructions of Creativity and Appropriation 1840–1940

Dev Gangjee
Relocating the Law of Geographical Indications

Andrew Kenyon, Megan Richardson and Ng-Loy Wee-Loon
The Law of Reputation and Brands in the Asia Pacific Region

Annabelle Lever
New Frontiers in the Philosophy of Intellectual Property

Sigrid Sterckx and Julian Cockbain
Exclusions from Patentability: How the European Patent Office Is Eroding Boundaries

Sebastian Haunss
Conflicts in the Knowledge Society: The Contentious Politics of Intellectual Property

Helena R. Howe and Jonathan Griffiths
Concepts of Property in Intellectual Property Law

Rochelle Cooper Dreyfuss and Jane C. Ginsburg
Intellectual Property at the Edge: The Contested Contours of IP

Normann Witzleb, David Lindsay, Moira Paterson and Sharon Rodrick
Emerging Challenges in Privacy Law: Comparative Perspectives

Paul Bernal
Internet Privacy Rights: Rights to Protect Autonomy

Peter Drahos
Intellectual Property, Indigenous People and Their Knowledge

Susy Frankel and Daniel Gervais
The Evolution and Equilibrium of Copyright in the Digital Age

Edited by Kathy Bowrey and Michael Handler
Law and Creativity in the Age of the Entertainment Franchise

Sean Bottomley
The British Patent System and the Industrial Revolution 1700–1852: From Privileges to Property

Susy Frankel
Test Tubes for Global Intellectual Property Issues: Small Market Economies

www.ingramcontent.com/pod-product-compliance
Lightning Source LLC
LaVergne TN
LVHW011522200926
848484LV00001B/114
* 9 7 8 1 1 0 7 0 1 3 1 4 8 *